YOUR FINANCIAL GUIDE

The Estate And Financial Planner For Federal And Postal Employees

From the Editors of the
FEDERAL EMPLOYEES NEWS DIGEST

© 1997 by Federal Employees News Digest, Inc.
Cover by Rick Clark Illustration & Design
Washington, DC

All rights reserved. No part of this publication may be reproduced, stored in a retrieval system, or transmitted in any form or by any means (electric, electronic, mechanical, photocopying, recording or otherwise) without the prior permission of the copyright owner.

We have attempted to compile information that is as accurate and current as possible. Federal policies, laws, regulations, statistics and addresses continually change, therefore no warranties are made as to the accuracy or completeness of the information in this book.

Published 1997 by
Federal Employees News Digest, Inc.
1850 Centennial Park Drive, Suite 520
Reston, VA 20191
Printed in the United States of America

ISBN 0-910582-35-1

TABLE OF CONTENTS

Introduction v

Chapter One - Building Your Estate 1
Federal Employees 'Investments'
Overcoming Inertia—Getting Started
Whose Investment Advice to Follow
Investment Information Resources

Chapter Two - Assessing Your Financial Status . 5
Determining Your Net Worth
Your Survivors' Monthly Support Obligations
How to Reduce Living Expenses

**Chapter Three - Planning for
Your Survivors** 11
Work Together to Make Preparations
Providing Short-term Funds for Your Survivors
Developing a Cash Reserve
Estimating Estate Settlement Expenses
Joint Bank Accounts
Credit Accounts—A Word for Women

**Chapter Four - Developing Sound
Estate Documents** 15
Why Estate Planning is Necessary
Singles Need Estate Planning, Too
The Need for an Attorney
What Your Gross Estate Includes
De Facto Estate Planning—Doing Nothing
Real Property Ownership Considerations
How Property Passes After Death of a Spouse
The Need for a Valid and Thorough Will
Using Trusts as Estate Planning Tools
Living Wills
Safeguarding Your Documents
Preparing Information Worksheets for Survivors
Settling Your Estate
How the Probate Process Works
The Executor/Administrator
The Importance of Witnesses
Legal Help
Helping Your Executor Now

**Chapter Five - Calculating Annuity
Benefits For Retirees (CSRS and FERS)** 23
Overview of CSRS Annuities
Calculating Your CSRS Annuity
CSRS Basic Annuity Computation Formula
A Word for CSRS-offset Employees
Special Annuity Systems
Potential Reductions in Your Annuity
Overview of FERS Annuity
Types of FERS Annuities
FERS Annuity Computation Formulas
FERS Combined Basic Annuity
Special Retirement Supplement
Special Annuity Systems

**Chapter Six - Survivor Payments Under
Federal Retirement Programs—CSRS** 35
Current Employees: CSRS Survivor Benefits
Retired Employees: Survivor Annuities
Disability Retirement
Cost-of-Living Adjustments (COLAs)
Death Benefits
How Your Survivor(s) Collect Benefits After You Die
Annuity Amounts Received After Your Death
What to Do If Your Spouse Dies Before You Do
What to Do If You Get Divorced
Taxability of Annuities
Where to Go for More Information
Survivor Questions & Answers

**Chapter Seven - Survivor Benefits Under
Federal Retirement Programs—FERS** 57
Current Employees: FERS Survivor Benefits
Retired Employees: Survivor Annuities
Disability Retirement
Cost-of-Living Adjustments (COLAs)
Death Benefits
How Your Survivors Collect Benefits After You Die
Annuity Amounts Received After Your Death
What to Do If Your Spouse Dies Before You Do
If You Get Divorced
Taxability of Annuities
Where To Go for More Information
Survivor Questions & Answers

**Chapter Eight - Social Security
Survivor Benefits** 79
What Social Security Provides
Eligibility Requirements
How Social Security Figures Your Benefits
When You Start Receiving Benefits
Benefits to Family Members
Survivor Annuity Benefits
Dual-Entitlement Provision
Lump-Sum Death Payment
Reductions in Retirement Benefits
Applying for Social Security Benefits
Taxability of Social Security Payments
Where to go for More Information
Social Security Survivor Benefits Questions & Answers

Chapter Nine - Other Survivor Benefits 87
Voluntary Contributions Program
Federal Employees' Compensation Act Death Benefits
Veterans Life Insurance
Veterans Survivor Pension

Chapter Ten - Insurance 93
Basic Insurance—For Employees
Basic Insurance—For Retirees
Optional Life Insurance
Estimating FEGLI Benefits

Designation of Beneficiary
Assignment of Benefits
Living Benefits
Filing an Insurance Claim
Discontinuing FEGLI Coverage
Converting to an Individual Policy
Where to Go for More Information
Private Insurance Considerations
Federal Employees Health Benefits Insurance
Temporary Continuation of Coverage
Medicare

Chapter Eleven - Thrift Savings Plan 105
TSP Account Withdrawals
Early Withdrawal Penalty
Types of Annuities
Calculating Your TSP Annuity
Purchasing an Annuity
Designation of Beneficiary
What Happens If You Don't Designate a Beneficiary
What Happens to Your TSP Account When You Die
Procedures Your Beneficiaries Must Follow in Order to Receive Your TSP Account
What Happens to Your TSP Annuity After You Die
Where to Go For More Information

Chapter Twelve - Funeral Considerations 111
Coffin and Burial Costs
How Much Funerals Cost
Body or Organ Donation Arrangements
Veterans Burial Benefits

Chapter Thirteen - Taxes 113
Federal Estate Taxes
State Death Taxes
Special State Inheritance and Estate Tax Laws

**Chapter Fourteen - Resources and
Other Information 123**
NARFE
AARP
Other Special Groups
Handy Telephone Numbers
Agency Obligations Concerning Death of Employee on Duty or Official Travel

Appendix 127

Figures

2-1 Determining Your Net Worth 5
2-2 Your Survivors' Estimated Monthly Income 6
2-3 Initial Monthly Support Plan Estimate 7
2-4 Projected Living Expense Reductions 8
3-1 Estimating Estate Settlement Expenses 12
4-1 How You Include Jointly Owned Real Property .. 19
5-1 Earned CSRS Retirement Percentages 24
5-2 Chart for Converting Unused Sick Leave Into Increased Servicetime Credit for Higher Annuities (CSRS Employees Only) 25
5-3 Service Branch Addresses 26
5-4 CSRS Retirement Table 27
5-5 Interest Charges 29
5-6 FERS Retirement Table 32
6-1 Insurable Interest Annuity Reductions 40
6-2 Retiree COLAs of Recent Years 41
6-3 CSRS Survivor Annuity Options at a Glance 47
7-1 Insurable Interest Annuity Reductions 62
7-2 Retiree COLAs of Recent Years 63
7-3 FERS Survivor Annuity Options at a Glance 69
8-1 Approximate Monthly Retirement Benefits If the Worker Retires at Normal Retirement Age and Had Steady Lifetime Earnings 80
8-2 Approximate Monthly Disability Benefits if the Worker Becomes Disabled in 1996 and Had Steady Earnings 81
8-3 Approximate Monthly Survivors' Benefits If the Worker Dies in 1996 and Had Steady Earnings 82
8-4 The Windfall Elimination Provision 84
9-1 Labor Department District Offices 89
10-1 Option A—Standard Insurance Withholdings 94
10-2 Option B—Additional Withholdings 94
10-3 Option C—Family 95
10-4 Life Insurance Worksheet 96
11-1 Comparison of TSP Annuity with Level and Increasing Payments 107
11-2 Monthly Annuity Factors Per $1,000 Account Balance 108
11-3 Amount of Initial Payments for Various Annuity Options 108
13-1 How to Calculate Your Federal Estate Taxes 113
13-2 Federal Gift and Estate Tax Table 114
13-3 State Death Tax Credit Table 115

INTRODUCTION

How much are you worth? How can you take hold of your finances and build a substantial estate? If you died tomorrow, on what would your survivors live?

The honest reply to these questions, for most people, would be "I'm not sure." Or, "I don't know."

This book is designed to help you find a solid answer to those questions and many more.

There are dozens and dozens of financial and estate planning books available, but this is the only one that focuses on you and the government-sponsored benefits that make up such a large part of your assets. You'll find that most financial advisors don't have a clue as to the wide variety of benefits to which you are entitled as either an active federal or postal employee or a federal annuitant. This book can go a long way toward helping you understand and take advantage of these benefits and in educating your spouse, financial planner, CPA and/or attorney on the subject.

Although personal situations vary, federal and postal employees and retirees share many of the same job benefits: health and life insurance, injury compensation coverage, civil service retirement and, in some cases, veterans benefits. This book will help you weigh and understand your options, assist you in keeping better records, and help you map out a plan that will secure your financial affairs, as well as the future of your loved ones.

It's easy to continue through a career and into retirement with only a generally hazy knowledge of the financial benefits you're entitled to by virtue of your government service. It's still easier to go through life avoiding the thought of your own demise. Yet it's unavoidable: some day you will cease being a person and become an "estate." As you must plan your finances in life, so must you prepare them for your death.

The book starts where you should start: with a look at your current financial situation, with an emphasis on your federally sponsored benefits. It is never too late to begin building an estate, and we give you the information and tools to do just that. We then show you how to estimate the needs of your survivors, as well as the assets that will be available on your death to fill those needs. You also will find copies of a number of the forms you'll need to apply for benefits or to notify particular agencies of your desires. You will learn what information you should be keeping in your records, and find assistance to help you fill them out.

There's a clear section on the ins and outs of estate planning. We show how to compute your own annuity payments, as well as the benefits that will go to your survivors, whether you die in service or after retirement. To make sure this information is relevant, we've separated the annuity-computation discussions into the various retirement programs to which you might be entitled, as well as the various marital and family situations that federal workers typically are involved in. We walk you through the government life and health insurance and thrift savings programs, outline the potential funeral and tax costs of settling your estate, and introduce you to the organizations that can provide valuable assistance and benefits.

Our approach throughout is to speak in plain English, providing practical tips, advice, and insights into what many consider an intimidating and confusing field. But the support isn't limited to intellectual help; we provide a range of practical financial and estate planning tools, including numerous worksheets and personal record organizers.

Once you have read the material and filled out the applicable worksheets in the back of the book, don't stop there. It's important to keep the information current. This doesn't mean reviewing it every week, or even every month, but taking the time periodically to make sure that your personal files and records are updated and in order will allow you to rest easier.

Our thanks to those who have helped in the preparation of this book, especially Reginald M. Jones, a current federal retiree and former chief of OPM's retirement and insurance policy division; John Sullivan of Sullivan & Company, Limited, an accounting firm in Reston, Va.; and Michael J. Sullivan, a congressional consultant on the design of the Thrift Savings Plan.

Here's hoping that this new edition of *Your Financial Guide* proves to be fruitful and rewarding reading.

FEND Editors

CHAPTER ONE

BUILDING YOUR ESTATE

Many federal employees believe they'll never have much of an estate. They maintain small savings accounts, purchase modest cars, own a home (with the bank holding the mortgage) and have government-sponsored life insurance policies. But they just don't get the feeling they have much to leave behind.

They have much more than they think.

In the not-too-distant past most federal workers had a pretty good idea of what they'd be worth based on their easily-projected retirement annuities and life insurance, as well as their outside holdings.

Things were much more predictable then.

But with the advent of the FERS retirement system and its Thrift Savings Plan all that changed.

The thrift plan has become one of the key wild cards in the federal employee's estate equation.

All employees hired since 1983 have a minimum one percent of salary invested in the tax-deferred thrift savings plan, whether they know it or not (the government automatically contributes this amount in thrift accounts that bear their names, and they become entitled to it after three years of service). For employees under the old CSRS retirement plan (generally, those hired before 1984) there is no automatic investment. But many of those employees also have committed funds to the plan. All who voluntarily invest their pay in the thrift plan expect their investments to grow, and by extension, help protect their loved ones after they die.

Whether they are successful in this goal depends on hard work and a thorough *and continuing* estate planning process.

They shouldn't trust luck to carry them through. And you shouldn't, either.

Well before the thrift plan appeared on the scene, the world of investments experienced an explosion in popularity. The old savings account gave way to new options. Mutual funds appeared and multiplied. Banks and savings and loans began offering certificates of deposit (CDs) to the public. The Individual Retirement Account (IRA) was born. Insurance companies greatly expanded the number of available investment vehicles. The price of gold and silver soared, then collapsed. More and more people accustomed to buying U.S. savings bonds through payroll deduction turned to other U.S. securities and government-backed mortgages. The days of one-stop investing are over. There are just too many variables.

The news business has kept pace with this well-documented trend and has even intensified it. There's nothing like the lure of quick money in either hard or booming times to stimulate investing. Newspapers have expanded their financial sections. Investment shows have sprouted like mushrooms on television and radio. Dozens of investment and business magazines have appeared on newsstands. Home computers can tap into investment news and people can buy and sell stocks with them, as well.

This trend will continue.

In some ways the Thrift Savings Plan alone has turned all post-1983 employees into investors.

Because you are reading this book you probably are one of those actively investing in the thrift plan. And you probably have a home and other outside investments, as well.

You already are building your estate.

Federal Employee 'Investments'

Virtually anything that can be converted into cash may be considered an investment. When you joined the federal or postal service, you "invested" your talents and work. In return, you were paid a salary and given entitlement to fringe benefits. Your retirement plan, life insurance, thrift savings account(s), voluntary retirement funding, and Social Security (in the case of FERS workers) all are worth money to you and your potential survivors. For the typical federal employee, they represent the greatest portion of his or her estate. A house may be your largest single asset, but over time these benefits can equal or exceed the value of even an extremely expensive home.

Don't underestimate this fact.

Your Financial Guide

Throughout this book you'll find detailed explanations of your federal employee "investments" and how they fit into your current finances, as well as your estate. As an overview, these investments include:

Retirement — Many private sector employees consider your federal employee retirement package to be too generous. Private company executives, a few members of Congress, and business lobby groups continually take potshots at your system, sometimes attempting to reduce or eliminate its advantages. If that makes you uncomfortable, it should. But it also should tell you something else. Your retirement system overall is one of the best in the nation. Its solvency is fully guaranteed by the government (the best insurance here is that members of Congress also are covered by it) and it offers inflation protection as well. There also is a survivor provision.

Thrift Savings Plan — Investing in the tax-deferred thrift savings plan is essential for FERS employees because it is needed to round out the eventual retirement payoff for post-1983 federal workers. In other words, since the regular civil service annuity component was reduced for FERS people, the thrift system was designed to make up for the lost ground. In practice, it can even permit FERS employees to exceed the eventual payout for employees under the older, CSRS retirement system. The thrift plan, however, also offers a fine opportunity for CSRS employees to maximize their federal employee retirement payout. You'll find more detail on this benefit in Chapter 11.

Social Security — All FERS employees are covered by Social Security. Their coverage can protect their survivors. Some CSRS employees are also covered by virtue of previous employment or their spouse's work.

Life Insurance — Uncle Sam provides you with a basic life insurance plan and optional coverage, as well. In many cases, private insurance companies can't beat the rates, although some insurance salespersons will say otherwise. You must judge for yourself if they are correct. The proper amount of insurance can help offset estate settlement costs.

Health Insurance — This is one of the most important advantages of federal employment. Look at any newspaper and you'll see that millions of Americans have no health insurance at all and are constantly in danger of financial ruin as a result of a serious illness. Your health insurance entitlement is one of the best in the country, according to leading authorities. You can even carry it into retirement—another advantage over many private company benefit packages. Your choice of plans and coverage optionsare many and varied. You can even protect your wife or husband if you have elected a survivor benefit under retirement. They'll be able to retain your federal health insurance if you have done so.

Voluntary (Retirement) Contributions — This is for CSRS employees only. The government allows you to set aside something extra for retirement. The investment is tax-deferred and the money can be withdrawn before retirement. The account is part of your estate.

Injury Compensation — The Federal Employees Compensation Act (FECA) serves as disability insurance for on-the-job injuries and illnesses, and has a death benefit to boot.

Veterans' Benefits — If you are a former member of the U.S. armed forces, you may be eligible for special benefits, including medical care, burial allowances, life insurance, low cost loans, and so on.

Overcoming Inertia — Getting Started

If you just can't seem to get going in the investment game, you are not alone. Many people have an understandable reluctance to commit money to mutual funds, stocks, bonds, and other such instruments. They could, after all, lose some of what they earned should these investments go sour. But it's not just the fear of financial risk. There also is a learning curve staring them in the face.

Investing can be complicated.

If you need just to get off dead center, try learning as much about your federal retirement thrift fund as you can. In Chapter 11, you'll find the basics to get you started in the TSP program.

Your personnel or payroll offices should have plenty of literature about this valuable investment opportunity, as well. The trio of funds under the TSP are well-managed and conservative in their approach.

Learn how to invest in the thrift program and you'll have the basics for investing in mutual funds (i.e., stocks, bonds, other securities, even cash, where you share risks and pool your buying power with other investors). From there, you can branch out to common stocks, U.S. Treasury securities, and beyond.

One of the thrift plan investment techniques is dollar-cost-averaging, that is, investing a set amount at regular intervals. The thrift fund allows you to do this through payroll deduction.

Another way is to invest up to $2,000 (another $250 for a non-working spouse) each year in an individual retirement account (IRA). As a federal employee, you may not be able to deduct your investment in an IRA (depending on your income level), but the money you put in will accumulate interest or capital gains without taxes. (However, you'll have to fork over taxes eventually when you begin withdrawing that money.) The

TSP also accumulates tax-deferred *and* allows you to deduct your investments from your gross income in the year you invested.

You'll find the TSP quite similar to mutual funds, although the amount the TSP "charges" you for managing the program usually is far less than commercial mutual funds charge for similar services.

The TSP and mutual funds both furnish you with periodic updates on your investment performance so you can keep good records.

Should you decide to begin buying stocks and bonds, you can get a broker to make the "trades" for you. There are "full-service" brokers who buy and sell them for you, provide advice, and help you keep records. They can even help you settle an estate by setting up estate accounts from which your executor or executrix can distribute estate assets. So-called "discount" brokers provide buying and selling help, hand out helpful brochures, but usually don't provide much in the way of advice.

Speaking of advice, it should be noted that a broker's advice isn't always good. In fact, some people who have lost a bundle or maybe all of their investments after following what they thought was sage advice from an established broker would argue that it's never any good. Some of it is, some of it isn't.

Whose Investment Advice to Follow

You may be surprised to find out that your own investment advice can be the most valuable. The emphasis is on the word "can." You have to be informed. Read all you can. Learn both by reading and doing. Take a small plunge initially, and as you learn more (and maybe lose a small amount) your expertise will develop. There are two kinds of investors—those who have lost money and those who haven't . . . yet.

Treat anyone's advice as just more to weigh before you invest more of your hard-earned cash.

Investment Information Resources

If you aren't one yet, you must become an investment "hunter." Like any other hunter, you have to stalk your prey while watching out for signs of danger. The newspapers are full of valuable information. So are TV and radio programs, books, magazines, newsletters, and the Internet.

Most can't tell you much about federal employee pay and benefits, but they do present plenty of investment information of a general nature. Your goal is to become a financial manager, either on your own or with the help of others. Well-intentioned friends can help inform you about investment opportunities, but if they aren't experts, take their suggestions with more than just a grain of salt. Always check things out for yourself. Avoid "hot tips" from self-proclaimed experts and unsolicited offerings of "sure-fire, 100 percent guaranteed" investment opportunities. The woods are full of unscrupulous "investment" peddlers.

You can try to leapfrog hard work and go for quick profits, but most people find that careful investing over the long haul is not only safer, but potentially more rewarding. You may not make a killing, but you won't get "killed" either, and you'll realize solid gains.

CHAPTER TWO

ASSESSING YOUR FINANCIAL STATUS

The first step in drafting a financial or estate plan is to make an honest assessment of how your finances stand now, the potential income of your survivors, and their potential future financial needs. Beginning with an examination of your financial picture now (Figure 2-1) will help everyone, especially those left behind.

Determining Your Net Worth

Estimating Your Assets
Cash $ _____
Bank Accounts - Checking _____
Bank Accounts - Savings _____
Money Market Funds _____
Cash Value of Government and Non-Government Life Insurance _____
Certificates of Deposit _____
Civil Service Retirement Fund Balance _____
Voluntary Retirement Account (if applicable) _____
Annuity Cash Values _____
Government Securities _____
Stocks/Mutual Funds _____
Thrift Savings Plan _____
Bonds - Municipal and Corporate _____
Owned Real Estate - Principal Residence _____
Owned Real Estate - Other _____
Business Interests _____
Hard Assets (Gold, Coins, etc.) _____
Furnishings _____
Collectibles and Antiques _____
Vehicles _____
Boats _____
Other (Specify) _____
Total Assets $ _____

Estimating Your Liabilities
Mortgage Balance - Principal Residence $ _____
Home Equity Loans _____
Mortgage Balance - Other Property _____
Life Insurance Policy Loans _____
Consumer Debt - Credit Cards _____
Department Store Credit Accounts _____
Bank Loans _____
Personal Loans _____
Other (Specify) _____
Total Liabilities $ _____

Current Net Worth = (Assets minus Liabilities) = $ _____

Figure 2-1

Your Financial Guide

Your Survivors' Estimated Monthly Income

Current Income of Potential Survivor
Before accounting for survivor benefits, determine the total amount of income that your spouse currently receives from all sources:

1. Employment (Wages or Salary) $ _____
2. Overtime (Average Monthly Amount)   _____
3. Part-Time Employment Wages or Salary   _____
4. Social Security Benefits (Now Receiving)   _____
5. Other Government Benefits (Now Receiving)   _____
6. Financial Investment Income *   _____
7. Rental Income - Owned Property   _____
8. Annuity Income (Now Receiving)   _____
9. Personal Loan Interest Payments   _____
10. Other income   _____

Total Current Income $ _____

Modified Income of Survivor
11. Survivor Benefits - Spouse   _____
12. Survivor Benefits - Dependent Child/Children   _____
13. Social Security Benefits   _____
14. Investment Income   _____
15. Lump-Sum Payments   _____

Total Survivor Income $ _____

* Dividends and Interest

Figure 2-2

Your Survivors' Monthly Support Obligations

Meeting Your Obligations

Before your estate can be settled, all debts must be paid. This may require your executor to exhaust your liquid assets, thus depriving your heirs of them. This is where life insurance can play a major role in your planning. You should estimate the debts that would exist if you were to die today and what sources would be used to satisfy them. In addition, you also may want joint debts, such as your home mortgage or car loans, to be liquidated. Add up the total amount of these debts and reduce them by any life insurance which is in place. This is the amount of life insurance you need to pay off all your debts. Reduce this by any amount of liquid assets that you want used for this purpose, and the amount remaining is the life insurance you need to meet this objective.

Assessing Your Survivors' Financial Needs

Your financial assessment should include determining: whether sufficient life insurance death benefits will be available to meet your estate's obligations while ensuring that adequate funds remain for meeting the monthly expenses of your survivors; whether plans for providing college educations for your children are still economically possible; and whether adequate provisions are available for meeting the other needs of your survivors. It's a good idea to eliminate any installment debt that your surviving spouse might have to face. It's a bad idea to be paying interest rates on installment credit accounts in the 18 to 21 percent range when your invested money is yielding returns of considerably less. After estimating the amount of money needed for settling your estate, if a significant amount of lump-sum insurance payment proceeds will still be available, it should be designated for this purpose (see Chapter 10 for insurance information).

Initial Monthly Support Plan Estimates

Take the time, in Figure 2-3, to estimate the optimum amount of funds needed by your survivors to continue their current lifestyle. (Use your check stubs to help you determine your average expense amounts.)

How does this total amount compare to your estimate of survivor monthly income in Figure 2.2? If it is too high, proceed to the next step in this chapter and make modifications needed to bring expenses into line. In fact, it makes good economic sense to review all of the expenses in this chapter to determine what economies can be achieved. Any economies yielded should be moved into the "Savings and Investment" category in the list.

Initial Monthly Support Plan Estimate

Housing Costs (Mortgage/Rental)	$ _____
Owned Home Maintenance, Repair, & Tax Costs	_____
Utilities — Gas/Electric/Water/Telephone	_____
Condominium Fees and Assessments	_____
Food	_____
Clothing Purchases, Dry Cleaning, & Laundry	_____
Furniture and Appliances (Purchase & Repair)	_____
Recreation and Entertainment	_____
Car Payments and Expenses (Gas, Repairs, etc.)	_____
Medical and Dental Expenses	_____
Prescription Drugs	_____
Insurance (Homeowners/Renters/Auto)	_____
Tax Obligations (Federal/State/Local)	_____
Credit Account and Loan Payments	_____
Child Care/Educational Expenses	_____
Contributions to Charity	_____
Life & Health Insurance Premiums	_____
Savings and Investments	_____
Other (Specify)	_____
Total Monthly Support Plan Obligations	$ _____

Figure 2-3

Strategies for Reducing Monthly Support Requirements and Revised Estimates

Make notations in each category (Figure 2-4) on actions that can be taken to reduce associated expenses, then modify the amount estimated for that category (see **How to Reduce Living Expenses** below).

How to Reduce Living Expenses

It makes little sense to plan an estate without considering how it will be used by your survivors. In addition to setting up your estate, discuss how your family can control expenses after you die. This may yield some interesting surprises. It could be that your spouse knows more than you do about handling money and you also may find that you both could do a better job of saving while you're still around to enjoy the dividends.

There are some fixed costs that are hard to reduce (your rent, for example). But there are other discretionary areas where real savings can be achieved without too much difficulty.

There are some actions that can be initiated by your survivor to reduce his or her expenses. You should discuss them now, while you're still in a position to help. They include:

- If you own your home, consider prepaying some of your mortgage. This single action can save you and your family tens of thousands of dollars over the life of the loan (typically, 15 or 30 years). If a homeowner with a $75,000 mortgage at 10 percent for 30 years includes just $25 more (as a prepayment on principal) with his or her $653 monthly mortgage payments, the savings would be more than $34,000 over the life of the loan. As a bonus, the number of monthly payments would drop by 64, thus shortening the time when you clear that debt.

- Consider refinancing your home. As a rule, if the going mortgage interest rate drops two or more percentage points lower than what you are paying, it's probably a good idea to refinance. There are variables, however, so a drop of slightly under two "points" also might make sense. Settlement costs and

loan fees also affect the equation. The length of time you expect to remain in your home, also must be considered. If you plan to move in only a year or two, it probably wouldn't make much sense to refinance.
- Homes need maintenance and repairs. Economy dictates your making the special efforts needed to shop around for contractors who have solid reputations and come with recommendations.
- Heating and air conditioning are major expenses—in all climates. Have your utility company make an inspection to recommend money-saving approaches.

- If your long distance telephone costs are unreasonable, check into alternative services and their wide variety of discount plans.
- If you belong to a condominium association, be active in its activities. Stay informed about plans for major improvements and associated assessments. They don't come cheap. Try to influence maintenance and other outlays if you believe they are out of control. Question projects that appear to be marginally essential. Make sure that those in charge are getting the best buys for your money when it comes

Projected Living Expense Reductions

Housing Costs (Mortgage/Rental)	$ _____
Owned Home Maintenance, Repair, & Tax Costs	_____
Utilities - Gas/Electric/Water/Telephone	_____
Condominium Fees and Assessments	_____
Food	_____
Clothing Purchases, Dry Cleaning, & Laundry	_____
Furniture and Appliances (Purchase & Repair)	_____
Recreation and Entertainment	_____
Car Payments and Expenses (Gas, Repairs, etc.)	_____
Medical and Dental Expenses	_____
Prescription Drugs	_____
Insurance (Homeowners/Renters/Auto)	_____
Tax Obligations (Federal/State/Local)	_____
Credit Account and Loan Payments	_____
Child Care/Educational Expenses	_____
Contributions to Charity	_____
Life & Health Insurance Premiums	_____
Savings and Investments	_____
Other (Specify)	_____
Total Revised Support Plan	$ _____

What amount of overall savings have you achieved through these revised strategies and spending plans?

Total Savings = $ _____

Percent of Savings as Compared to Initial Estimate = _____ %

Figure 2-4

to all of the costs involved in running the property.
- Food costs continue to rise. The only way to make ends meet is to become a dedicated bargain hunter. Go after the sale items even if it means going to a number of stores. Plan ahead and buy items on sale in bulk that you know you will need in the future. If there is a discount food warehouse operation in your area, one where you have to pack your own bags and don't have a lot of fancy fringes, don't hesitate to be one of its best customers. You can save 15-25 percent on groceries. Use money-saving coupons to further reduce your costs.
- Pay with cash. If you can't afford the $25 meal, consider a cheaper one, or cook at home.
- Buy clothing only when it's on sale. Be conservative in your dry cleaning requirements; if you shop around, you might be able to find a discount dry cleaning operation such as those that offer a fixed price for any item.
- When you receive a monthly bill from a department store or one of your credit card companies, check it against your receipts to make sure that all charges are proper. A pain in the neck? You bet. But it could save you hundreds of dollars. If you find a problem, immediately call the number provided on the invoice and explain that it is an erroneous charge. Many companies will issue an immediate credit and then investigate the matter. If their investigation verifies your contention, the credit will stand. Some will ask you to send a letter explaining the nature of your dispute. Do whatever it takes to avoid paying for merchandise that you did not purchase.

You also can significantly reduce your expenses by paying off your credit card balances. These seemingly innocent debts eat up far more money than many realize. The more you pay off, the less interest is building. This gives you more money. Think of it as a raise. A small purchase—say $25—on a credit card if left unpaid for many months can result in a total cost of $50-100. Is that $25 meal you charged worth $100?

These are just a few tips for cutting down on your spending when the money needed to do all that you would like to do is not available. Get in the habit of reading the financial pages of newspapers and magazines. They are full of similar advice.

CHAPTER THREE

PLANNING FOR YOUR SURVIVORS

If you are like most people, you would rather not plan for the inevitability of death. What could be more unpleasant to contemplate? But plan you must, if you hope to provide a comfortable future for your loved ones—a future free from financial worry.

You need a thorough understanding of the assets and entitlements that will be available to your survivors at your death. You must determine if they'll be sufficient to meet your survivors' needs after expenses arising from your death are paid. These expenses include your tax liabilities, debts, funeral and burial charges, and the array of costs associated with administering and settling your estate.

Work Together to Make Preparations

It's vital that you and your spouse and other heirs work together to plan the disposition of your estate. You don't want a grieving loved one to have to start from scratch. Imagine the consequences. This thought alone should spur you to discuss these important matters just as soon as possible.

Time seems to move more quickly as you get older. You continue to focus on solving daily problems and, regardless of your age, keep on making long-term plans. It's good to think positively about the future, and healthy, too.

But if you ignore the need to plan your estate, you are doing your family a major disservice.

You may find it wise to spend some money on expert advice once you get a handle on your finances and the benefits available to you from the federal government. Bring your spouse along when you confer with these experts. It's a good idea to make sure everyone is reading from the same script.

Find an attorney who specializes in estate settlements and knows how to prepare wills properly. If you don't know where to begin your search, look up the state or local bar association in the telephone book and ask for a lawyer who is known to have that expertise. Some attorneys don't charge for the initial half-hour or so of consultation.

Once you have an attorney, you should seek out a certified public accountant (CPA) who will help you anticipate tax consequences of your estate plan. You might consult a professional financial adviser, as well.

The hourly fees for these professionals, ranging from $100 to $200 in many cases, can save you many thousands of dollars in future taxes and ensure that your loved ones won't be caught financially flat-footed when you die.

Look upon these fees as part of your investment strategy.

Providing Short-Term Funds For Your Survivors

During the period immediately following your death, your survivors will face a time when cash flow problems may significantly impair their ability to meet obligations. You need to carefully plan to ensure that sufficient cash will be available to your survivors for meeting their needs until your estate is settled. It will probably take at least two months to obtain insurance settlements and perhaps longer to receive survivor benefit payments.

Developing a Cash Reserve

Your personal representative (executor or administrator) will need a source of cash to meet the expenses of settling your estate, which must be paid shortly after your death. Detailed explanations are provided in sections of this book concerning:

- *Funeral and burial expenses* — These widely varying costs can gouge your survivors' finances.
- *Administrative expenses* — These are the costs of opening, administering, and closing estates. The process usually takes a year, although it can take much longer if your estate is large or complicated. Much of the expense consists of fees paid to the executor and in many cases an attorney and accountant. There are court costs, as well. In cases where heirs contest the provisions of the will, (i.e., take legal action to overrule the distribution of assets specified in the will) the expenses can increase significantly.

Your Financial Guide

Defending against these suits can be very costly. That's a key reason to make sure you and your legal advisers develop a rock solid will.
- *Miscellaneous estate settlement costs*— The cost of appraising real estate and other tangible property and the cost of insuring and maintaining property while the estate is open can be high. Your survivors face an array of such costs, as well as required accountings, estate inventories, and tax returns, which must be filed with the court and tax authorities. See Figure 3.1 to estimate your estate settlement expenses.
- *Debts*— Any debts you owe at the time of your death, such as loans, must be paid. Creditors have a limited period to make these claims against the estate, and the executor usually has about six months to verify their validity and make payments.
- *Death taxes*—Many federal employees, as explained in this book, will not be subject to federal transfer taxes because these taxes generally apply only to estates of $600,000 or more. But others have estates well above that threshold. This book includes a section for computing your *potential* federal tax obligations, if any. In many states, there may be a death tax obligation, as well.
- *Contingency funds*— These are for unexpected expenses, which are inevitable. It's wise to factor in an extra amount to cover *unanticipated* charges, fees and so on when planning the amount needed to handle all contingencies. Add 3 to 5 percent to your "bottom line" estimate for settling your estate to account for the unexpected.

If there won't be a sufficient amount of cash readily available to meet the expenses involved in settling your estate and to provide income for your survivors, you may want to consider purchasing a life insurance policy to provide essential funds.

Life insurance is payable at the time of death and can be a good source of cash to meet these expenses until annuity and other payments begin. The alternative for your family may be to borrow money at potentially high interest rates or to dispose of personal property at possibly distressed prices in order to meet these obligations. You could spend 30 years paying off a home loan only to have your survivor be forced to sell the house to satisfy estate-related costs and taxes.

Estimating Estate Settlement Expenses

Step 1 - Calculate Your Total Liabilities
Use the chart provided for assessing your net worth (Figure 2.1). Only include your share of the value of the items listed to determine your "Gross Estate."

Step 2 - Calculate Your Total Estate Settlement Expenses

GROSS ESTATE	$ _____
Minus Funeral Expenses	(_____)
Minus Administrative Expenses	(_____)
Minus Debts	(_____)
= ADJUSTED GROSS ESTATE	$ _____
Minus Marital Deduction	(_____)
Minus Charitable Deduction	(_____)
= TAXABLE ESTATE	$ _____
TENTATIVE TAX (See Chapter 13)	$ _____
Minus Unified Credit	(92,800)
Minus State Death Tax Credit	(_____)
= FEDERAL ESTATE TAX	$ _____

Step 3 - Summary

Plus Federal Estate Tax	$ _____
Plus State Death Tax	$ _____
Plus Funeral Expenses	$ _____
Plus Administrative Expenses	$ _____
Plus Debts You Wish to Liquidate	$ _____
= TOTAL ESTATE SETTLEMENT EXPENSES	$ _____

Figure 3-1

Joint Bank Accounts

Do not rely on a joint bank account to provide the funds needed by your spouse during this interim period. Legally, the money in a joint account belongs to either of you, so either can empty the account. However, upon your death each of you is assumed to own one-half of any joint asset. In some states, your widow or widower may find that the entire account has been frozen pending processing of your estate.

You may find it necessary or desirable to have a special bank account in your spouse's name if you live in a state where a joint account can be partially (one-half) or fully frozen when the joint owner dies. This account should include checking and cash card features and enough funds to meet projected expenses.

It's strongly recommended that you check with your attorney concerning the laws that apply in these situations.

Credit Accounts—A Word for Women

The Equal Credit Opportunities Act includes provisions for a married woman to establish a credit history of their own. However, the law states that should she become divorced, separated, or widowed, the creditors cannot automatically terminate the existing line of credit but can ask her to reapply. Such a procedure could lead to a reduction of credit limits below the current amount carried on the cards. Therefore, a surviving spouse could find him/herself without available credit until the outstanding balance is reduced.

Accordingly, each spouse should establish credit in his or her own name to avoid this potential complication.

CHAPTER FOUR

DEVELOPING SOUND ESTATE DOCUMENTS

It can take years to build an estate, but only a short time to destroy it. That's the primary reason that you must document your holdings and entitlements and then instruct authorities on what to do with them when you die. Without legally valid instructions, you are leaving it up to strangers or others you haven't chosen to dispose of your money and property. Necessary documents include not only your Last Will and Testament, but insurance policies, personnel and retirement records, and other types of information, such as burial instructions, previous addresses, education, entitlements, and other relevant papers.

Why Estate Planning Is Necessary

The purpose of estate planning is to ensure that your death will not create unnecessary financial hardships for your family. This cannot be overstated. Nor is it an issue that can be postponed. Too many young people die in accidents or from sudden illnesses.

Your objective is to develop a plan that will allow maximum preservation of your assets and minimize the costs associated with your death. You want as much of your assets as possible to pass on to your survivors with minimum delay. And you want to keep your tax obligations at the lowest possible level.

To do this, you need a viable plan for the orderly settlement of your estate.

Effective estate planning requires knowledge of the laws and procedures that relate to wills, the ownership of property, estate administration, and the payment of gift, income, and death taxes.

Again, depending upon the complexity of your estate planning requirements, you may require the services of professionals such as an attorney, accountant, and a trust officer or financial planner.

- An attorney's role is to assist you in preparing legal documents such as a will or a trust agreement, and to suggest strategies to ease the transfer of assets to your survivors.
- An accountant's detailed knowledge of your financial situation and the associated tax consequences allows you to make the plans required for minimizing expenses.
- Assistance from a trust officer or financial planner may be needed if a substantial and complicated estate is involved.

Singles Need Estate Planning Too

A married person can pass his or her entire estate to a spouse without paying federal estate taxes by using the unlimited marital deduction. But single persons, even those who are divorced or widowed, don't have this tax advantage.

If you are single, your estate planning begins with goals such as making provisions for any children you might have from a previous marriage, for partners, other loved ones, and charities. You must have a will that specifies your intentions. If you are sharing your life with a legally unrelated person, a will helps make it possible to bypass legally entitled heirs and pass property on to the non-related individual. To ensure this, your attorney can prepare property agreements and include a "no contest" clause in your will. This type of clause typically provides that anyone who challenges the will is excluded from inheriting via that will.

The Need for an Attorney

An experienced attorney is essential to the process of developing proper documents. You can't be assured that your will and other legal documents are properly prepared without competent legal assistance from an attorney *familiar with the laws of your state*. He or she understands the special techniques that are required under state law to ensure that the documents will carry out your objectives.

Although you may be able to use a computer program or boilerplate form to draft your own will, you should be aware that this can be very risky. There simply is no generic form that can cover all laws pertaining to your estate.

But you may find it useful to work with fill-in-the-blank forms or other materials as a way to prepare for your meetings with an attorney. This exercise can help you organize your thoughts and reduce the billing time once you begin consulting a lawyer.

Your Financial Guide

What Your Gross Estate Includes

Your *gross* estate includes any property you own or control at the time of your death—even life insurance that is payable to you or a designated beneficiary. The valuation of life insurance in your gross estate is its face value, while the value of other personal possessions is their *fair market value* (the amount you actually could get if you sold them today). Any of the following items that are in your name will be included in your estate:

- Money in your checking or saving accounts
- Bank certificates of deposit (CDs)
- Stocks
- Corporate or government bonds
- Assets in a living trust
- Mutual fund shares
- Money market assets
- Personal residence that you own
- Other real estate that you own
- Checking accounts
- Thrift plan balance
- Art objects and antiques
- Coin, stamp, or other *valuable* collections
- Jewelry
- Household furnishings
- Vehicles
- Boats
- Other personal property

Most of these items pass to your survivors through provisions of your will. Exceptions would be bank account proceeds that are payable directly to joint owners. Certain other assets are payable to your survivors by law or under the terms of a contract; they go directly to your survivors. These assets include Social Security benefits, veterans' benefits, life insurance proceeds that were made payable to the survivor rather than the estate, government annuity benefits, and workers' compensation death benefits.

Jointly-owned real estate is included in the valuation of your estate. See below and Figure 4.1, "How You Include Jointly Owned Real Property."

De Facto Estate Planning — Doing Nothing

If you do nothing, you already have done something. You have placed your estate planning in the hands of strangers. You will die subject to the laws of "intestate succession," which means that you did not leave a will.

If you die without a will and are married, most states specify that your spouse and children will inherit your estate. If you are single, your brothers and sisters and parents will share your estate. A dismal scenario would be if your only relative is someone who you would not want to receive your estate, a person you could have specifically excluded in a will.

If no legal heirs can be found, the state becomes your heir. The operative term is *escheat*, which means that all you own is forfeited to the state. Taking the time to prepare a will allows you to leave your funds to those you choose.

If you die without a will, the state will appoint an administrator through the probate court (which is responsible for dealing with wills). This person will be an attorney who is entitled to fees for his or her services. These fees usually are substantial, and will be deducted from the inheritance that your heirs receive. Attorneys' fees, court costs, and other expenses can consume a large chunk of your survivors' inheritance.

Real Property Ownership Considerations

How property is owned can make a major difference in the tax owed on that property during the settlement of an estate. There are different ways to own real property:

Outright Ownership of Real Estate

- This is the so-called "fee simple" type of ownership, which permits the owner to sell or exchange the property without the consent of anyone else. Any income or other gain from the sale or exchange belongs to the owner. The owner (which could be your estate, for example) is responsible for paying all of the expenses of the property: taxes, maintenance, repairs, and so on.

Joint Ownership of Property

- There are three forms of joint ownership commonly used in holding title to real estate: (1) joint tenants with rights of survivorship, (2) tenants by the entirety, and (3) tenants in common. Joint tenants and tenants by the entirety essentially are the same, except that a tenants-by-the-entirety relationship can exist only between a husband and wife. Under these forms of ownership, when one owner dies, his or her share is immediately transferred to the remaining owners by operation of law. An ownership interest under these forms of titling can be transferred only after a property has been legally divided. Ownership under a tenancy in common, on the other hand, has no survivorship rights, and each owner may dispose of his or her share at any time during his or her lifetime or under the terms of a will at death. (See Figure 4.1.)

In computing your gross estate, any part interest you have in real estate must be considered. For example, if you and your brother own a home as joint tenants, it is essential to be able to prove who contributed what proportionate amounts to the property. In the absence of such proof, 100 percent of the fair market value of the property must be included in your estate if you die before your brother. However, documentation showing that you contributed equally would result in your estate having to declare only one-half of the property's fair market value. If this joint property ownership arrangement continues until your death, your interest in the property would automatically pass on to your brother by right of survivorship.

How Property Passes After the Death of a Spouse

There are four ways that property can be transferred to a surviving spouse; i.e., by a will, by contract, as a gift, or through the operation of law.

All individually owned property, such as stocks, personal items, or cash, that is not passed on by law or contract can be transferred by a will. For example, family heirlooms may be left to specific individuals by making provisions in one's will.

Life insurance, annuity contracts, and trust agreements are contracts for transferring property. In a life insurance policy, the contract identifies the beneficiary who is to receive the proceeds of the policy. The same concept applies to the designation of a beneficiary to receive survivor benefits in an annuity contract. A trust agreement is an agreement between a grantor and a trustee on how to manage property. It can contain separate instructions for management before and after the grantor's death. In many ways, this trust serves as a substitute for a will (although it cannot ever fully satisfy this need).

In community property states, the settlement and distribution of estate assets are subject to additional rules.

There are several states where property acquired during a marriage is owned 50/50 by the wife and husband, regardless of the relative amount of financial contributions to the purchase of the property. They include Arizona, California, Idaho, Louisiana, New Mexico, Nevada, Texas, Washington, and Wisconsin. In these states, when one spouse dies, no more than one-half of the property may be disposed of by the deceased individual's will. The surviving spouse does not receive that one-half interest in the property unless the deceased spouse provides for this in his or her will, or unless state law provides for this type of action in the absence of a will. Two exceptions apply: (1) Property received by one spouse as a gift or an inheritance is separate; it does not become community property unless the recipient mixes it with marital assets. (2) Similarly, property acquired by one of the parties prior to the marriage also is excluded as long as it is kept separate after the marriage.

The Need for a Valid and Thorough Will

If you do not have a will, you are being foolish. Work with your attorney and have one prepared immediately. The creation of a thorough last will and testament ensures that your estate plan suits your needs. It also permits you to designate your own executor to administer your estate. Your spouse or a trusted friend can serve as executor, if you desire.

Your will provides the basis for leaving all of your assets to your spouse. Without a will, many state laws require proportional distribution of your assets between your spouse and children. It is important to note that the terms of a will are not fixed. A will is a living document that can be changed as your needs change over time. For example, you subsequently may decide to add special provisions for your grown children. Similarly, you may want to add provisions for assisting in the education of grandchildren. Your attorney has the expertise to create the wording needed to expedite the economical transfer of your estate to your survivors.

Most wills contain some or all of the following basic framework:

- *Introduction* — Specifies that you are the "testator" of the will, and includes a statement to the effect that you are of sound mind and are executing the document without coercion or restraint. It also gives details, such as your full name, address, marital status, and the identity of individuals covered by the stipulated provisions.
- *Specific Property Dispositions* — The purpose of the will is to dispose of property. (Joint property passes automatically.) Property dispositions involve clauses such as one specifying that your gold watch goes to your eldest son, etc.
- *Formula Disposing of Property* — Percentages of your gross estate that you want to go to a designated beneficiary (for example, 50 percent to your spouse and 25 percent for each of your two kids).
- *Residuary Clause* — How the rest of your property is to be distributed.
- *Simultaneous Death Provision* — Should you and your spouse die at the same time, a simultaneous death provision can help avoid the need for having the same property administered as part of two separate estates by creating a presumption that one spouse predeceased the other and that the survivor ended up with everything.
- *Guardianship Provision* — Identifies who cares for minor children.

Your Financial Guide

- *Names of Executors* — Who will be settling your estate.
- *Testamentary Trust* — Arrangement under which property other than money goes into a special trust that gives someone the benefit of its use for a period. It then passes directly to your children or other designated heirs without going through one more expensive estate settlement or a probate proceeding.
- *Signatures* — Testator (you) and witnesses sign the document in front of each other. A valid will requires either two or three witnesses depending on state law. It's best to have disinterested parties (who would be available in the future to certify that the will is valid) serve in this capacity. For extra legal protection, the signing should be witnessed by a notary public.

Since a will is so important to the future of your loved ones, secure it by keeping one copy at home with other important papers. You also should have another copy retained by your lawyer, and provide a third copy to the executor who has agreed to serve in this capacity.

Keep the original in your safety deposit box.

Using Trusts as Estate Planning Tools

A trust is a legal device for managing property. You can give property to another person (the trustee) to hold for you or for the benefit of another individual or individuals (the beneficiary/beneficiaries). There are numerous types of trusts to consider depending on the unique needs of your estate. A trust can be created during your lifetime or at death through your will. Your estate planner and attorney can explain the various types of trust arrangements and their respective advantages.

A "Living Trust" technique is becoming more popular as a means of avoiding probate. These so-called *inter vivos* trusts offer a great deal of flexibility. You or someone else creates the trust during your lifetime and he or she becomes the initial trustee. This gives you the option of changing its terms or canceling it. You retain control until you die or lose capacity, and then the person you named as successor trustee takes control. Even though transfer of control begins at the moment of death or incapacity, property in such a trust is not subject to probate because the property passes by the terms of the agreement, not by order of a court.

For many people, use of such a trust can be highly advantageous because the probate estate settlement process can be extremely time-consuming and expensive and can leave survivors in an unfavorable financial position for a long time. The problem is that in settling an estate through the probate process, final distributions aren't made to your survivors until all of your obligations are satisfied and the probate court approves the executor's or administrator's *final accounting*.

Property also may be left to your spouse in a "bypass" or family trust. This means that your spouse has an income interest in the property but never actually owns it. This trust is created in your will and, if properly drafted, allows the property within it to escape taxation as part of the estate of the second person to die. At the death of your spouse, the property can either be distributed to its ultimate beneficiaries or it can remain in trust until some later date specified in the trust document. When the spouse dies, the property goes to those next in line, typically the decedent's children.

An irrevocable life insurance trust created during your lifetime also can be used to pass money or property to your survivors. Your trustee buys a policy on your life based on premium contributions, which you provide for via annual gifts. When properly established, the contributions to the trust for premium payments do not generate a gift tax, if the beneficiaries have a right to withdraw the premiums that does not expire for at least 30 days after the gifts are made to the trust. When you die, the insurance proceeds are paid to the trust. The income from the trust is usually paid to the spouse for life and then to the children. If the children are still minors at the second death, the trust usually is kept in existence until the last child reaches the age of majority.

Property also may be left to a spouse in what is commonly referred to as a "Q-TIP" trust. This type of trust usually is used where there is a second marriage or where the spouse is a poor money manager. Under this arrangement, all property passing into the trust will not be taxed until the death of the surviving spouse. At that time the property will pass to designated heirs. Usually, these heirs are children of a prior marriage. Until the second death, the survivor receives all of the income of the trust and, depending on your wishes, may or may not invade the principal. Under no circumstances can the principal be distributed to anyone other than the surviving spouse.

Living Wills

A "living will" is a document that states your wishes for continued life-sustaining medical treatment if you suffer a terminal illness or injury. Most states allow an adult to make such an advance declaration instructing that life-sustaining procedures be withheld or withdrawn.

Should you wish to make such a declaration, be sure the language you use is clear and specific because it may be subject to interpretation later by doctors, your family, and possibly even the legal system. For example, you should define what you consider a "terminal condition" and what you consider to be "life-sustaining" care. You can obtain standard "living will" forms from many senior citizen centers, legal stationery stores, and medical and hospital associations.

Safeguarding Your Documents

Once you develop the documents, you must keep them in a secure place. One of the best places is a safety deposit box in a bank or other savings institution. It might be a good idea to arrange for your administrator, *if he or she also is an heir,* to have access to it. Otherwise, after your death, access might be delayed by legal requirements. In some states, for example, an officer of the court (usually a clerk) is required to be present when an executor without a safety deposit "signature card" opens the box.

Of course, you have to decide if you are comfortable with someone else having access to your safety deposit box while you are alive. Fortunately, the cost of renting a safety deposit box is tax deductible.

Preparing Information Worksheets for Survivors

Please take the time to complete the information worksheets included in the Appendix. In filling out these worksheets, you will be providing essential information needed by your survivors and executor. This will help avoid a time-consuming and possibly expensive search for information when you are no longer around to provide it. The information also may be helpful to your lawyer who could be unfamiliar with the complex laws and regulations governing your federal benefits. You might consider giving him or her a copy of this book to help in your estate planning process. You also may want to obtain related publications from *Federal Employees News Digest* that can be beneficial in this regard. You'll find a list of these FEND publications in the back of this book for your convenience.

You'll find that taking the time to compile this information also will help you in other ways. Knowing just what your assets and liabilities are can come in handy for other purposes, such as investing or planning for a major purchase or expense.

Protect the original copies of all your worksheets, including your personal estate inventory, net worth, location of assets, bank and CD serial numbers, insurance policy value, and stock and company names, etc., by storing them in your safety deposit box.

How You Include Jointly Owned Real Property
The following table shows how jointly owned real property is included in the valuation of your gross estate.

Type of Ownership	Definition	What's Included
UNMARRIED PERSONS		
Tenants in Common	Property owned by 2 or more persons in equal or unequal shares without rights of survivorship. Interest may be transferred during life or at death without consent of other owners.	Same percentage as you owned.
Joint	Property owned by two or more persons in equal shares with right of survivorship. Interest may be transferred during life without consent of other joint owners.	100 percent unless survivor's contribution is proven. If proven, your percentage of contribution is included
MARRIED PERSONS		
Tenants by the entirety	Property owned by married persons in equal shares with right of survivorship. Interest cannot be transferred during life without consent.	50 percent of value regardless of your contribution.
Community property	Property owned by married person in community states with right of survivorship.	50 percent of value regardless of your contribution.

Figure 4-1

Your Financial Guide

Settling Your Estate

"Probate" is the legal term used to describe the process of transferring your property to the heirs named in your will (or to others if you don't have a will). If you don't have a will, *intestate succession* laws apply.

The probate process is performed under supervision of the probate court of the city or county where you live. You should realize, however, that your executor will be dealing mainly with the court's clerical staff. The court certifies the will, examines the inventory of your property, and supervises its transfer to your heirs. The idea is to ensure that someone is accountable for your assets.

How the Probate Process Works

The probate process is designed to ensure that the deceased individual's assets are collected, debts are paid, and any remaining property is distributed according to law. Depending on the complexity of the estate and whether any legal challenges are filed, this process might last as little as a few months or it might take as long as several years. Should a legal challenge be brought—for example, by a potential inheritor questioning the validity of the will—formal proceedings likely will be conducted in court before a judge. In the absence of such challenges, the proceedings are more informal. They normally require only that the executor coordinate with court personnel; appearances before a judge usually are not required.

The Executor/Administrator

The executor, also called the administrator or personal representative, is named in your will. After you die, he or she (or they) will be responsible for managing your estate during probate. The executor acts on behalf of the deceased until all obligations are met and all property is transferred.

A person you designate as executor may, for some reason, be unable or unwilling to serve in that role. In such a case, a member of your family or a friend may ask the probate court to appoint one. Most states have laws setting priorities in the order of appointments in such cases. For example, a surviving spouse or adult children probably would have priority over parents or brothers and sisters. Some states also require the executor to be a resident of that state.

Trustworthiness and competence are the two most important attributes of an executor. It can take a surprisingly short time for a less than honest or incompetent executor to wipe out even large estates. The law may provide stiff penalties for a dishonest or poor administration of an estate, but this won't help your loved ones if the damage already has been done. Choose wisely.

The Importance of Witnesses

If your will is contested, the executor will have to attempt to locate surviving witnesses to the will. It is a good idea, therefore, to have your will witnessed by people well known to your family and friends. Also, it would be a good idea to include with your estate documents the latest addresses of your witnesses.

Witnesses may be required to provide testimony or affidavits to help establish the validity of the will. If the witnesses cannot be located, the judge may call other witnesses to verify that the signature on the will is yours and that you were competent at the time you signed the will.

A will can't be accepted for probate unless the court is satisfied that is authentic. If it can't be authenticated, the court probably will determine that you died without a will. The court then would appoint an administrator to perform the same duties that the executor would have accomplished. This is a time-consuming and potentially expensive process that may not end with your estate being settled as you wish. This is yet another good reason to make sure your will is properly prepared and can't be successfully contested.

Legal Help

Settling an estate frequently requires the services of an attorney. This is often the case—even where the estate is a relatively simple one—if the executor is a friend or family member who has little or no experience in such matters. In situations where estates are substantial or complicated, attorneys are hired regularly. While the attorney would be hired by and work with the executor, it is a good idea to prepare for this beforehand.

You should discuss the situation with your executor and may wish to designate an attorney in advance whom you want to help handle your estate, the settlement, or both. When engaging an attorney, it's a good idea to obtain a written agreement regarding the fees. Legal costs can mount quickly, much to the surprise of those unfamiliar with legal proceedings. Some states require court approval of such fees before the executor is permitted to compensate the attorney. The estate pays the legal fees.

Helping Your Executor Now

Being the executor of an estate is a complicated and time-consuming responsibility. Initially, the most important function of the executor is to locate, collect, and protect the deceased person's assets. Only then will the full extent of the estate be known. If the deceased had a claim against another individual, the executor must take action to recover the funds in question or to pay any debts owed. All funds recovered are placed into the estate.

You should bear in mind this range of responsibilities when choosing your executor, and should be sure to discuss any such issues with him or her before you make the formal designation. That person may not have the ability or the time to carry out all the duties that will arise.

You also should take steps now to make it as easy as possible for your executor to carry out these responsibilities. Among the most important duties the executor will be carrying out are:

- Filing the Will. The executor must file the last known valid will and any codicils or amendments with the probate court in the county or city where you resided.
- Posting a Performance Bond. The executor probably will be required to post a performance bond, which protects the heirs from mismanagement in the administration of the estate. The value of the bond is based on the size of the estate, the type of assets involved, etc., and will be determined at the time the will is filed. The bond is purchased at that time from a bonding company; they typically have required application forms available at probate court offices. The cost is borne by the estate.
- Notifying Interested Parties. The executor must provide notice to all interested parties who are named in the will or who otherwise are entitled to a share of your estate that the will has been filed. The purpose is to give such parties an opportunity to inspect the will by visiting the probate court office. This can involve a great deal of paperwork and phone calls on the executor's part.
- Notifying Known Creditors. The executor must send notice of the death to all known creditors, including banks, credit card companies, landlords, etc. Leases may have to be terminated and utilities may have to be disconnected or transferred.
- Advertising to Identify Unknown Creditors. The executor likely will have to notify any potential unknown creditors that the estate is being probated. This is typically done by publishing a notice in a local newspaper for a number of weeks. The notice should indicate that the individual has died and that any creditors must file claims with the executor.
- Making Deposits and Disbursements. This is accomplished by opening an estate checking account for making deposits and disbursements. The proceeds of insurance policies payable to the estate are deposited in the account, as are debts recovered from creditors. The executor also uses the account to pay valid debts owed by the estate, such as funeral expenses and disbursements for federal and state income, estate, or inheritance tax payments.
- Filing Tax Returns. The executor is responsible for filing tax returns on the estate's assets. Returns must be filed for any years or parts of a year in which the estate is still open.
- Making a Final Accounting to Probate Court. The executor must make an inventory of your assets and their estimated market values, and file this information with the probate court. This filing must include an accounting of all property sold or disposed of in some other manner, disbursements, and gains and losses, as well as details on distributions made to heirs or beneficiaries.

When the final accounting is submitted to the probate court, the executor applies for the termination of his or her appointment. At this time, the executor may submit an application for the payment of his or her reasonable fees and a detailed accounting of reimbursable expenses that were incurred. The executor need not make such a request, however. Spouses who serve as executors, for example, frequently do not apply for fee compensation.

CHAPTER FIVE

CALCULATING ANNUITY BENEFITS FOR RETIREES (CSRS AND FERS)

Whichever federal retirement system you are covered under, the annuity payments you and your survivors are entitled to represent one of the most valuable benefits related to your federal employment. Whether you are entitled to benefits under the Civil Service Retirement System, the Federal Employees' Retirement System, or both CSRS and FERS, the amount of your annuity (as well as the amount of your survivors' annuity payments) generally will be based on your age at retirement, years of service, and earnings.

Under either CSRS or FERS coverage, employees also should keep in mind that an extremely significant benefit of federal employment is the ability of a retiring worker to provide a survivor annuity for his or her spouse. CSRS survivor benefits generally amount to 55 percent of your own annuity, while full FERS survivor benefits generally amount to 50 percent of your annuity. Such an annuity not only provides a steady stream of income for your spouse, it also keeps up with inflation through annual COLAs as well.

Following is a closer look at how retirees' annuity amounts are calculated under the two main federal retirement systems. Although there are a few instances in which the CSRS and FERS rules are identical or similar (e.g., determining an individual's "high-3 average salary), to avoid confusion, all relevant annuity-calculation information is provided in the following separate discussions of the CSRS and FERS general benefit calculation procedures.

Overview of CSRS Annuities

If covered under CSRS, the retirement benefits you receive are purchased by the contributions you and your agency have made to the Civil Service Retirement Fund, which is administered by OPM. Generally, there are three types of retirement benefits available under CSRS:

Standard Retirement Benefits — These are available under CSRS to workers at age 55 with 30 years of service, at age 60 with 20 years, or at age 62 with five years. With any of these combinations of age and service, you may retire voluntarily at any time. Of course, the more years of service you have, the more you will receive in monthly annuity payments. While 30 years of service will produce an annuity that is 56.25 percent of your highest three years of average salary, 20 years will yield only 36.25 percent, and five years, only 7.5 percent (see Figure 5-1).

Early Retirement — Workers who are involuntarily separated from their jobs (such as in a reduction-in-force) are eligible for a retirement annuity if they: (1) have been employed under CSRS coverage for one year out of the last 2-year period immediately preceding the separation on which the annuity is based, and (2) meet either of the following requirements:

- They are at least age 50 and have 20 years of creditable service, including five years of civilian service; or
- Regardless of age, they have at least 25 years of creditable service, including five years of civilian service.

While leaving government on an "early out" before you are age 55 has its attractions, it also has its downside. Your annuity will be reduced by 2 percent (i.e., one-sixth percent per month) for every year that you are under 55. And, as noted under Standard Retirement (above), the fewer years' service you have, the smaller your annuity will be.

Deferred Retirement — Workers who leave their federal jobs after having completed at least five years of CSRS-covered service are eligible for benefits once they reach age 62. The amount of this deferred retirement benefit will be based on your years of service and highest three years of average salary at the time you separate from service. Of course, the longer the time between separation and age 62, the more inflation will have eroded the benefit's value. Another potential downside of deferred retirement is that your federal health benefits coverage will end on your separation. In addition, separated employees have no survivor protections if they die before they begin receiving a deferred annuity.

Calculating Your CSRS Annuity

Knowing the value of the annuity to which you will be entitled is important not only for determining your retirement income but also for estimating the amount of survivor benefits your spouse and dependent children would receive if you die after retiring. That's because the amount of survivor benefits is based on percentages of the standard basic retirement benefit.

To calculate your CSRS annuity, you first need to determine two things: your "creditable service" and your "high-3 average salary." Below are guidelines for making those determinations.

Creditable Service

To estimate the value of your annuity, the first thing you need to do is determine the years of creditable service you expect to have completed when you retire. Creditable service under CSRS includes:

- All federal civilian service during which retirement deductions were taken.
- Unused sick leave (see Figure 5-2). Accrued sick leave may be added, however, only after you have met the minimum creditable service requirements. It may not be used to meet those minimums. For example, if you are 55 and only have 29 years and six months of creditable service, you could not use six months of accumulated sick leave to meet the 30-year requirement for an immediate annuity.
- Most military service, as long as it was active service, terminated under honorable conditions, and performed before separation for civilian retirement. However, there are two exceptions to this general rule for crediting periods of military service:

  1. *Post-1956 military service* — If you were first employed under CSRS *before* October 1, 1982, you can either: a) make a 7 percent deposit for such service to avoid an annuity reduction at age 62 (and for your survivor as well), or b) decide not to pay the deposit and have your annuity reduced at age 62 if you are then eligible for Social Security benefits. For information on earnings during military service, write your branch of service. (See Figure 5-3 for a list of these addresses.)

  If you were first employed under CSRS *after* September 30, 1982, you will not receive credit for post-1956 military service for any purpose, unless you make a deposit covering that service prior to your separation from federal employment. If you choose not to make this deposit, you will not receive credit for that time for purposes of either annuity computations or retirement eligibility.

  Note: If you die and have not made a deposit for post-1956 military service, your survivor will be given an opportunity to do so. OPM will provide information that will help your survivor decide whether the additional annuity gained will be worth making the payment.

  2. *Military retiree pay* — If you are an employee receiving military retired pay and wish to have those years added to your civilian service, you must waive the military retired pay unless you were awarded that pay: a) on account of a service-connected disability incurred either in combat with an enemy of the United States or caused by an instrumentality of war and in the line of duty during a period of war; or b) under the provisions of Chapter 1223, Title 10, U.S. Code, which pertains to retirement from a reserve component of the Armed Forces.

Although it is possible to receive credit for periods of service for which no retirement deductions were made, in general, the circumstances that led to such service credits were eliminated at the time the Federal Employees' Retirement System was enacted. In most cases, if you do have such service and want it credited, you will be required to make a deposit covering the outstanding amounts, plus applicable interest.

Once you have added up your creditable years of service (plus sick leave), there is only one thing more you need to know before you can estimate your retirement annuity. That is your "high-3" average salary.

High-3 Average Salary

This term of art refers to the three consecutive years in which you received the highest level of civilian pay. For virtually all employees, these are their last 36 months of federal government employment. If you are ready to retire now, figuring out your "high-3" average salary is a snap.

If you are some years away from retirement, you will have to estimate your "high-3" salary. The easiest way to do that is to increase your salary by a percentage factor that you believe will best approximate future annual increases.

Earned CSRS Retirement Percentages
Based on Years of Service

Years of Service	Percent of High 3-Year Avg Earnings	Years of Service	Percent of High 3-Year Avg Earnings	Years of Service	Percent of High 3-Year Avg Earnings	Years of Service	Percent of High 3-Year Avg Earnings
5	7.50%	15	26.25%	25	46.25%	35	66.25%
6	9.25%	16	28.25%	26	48.25%	36	68.25%
7	11.00%	17	30.25%	27	50.25%	37	70.25%
8	12.75%	18	32.25%	28	52.25%	38	72.25%
9	14.50%	19	34.25%	29	54.25%	39	74.25%
10	16.25%	20	36.25%	30	56.25%	40	76.25%
11	18.25%	21	38.25%	31	58.25%	41	78.25%
12	20.25%	22	40.25%	32	60.25%	42	80.00%
13	22.25%	23	42.25%	33	62.25%	43	80.00%*
14	24.25%	24	44.25%	34	64.25%		

* Annuity in excess of 80%, which is produced by credit for unused sick leave, is payable in the case of CSRS employment.

Figure 5-1

Example
Current salary: $40,000
Estimated annual salary increases: 3 percent
Years to retirement: 3

- Year 1: $40,000
- Year 2: $41,200 ($40,000 x 3% = $1,200 + $40,000)
- Year 3: $42,436 ($41,200 x 3% = $1,236 + $41,200)

Estimated "high-3" average salary: $41,212

If you believe you will be promoted to a higher grade or grades along the way, you will want to factor those higher salary levels in as well.

CSRS Basic Annuity Computation Formula

The basic CSRS annuity computation formula is a rather simple one. However, there are numerous special circumstances, which may or may not apply to you, that can either increase or decrease that basic amount. These circumstances are described below.

To compute your basic annuity under CSRS, follow these steps:

- Take 1.5 percent of your "high-3" average pay and multiply the result by service up to 5 years.
- Take 1.75 percent of your "high-3" average pay, multiplied by all service over 5 and up to 10 years.
- Take 2 percent of the "high-3" average pay, multiplied by all service over 10 years.

Adding the amounts derived from each of the three steps will give you your annual annuity. In turn, dividing that sum by 12 will produce your monthly benefit amount.

Example
Age 56
30 years of service
$40,000 "high-3" average salary

A. 1.5 % x $40,000 x 5 years = $3,000
B. 1.75 % x $40,000 x 5 years = $3,500
C. 2 % x $40,000 x 20 years = $16,000

Chart for Converting Unused Sick Leave Into Increased Servicetime Credit for Higher Annuities (CSRS Employees Only)

No. of Days	1 Day & Up	1 Mo. & Up	2 Mo. & Up	3 Mo. & Up	4 Mo. & Up	5 Mo. & Up	6 Mo. & Up	7 Mo. & Up	8 Mo. & Up	9 Mo. & Up	10 Mo. & Up	11 Mo. & Up
0	-	174	348	522	696	870	1044	1217	1391	1565	1739	1913
1	6	180	354	528	701	875	1049	1223	1397	1571	1745	1919
2	12	186	359	533	707	881	1055	1229	1403	1577	1751	1925
3	17	191	365	539	713	887	1061	1235	1409	1583	1757	1930
4	23	197	371	545	719	893	1067	1241	1415	1588	1762	1936
5	29	203	377	551	725	899	1072	1246	1420	1594	1768	1942
6	35	209	383	557	730	904	1078	1252	1426	1600	1774	1948
7	41	214	388	562	736	910	1084	1258	1432	1606	1780	1954
8	46	220	394	568	742	916	1090	1264	1438	1612	1786	1959
9	52	226	400	574	748	922	1096	1270	1444	1617	1791	1965
10	58	232	406	580	754	928	1101	1275	1449	1623	1797	1971
11	64	238	412	586	759	933	1107	1281	1455	1629	1803	1977
12	70	243	417	591	765	939	1113	1287	1461	1635	1809	1983
13	75	249	423	597	771	945	1119	1293	1467	1641	1815	1988
14	81	255	429	603	777	951	1125	1299	1472	1646	1820	1994
15	87	261	435	609	783	957	1130	1304	1478	1652	1826	2000
16	93	267	441	615	788	962	1136	1310	1484	1658	1832	2006
17	99	272	446	620	794	968	1142	1316	1490	1664	1838	2012
18	104	278	452	626	800	974	1148	1322	1496	1670	1844	2017
19	110	284	458	632	806	980	1154	1328	1501	1675	1849	2023
20	116	290	464	638	812	986	1159	1333	1507	1681	1855	2029
21	122	296	470	643	817	991	1165	1339	1513	1687	1861	2035
22	128	301	475	649	823	997	1171	1345	1519	1693	1867	2041
23	133	307	481	655	829	1003	1177	1351	1525	1699	1873	2046
24	139	313	487	661	835	1009	1183	1357	1530	1704	1878	2052
25	145	319	493	667	841	1015	1188	1362	1536	1710	1884	2058
26	151	325	499	672	846	1020	1194	1368	1542	1716	1890	2064
27	157	330	504	678	852	1026	1200	1374	1548	1722	1896	2070
28	162	336	510	684	858	1032	1206	1380	1554	1728	1901	2075
29	168	342	516	690	864	1038	1212	1386	1559	1733	1907	2081

HOW TO USE THIS CHART - To find the increased service time credit for unused sick leave, use the following formula: find the number of hours of unused sick leave. In the horizontal column you will find the number of months and in the vertical column the remaining number of days. For example, 441 hours equals two months and 16 days. Another example: 1455 hours equals eight months and 11 days.

Note: For retirement credit purposes, sick leave days are generally six hours long. By law there are 2,087 hours in a work year. Since OPM calculates annuities on a 360-day year (12 equal months of 30 days length), 360 divided into 2,087 equals roughly six hours.

Figure 5-2

Your Financial Guide

Basic Annuity = $22,500 ÷ 12 = $1,875 per month

Following is an overall summary of the step-by-step process you should take to determine the amount of your basic monthly annuity (before any required or voluntary reductions):

1. Determine your estimated age at retirement _____

2. Calculate your estimated years of service _____

3. Compute your estimated "high-3" average salary
   $_____

   A. 1.5% x $_____ x 5 years = $ _____
   B. 1.75% x $_____ x 5 years = $ _____
   C. 2% x $_____ x _____ years = $_____
   Basic Annuity = $ (Sum of A, B, and C) ÷ 12
                 = $ _____ per month

(For a quick method of determining your CSRS monthly annuity, see the "CSRS Retirement Table" found in Figure 5-4.)

A Word for CSRS-Offset Employees

The calculation for CSRS-Offset employees is identical to that for employees whose whole government career is based on CSRS coverage alone. However, since CSRS-Offset employees also are covered by Social Security, their CSRS annuity at age 62 will be reduced ("offset") by the estimated amount of their Social Security benefit that is attributable to Offset service. Although the process by which this is done is not precise, by legislative intent it should not work to the disadvantage of retirees. In fact, it generally results in a slightly higher retirement benefit.

To determine a CSRS-Offset annuity, compute your CSRS annuity entitlement based on your high-three year average salary and length of service, plus any other pertinent adjustments, as if you were covered by CSRS alone. When you become eligible for Social Security benefits, usually at age 62, the CSRS annuity will be reduced by the amount of Social Security earned in federal service.

To accomplish this, the Social Security Administration takes the earnings for the time you were covered by both Social Security and CSRS and computes a Social Security benefit two ways: with the earnings included and with them excluded. It then sends this information to OPM to determine the offset amount. The amounf of the offset reduction will be the lesser of the following two figures:

1) The difference between the Social Security monthly benefit amount with and without CSRS-Offset service; or
2) The product obtained by multiplying the Social Security monthly benefit amount (with federal earnings) by a fraction whose numerator is the employee's total amount of CSRS-Offset service (rounded to the nearest whole number of years) and whose denominator is 40. As a formula, this can be expressed as Social Security Benefit x (Years of Offset Service ÷ 40).

Example
Assume that you retire at age 61 with a high-3 average salary of $40,000 and 30 years of federal service, including 10 years of CSRS-only coverage and 20 years of Offset coverage, plus 10 more years of Social

---

Service Branch Addresses

Army
DFAS - Indianapolis Center
Fort Benjamin Harrison
Indianapolis, IN 46249-0001

Navy
Director
DEAS -Cleveland Center
Anthony J. Celebreeze Federal Building
Cleveland, OH 44199-2055

Air Force
DRAS - Denver Center
Lowry AFB
Denver, CO 80279-5000

Coast Guard
Commanding Officer (SIR)
Settlements and Records
Military Pay and Personnel Center
444 SE Quincy Street
Topeka, KS 66683-3591

Public Health Service
Division of Commissioned Personnel
Compensation Branch
Parklawn Building, Room 4-50
5600 Fisher's Lane
Rockville, MD 20857

Figure 5-3

CSRS Retirement Table

Monthly Annuities Computed Under Basic Formulae

(Second line of each salary level reflects annuity with survivor deduction.)

Basic annuity is subject to reduction if (a) deductions are not in the fund for any service since August 1, 1920, (b) retirement—except for disability—is before age 55, (c) a survivor-type annuity is elected at retirement.

Highest 3 Year Average Salary	5	10	15	16	17	18	19	20	21	22	23	24	25	30	35	40	42	Amounts For Each Addl Yr. Unlisted
20,000	125	271	438	471	504	538	571	604	638	671	704	738	771	938	1,104	1,271	1,338	33
	122	264	416	446	476	506	536	566	596	626	656	686	716	866	1,016	1,166	1,266	
23,000	144	311	503	541	580	618	656	695	733	771	810	848	886	1,078	1,270	1,461	1,538	38
	140	304	475	510	544	579	613	648	682	717	751	786	820	993	1,165	1,338	1,407	
26,000	163	352	569	612	655	699	742	785	829	872	915	959	1,002	1,219	1,435	1,652	1,739	43
	158	339	534	573	612	651	690	729	768	807	846	885	924	1,119	1,314	1,509	1,587	
30,000	188	406	656	706	756	806	856	906	956	1,006	1,056	1,106	1,156	1,406	1,656	1,906	1,006	50
	183	388	613	658	703	748	793	838	883	928	973	1,018	1,063	1,288	1,513	1,738	1,828	
33,000	206	447	722	777	832	887	942	997	1,052	1,107	1,162	1,217	1,272	1,547	1,822	2,097	2,207	55
	201	425	672	722	771	821	870	920	969	1,019	1,068	1,118	1,167	1,415	1,662	1,910	2,009	
36,000	225	488	788	848	908	968	1,028	1,088	1,148	1,208	1,268	1,328	1,388	1,688	1,988	2,288	2,408	60
	219	461	731	785	839	893	947	1,001	1,055	1,109	1,163	1,217	1,271	1,541	1,811	2,081	2,189	
40,000	250	542	875	942	1,008	1,075	1,142	1,208	1,275	1,342	1,408	1,475	1,542	1,875	2,208	2,542	2,675	66
	244	510	810	870	930	990	1,050	1,110	1,170	1,230	1,290	1,350	1,410	1,710	2,010	2,310	2,430	
43,000	269	582	941	1,012	1,084	1,156	1,227	1,299	1,371	1,442	1,514	1,586	1,657	2,016	2,374	2,732	2,876	72
	262	547	869	934	998	1,063	1,127	1,192	1,256	1,321	1,385	1,450	1,514	1,837	2,159	2,482	2,611	
46,000	288	623	1,006	1,083	1,160	1,236	1,313	1,390	1,466	1,543	1,620	1,696	1,773	2,156	2,540	2,923	3,076	76
	280	583	928	997	1,066	1,135	1,204	1,273	1,342	1,411	1,480	1,549	1,618	1,963	2,308	2,653	2,791	
50,000	313	677	1,094	1,177	1,260	1,344	1,427	1,510	1,594	1,677	1,760	1,844	1,927	2,344	2,760	3,177	3,344	83
	304	632	1,007	1,082	1,157	1,232	1,307	1,382	1,457	1,532	1,607	1,682	1,757	2,132	2,507	2,882	3,032	
53,000	331	718	1,159	1,248	1,336	1,424	1,513	1,601	1,689	1,778	1,866	1,954	2,043	2,484	2,926	3,368	3,544	88
	323	668	1,066	1,145	1,225	1,304	1,384	1,463	1,543	1,622	1,702	1,781	1,861	2,258	2,656	3,053	3,212	
56,000	350	758	1,225	1,318	1,412	1,505	1,598	1,692	1,785	1,878	1,972	2,065	2,158	2,625	3,092	3,558	3,745	93
	341	705	1,125	1,209	1,293	1,377	1,461	1,545	1,629	1,713	1,797	1,881	1,965	2,385	2,805	3,225	3,393	
60,000	375	813	1,313	1,413	1,513	1,613	1,713	1,813	1,913	2,013	2,113	2,213	2,313	2,813	3,313	3,813	4,013	100
	366	754	1,204	1,294	1,384	1,474	1,564	1,654	1,744	1,834	1,924	2,014	2,104	2,554	3,004	3,454	3,634	
63,000	394	853	1,378	1,483	1,588	1,693	1,798	1,903	2,008	2,113	2,218	2,323	2,428	2,953	3,478	4,003	4,213	105
	384	790	1,263	1,357	1,452	1,546	1,641	1,735	1,830	1,924	2,019	2,113	2,208	2,680	3,153	3,625	3,814	
66,000	413	894	1,444	1,554	1,664	1,774	1,884	1,994	2,104	2,214	2,324	2,434	2,544	3,094	3,644	4,194	4,414	110
	394	827	1,322	1,421	1,520	1,619	1,718	1,817	1,916	2,015	2,114	2,213	2,312	2,807	3,302	3,797	3,995	
70,000	438	948	1,531	1,648	1,765	1,881	1,998	2,115	2,231	2,348	2,465	2,581	2,698	3,281	3,865	4,448	4,681	116
	416	876	1,401	1,506	1,611	1,716	1,821	1,926	2,031	2,136	2,241	2,346	2,451	2,976	3,501	4,026	4,236	
73,000	456	989	1,597	1,719	1,840	1,962	2,085	2,205	2,327	2,449	2,570	2,692	2,814	3,422	4,030	4,639	4,882	122
	433	912	1,460	1,569	1,679	1,788	1,898	2,007	2,117	2,226	2,336	2,445	2,555	3,102	3,650	4,197	4,416	
76,000	475	1,029	1,663	1,789	1,916	2,043	2,169	2,296	2,423	2,549	2,676	2,803	2,929	3,563	4,196	4,829	5,083	126
	450	949	1,519	1,633	1,747	1,861	1,975	2,089	2,203	2,317	2,431	2,545	2,659	3,229	3,799	4,369	4,597	
80,000	500	1,083	1,750	1,883	2,017	2,150	2,283	2,417	2,550	2,683	2,817	2,950	3,083	3,750	4,417	5,083	5,350	133
	473	998	1,598	1,718	1,838	1,958	2,078	2,198	2,318	2,438	2,558	2,678	2,798	3,398	3,998	4,598	4,838	
83,000	519	1,124	1,816	1,954	2,092	2,231	2,369	2,507	2,646	2,784	2,922	3,061	3,199	3,891	4,582	5,274	5,551	138
	489	1,034	1,657	1,781	1,906	2,030	2,155	2,279	2,404	2,528	2,653	2,777	2,902	3,524	4,147	4,769	5,018	
86,000	538	1,165	1,881	2,025	2,168	2,311	2,455	2,598	2,741	2,885	3,028	3,171	3,315	4,031	4,748	5,465	5,751	143
	506	1,071	1,716	1,845	1,974	2,103	2,232	2,361	2,490	2,619	2,748	2,877	3,006	3,651	4,296	4,941	5,199	
90,000	563	1,219	1,969	2,119	2,269	2,419	2,569	2,719	2,869	3,019	3,169	3,319	3,469	4,219	4,969	5,719	6,019	150
	529	1,119	1,794	1,929	2,064	2,199	2,334	2,469	2,604	2,739	2,874	3,009	3,144	3,819	4,494	5,169	5,439	
93,000	581	1,259	2,034	2,189	2,344	2,499	2,654	2,809	2,964	3,119	3,274	3,429	3,584	4,359	5,134	5,909	6,219	155
	546	1,156	1,853	1993	2,132	2,272	2,411	2,551	2,690	2,830	2,969	3,109	3,248	3,946	4,643	5,341	5,620	
96,000	600	1,300	2,100	2,260	2,420	2,580	2,740	2,900	3,060	3,220	3,380	3,540	3,700	4,500	5,300	6,100	6,420	160
	563	1,193	1,913	2,057	2,201	2,345	2,489	2,633	2,777	2,921	3,065	3,209	3,353	4,073	4,793	5,513	5,801	
100,000	625	1,354	2,188	2,354	2,521	2,688	2,854	3,021	3,188	3,354	3,521	3,688	3,854	4,688	5,521	6,354	6,688	167
	585	1,241	1,991	2,141	2,291	2,441	2,591	2,741	2,891	3,041	3,191	3,341	3,491	4,241	4,991	5,741	6,041	
110,000	688	1,490	2,406	2,590	2,773	2,956	3,140	3,323	3,506	3,690	3,873	4,056	4,240	5,156	6,073	6,990	7,356	183
	641	1,363	2,188	2,353	2,518	2,683	2,848	3,013	3,178	3,343	3,508	3,673	3,838	4,663	5,488	6,313	6,643	

The above figures are rounded to the nearest dollar

Example illustrating computations: Assume an Average Salary of $40,000 at 24 years of service:

For 1st 5 years use:	1 1/2% x $40,000 x 5 = $3,000.00
For 2nd 5 years use:	1 3/4% x $40,000 x 5 = 3,500.00
For balance of 14 years use:	2% x $40,000 x 14 = 11,200.00
	Total annual annuity $17,700.00

Divide by 12 (months) = $1,475 a month. If a survivor annuity is elected, the monthly annuity would be reduced to $1,350.

Figure 5-4

Your Financial Guide

Security coverage from private-sector work. At retirement, your annual CSRS annuity would be $22,500 under the CSRS general formula. At age 62, you also would be eligible for a Social Security benefit of $7,000 (for purposes of this example). Of this $7,000, let's assume that $5,000 is attributable to your Offset service time and $2,000 to your private-sector work.

The CSRS benefit is reduced by the Social Security amount attributable to Offset service, limited by the Offset formula. In this case, the formula calls for multiplying the Social Security benefit ($7,000) by the years of Offset service (20), and then dividing that result by 40, which equals $3,500. Thus the CSRS benefit of $22,500 is reduced by $3,500, leaving $19,000.

However, since you are eligible for the full Social Security benefit of $7,000, your total benefit at age 62 will be $26,000 ($19,000 plus $7,000).

If you had only CSRS time and the 10 years of private-sector Social Security coverage, your benefit at age 62 would be $22,500 in CSRS, plus the $2,000 in Social Security from the private-sector coverage, for a total of $24,500. Thus, because of the Offset formula, your status as on Offset plan employee means that you would end up slightly better off than an employee with pure CSRS coverage.

Note: *If you have Social Security coverage in the private sector, the amount of reduction in the CSRS benefit generally will be less than the Social Security benefit to which you will be entitled. If ineligible for Social Security benefits at age 62, you will continue to receive your full CSRS benefits.*

Special Annuity Systems

Employees in certain positions, including law enforcement, firefighter, and air traffic controller jobs, are subject to special CSRS annuity rules.

Law enforcement and firefighter personnel may voluntarily retire if they are age 50 or over and have completed at least 20 years of such service. In addition, there are special provisions for computing their annuities. If you fit into one of these categories, under CSRS you are entitled to 2.5 percent times your average "high-3" salary, multiplied by the number of years you served in a law enforcement or firefighter position (not to exceed 20 years). To this, you add 2 percent times your average "high-3" salary for years served in excess of 20 (or in a position that did not involve law enforcement or fire fighting), as well as credits for unused sick leave.

Note: *There is no reduction in annuity for employees retiring under age 55.*

Air traffic controllers must generally be separated from service on the last day of the month in which they turn age 56. However, this law does not apply to anyone appointed by the Department of Transportation before May 16, 1972, or by the Department of Defense before September 12, 1980.

If you are an air traffic controller, you are entitled to optional retirement at age 50 with 20 years of ATC service or at any age with 25 years as an ATC.

Although there is no special annuity computation, if you retire under this provision you are guaranteed an annuity of not less than 50 percent of your "high-3" average pay.

Potential Reductions in Your CSRS Annuity

Once a basic annuity has been computed it may be reduced for several reasons. These include:

- *Reduction for Age* — This applies if you retire under early retirement or optional retirement based on a combination of age and length of service. It equals one-sixth of one percent for each full month under age 55. (Remember, this reduction does not apply to those under a 20-year retirement system.) This reduction will not end when you reach age 55.

- *Reduction for Unpaid Deposits* — The reduction equals 10 percent of the unpaid deposits for service prior to October 1, 1982. No credit can be given for non-deduction service after October 1, 1982, unless a deposit is made to OPM.

- *Reduction for Unpaid Redeposits* — In most cases, if you received a refund of your retirement contributions and have not made a redeposit, you may either repay it when you retire or, if the refunded service ended before October 1, 1990, have your annuity reduced by an actuarial formula. Repayment allows you to get full credit for the years of service for which you received the refund.

- *Reduction for Survivor Annuity* — The reduction for a full survivor election is around 9 percent of the retiree's basic annuity after it has been reduced for age and unpaid deposits. For a partial survivor election, the reduction is usually less. How much less depends on the amount of annuity you and your spouse select as a base for the computation. A court-ordered survivor annuity results in a deduction of 10 percent of the court-ordered base.

- *Reduction for Post-1956 Military Service* — If you were first hired on or after October 1, 1982, you can only receive credit for military service performed after 1956 if you pay a percentage (generally, 7 percent) of the military pay you earned, plus interest to your employing agency. If you were hired before October 1, 1982, you have the option of making a deposit. If you don't make this deposit and become eligible for a Social Security retirement benefit at age 62, those years of service and the money associated with them will be subtracted from your CSRS annuity. (See Figure 5-3 for a list of addresses you may use to get information about your post-1956 military service earnings.)

- *Reduction for Alternative Annuity* — If you are eligible for retirement and suffer from an illness or condition that generally would limit your life to two years, you have the right to choose a lump-sum payment equal to the amount of your contributions to the retirement system and a reduced monthly annuity (the amount of which will be determined by an actuarial formula).

Interest Charges

To capture non-deposit service, the full amount must be paid with interest. The amount of interest charged varies depending on the time and circumstances of the contribution. On the other hand, service for which a refund of contributions has been made can be credited by making a redeposit payment with interest (without such a redeposit, the annuity will be reduced actuarially).

In most cases, interest on redeposits is charged at the rates shown in Figure 5-5.

Interest Charges	
Prior to 12/31/47	4.000%
1/1/48 to 12/31/84	3.000
1985	13.000
1986	11.100
1987	9.000
1988	8.400
1989	9.100
1990	8.750
1991	8.625
1992	8.125
1993	7.125
1994	6.250
1995	7.000
1996	6.875
1997	6.875

Exceptions to the above rates are: (1) Nondeduction service earned before October 1, 1982, and redeposits of refunds made before October 1, 1982: Interest is charged at 3% in all years; and (2) Military service — Interest is only charged beginning two years after the beginning of civilian employment. In any event, interest is not charged before October 1985.

Figure 5-5

Maximum CSRS Annuity Amount

The basic annuity for CSRS retirement cannot exceed 80 percent of your "high-3" average salary. To qualify for the top amount you would need to accumulate 41 years and 11 months of service. Should you work more than 41 years and 11 months, your excess deposits will be applied to any redeposits you may owe. If you don't owe any, the excess deposits will be returned to you in a lump-sum payment at retirement.

Note: The 80 percent limitation does not apply to credits given for unused sick leave or subsequent increases in your annuity as a result of cost-of-living adjustments (COLAs).

Overview of FERS Annuities

If you are covered by the Federal Employees' Retirement System, your FERS benefits are the first element making up your basic retirement and survivor benefits package. The other two pieces of your basic retirement package are Social Security benefits and contributions to your Thrift Savings Plan account.

Like CSRS benefits, the amount of FERS benefits paid to federal retirees and their survivors generally depends on an employee's age, years of service, and earnings. Similarly, as with CSRS coverage, one of the most valuable benefits of FERS coverage is your ability to provide a survivor annuity for your spouse at retirement. Full FERS survivor benefits are 50 percent of your own annuity. Reduced survivor benefits are 25 percent of your own annuity and may be elected *only* with the concurrence of your spouse.

Types of FERS Annuities

There are three categories of retirement benefits in FERS: Standard, Early, and Deferred.

Standard Retirement – Eligibility for a standard FERS annuity usually is determined by your age and number of years of service. In some cases, you must have reached the Minimum Retirement Age (MRA) to receive retirement benefits. You can determine your Minimum Retirement Age by referring to the following chart:

Minimum Retirement Age

If you were born before 1948	Your MRA is 55
in 1948	55 and 2 months
in 1949	55 and 4 months
in 1950	55 and 6 months
in 1951	55 and 8 months
in 1952	55 and 10 months
In 1953 through 1964	Your MRA is 56
in 1965	56 and 2 months
in 1966	56 and 4 months
in 1967	56 and 6 months
in 1968	56 and 8 months
in 1969	56 and 10 months
In 1970 and after	Your MRA is 57

The amount of standard retirement benefits you will receive under FERS is determined by your age and length of service. Since the amount of your annuity is based on years of service, the more years you have, the higher your annuity will be. If you meet one of the following sets of age and service requirements, you are entitled to retire on an immediate annuity:

Age	Years of Service
62	5
60	20
MRA	30
MRA	10*

* With reduced benefits. Reduced benefits means that if you retire at the MRA with at least 10 but less than 30 years of service, your benefit will be reduced by 5 percent a year for each year you are under age 62 (unless you have 20 years of service and your annuity begins at age 60 or later).

Early Retirement — Early retirement is available to most individuals who are involuntarily separated and to those voluntarily separated during a major reorganization or reduction-in-force (RIF). To be eligible, you must meet the following requirements:

Age	Years of service
50	20
Any Age	25

While leaving government on an "early out" has its attractions, it also has a downside. As noted under Standard Retirement (above), the fewer years of service you have, the smaller your annuity will be.

Deferred Retirement — If you leave federal service before you meet the age and service requirements for an immediate annuity, you may be eligible for deferred retirement benefits. To be eligible, you must have completed at least five years of creditable civilian service. You may then receive benefits when you reach one of the age and service combinations shown under Standard Retirement (see above). Of course, the longer the time between the dates you leave government service and your annuity comes due, the more inflation will have eroded the value of your retirement benefit.

Warning: *By law, if you withdraw your FERS contributions when you leave government, the service covered by those contributions is lost and cannot be recaptured.*

Calculating Your FERS Annuity

Similar to an employee with CSRS coverage, the ability to calculate the value of the FERS annuity to which you will be entitled is important not only for determining your retirement income, but also for estimating the amount of survivor benefits your spouse and dependent children would receive if you die after retiring. That's because the amount of survivor benefits is based on percentages of the standard basic retirement benefit.

To calculate your FERS annuity, you first need to determine two things: your "creditable service" and your "high-3 average salary." Below are guidelines for making those determinations.

Creditable Service

To estimate the value of your annuity, the first thing you need to do is determine the years of creditable service you expect to have completed when you retire. For FERS coverage purposes, creditable service generally includes:

- Federal civilian service for which contributions have been made or deposited;
- Most military service, as long as it was active service that was terminated under honorable conditions and performed before separation for civilian retirement. However, there are two exceptions to this general rule:

1. Post-1956 military service—To receive credit for post-1956 military service before you were covered by FERS, you must deposit 3 percent of your military base pay. Interest begins two years after you are hired, or January 1, 1989, whichever is later. For information on earnings during military service, write your branch of service. (See Figure 5-3 for the addresses.)

   Note: If you die without making a deposit for post-1956 military service, your survivor will be given an opportunity to do so. OPM will provide information that will help your survivor decide whether the additional annuity gained will be worth making the payment.

2. Retired military — If you are an employee receiving military retired pay and wish to have those years added to your civilian service, you must waive the military retired pay unless you were awarded that pay: a) on account of a service-connected disability either incurred in combat with an enemy of the United States or caused by an instrumentality of war in the line of duty during a period of war, or b) under the provisions of Chapter 1223, Title 10, U.S. Code, which pertains to retirement from a Reserve component of the Armed Forces.

- Leaves of absence for performing military service or while receiving workers' compensation.
- Unused sick leave (CSRS component only, if you have one). Unused sick leave may be added to the CSRS component only after you have met the minimum creditable service requirements for retirement. It may not be used to meet those minimums. Nor may it be added to the FERS component.

Although it also is possible to receive credit for service for which no retirement deductions were made, the circumstances that led to such service generally were eliminated at the time FERS was enacted. If you do have such service, you normally must make a deposit to cover the outstanding amounts, plus applicable interest.

Once you have added up your creditable years of service (plus sick leave if you have a CSRS component), there is only one thing more you need to know before you can estimate your retirement annuity. And that is your "high-3" average salary.

High-3 Average Salary

This term of art refers to the three consecutive years in which you received the highest level of civilian pay. For virtually all employees, these are their last 36 months of federal government employment. If you are ready to retire now, figuring out your "high-3" average salary is a snap.

If you are some years away from retirement, you will have to estimate your "high-3." The easiest way to do that is to increase your salary by a percentage factor that you believe will best approximate future annual increases.

Example

Current salary: $40,000
Estimated annual salary increase: 3 percent
Years to retirement: 3

- Year 1: $40,000
- Year 2: $41,200 ($40,000 × 3% = $1,200 + $40,000)
- Year 3: $42,436 ($41,200 × 3% = $1,236 + $41,200)

Estimated "high-3" average salary: $41,212

If you also believe you will be promoted to a higher grade or grades along the way, you will want to factor those dollar amounts in, too.

FERS Annuity Computation Formulas

If you are under age 62 when you retire—or have fewer than 20 years of creditable service—the basic computation formula for calculating the annual amount of your FERS annuity is:
1% × "high-3" average salary × length of service

In turn, dividing this amount by 12 will produce your monthly FERS annuity. For a quick method of calculating your FERS annuity, see Figure 5-6.

Example 1— Standard Retirement
Age 60
25 years of total service
$40,000 "high-3" average salary
1% × $40,000 × 25 = $10,000 ÷ 12 = $833.33 per month

Example 2 — Early Retirement
Age 57
18 years of total service
$35,000 "high-3" average salary
1% × $35,000 × 18 = $6,300 ÷ 12 = $525 per month

FERS Multiplier — If you are at least age 62 and have performed at least 20 years of creditable service, the percentage multiplier for determining a FERS annuity is raised from 1 percent to 1.1 percent.

Example 3 — Higher Multiplier
Age 62
30 years of total service
$45,000 "high-3" average salary
1.1% × $45,000 × 30 = $14,850 ÷ 12 = $1,237.50/month

FERS Combined Basic Annuity

This type of "combined" annuity is paid to people who have service covered under both CSRS and FERS. Many FERS employees have CSRS service in their work histories. For those employees, their basic annuity is the sum of the CSRS and FERS annuity components. The following example shows how that is done.

Example

20 years applied to the CSRS component
10 years applied to the FERS component
$45,000 "high-3" average salary

Step 1 — Compute the CSRS Annuity Component

1.5% × $45,000 × 5 years of service	= $3,375
1.75% × $45,000 × 5 years of service	= $3,938
2% × $45,000 × 10 years of service	= $9,000
Sum of above lines	= $16,313

Step 2 — Compute the FERS Annuity Component

1% × $45,000 × 10 = $4,500

Step 3 — FERS Combined Annuity = $20,813

(Add Step 1 to Step 2, divide by 12) = $1,734.42 per month

For a quick method of calculating your CSRS component, see Figure 5-4.

Special Retirement Supplement

If you meet certain requirements, you will receive a special retirement supplement, which is paid as an annuity until you reach age 62. This supplement approximates the Social Security benefit earned while you were employed under FERS. You will be eligible for the supplement if you:

- Retire after the Minimum Retirement Age (MRA) with 30 years of service.
- Retire at age 60 with 20 years of service.

FERS Retirement Table

Monthly Basic Annuity Amounts Based on "High-3" Salary And Years of Service For Employees

(Second line of each salary level reflects annuity *with* survivor deduction.)

Highest 3 Year Average Salary	5	10	15	16	17	78	19	20	21	22	23	24	25	30	35	40	42	Amounts For Each Addl Yr. Unlisted
20,000	83	167	250	267	283	300	317	333	350	367	383	400	417	500	583	667	700	16
	75	150	225	240	255	270	285	300	315	330	345	360	375	450	525	600	630	
23,000	96	192	288	307	326	345	364	383	403	422	441	460	479	575	671	767	805	19
	86	173	259	276	293	311	328	345	362	380	397	414	431	518	604	690	725	
26,000	108	217	325	347	368	390	412	433	455	477	498	521	542	650	758	867	910	21
	98	195	293	312	332	351	371	390	410	429	449	468	488	585	683	780	819	
30,000	125	250	375	400	425	450	475	500	525	550	575	600	625	750	875	1,000	1,050	25
	113	225	338	360	383	405	428	450	473	495	518	540	563	675	788	900	945	
33,000	138	275	413	440	468	495	523	550	578	605	633	660	688	825	963	1,100	1,155	27
	124	248	371	396	421	446	470	495	520	545	569	594	619	743	866	990	1,040	
36,000	150	300	450	480	510	540	570	600	630	660	690	720	750	900	1,050	1,200	1,260	30
	135	270	405	432	459	486	513	540	567	594	621	648	675	810	945	1,080	1,134	
40,000	167	333	500	533	567	600	633	667	700	733	767	800	833	1,000	1,167	1,333	1,400	33
	150	300	450	480	510	540	570	600	630	660	690	720	750	900	1,050	1,200	1,260	
43,000	179	358	538	573	609	645	681	717	753	788	824	860	896	1,075	1,254	1,433	1,505	36
	161	323	484	516	548	581	613	645	671	710	742	774	806	968	1,129	1,290	1,355	
46,000	192	383	575	613	652	690	728	767	805	843	882	920	958	1,150	1,342	1,533	1,610	38
	173	345	518	552	587	621	656	690	725	759	794	828	863	1,035	1,208	1,380	1,449	
50,000	208	417	625	667	708	750	792	833	875	917	958	1,000	1,042	1,250	1,458	1,667	1,750	41
	188	375	563	600	638	675	713	750	788	825	863	900	938	1,125	1,313	1,500	1,575	
53,000	221	442	663	707	751	795	839	883	928	972	1,016	1,060	1,104	1,325	1,546	1,767	1,855	44
	199	398	596	636	676	716	755	795	835	875	914	954	994	1,193	1,391	1,690	1,670	
56,000	233	467	700	747	793	840	887	933	980	1,027	1,073	1,120	1,167	1,400	1,633	1,867	1,960	46
	210	420	630	672	714	756	798	840	882	924	966	1,008	1,050	1,260	1,470	1,680	1,764	
60,000	250	500	750	800	850	900	950	1,000	1,050	1,100	1,150	1,200	1,250	1,500	1,750	2,000	2,100	50
	225	450	675	720	765	810	855	900	945	990	1,035	1,080	1,125	1,350	1,575	1,800	1,890	
63,000	263	525	788	840	893	945	998	1,050	1,103	1,155	1,208	1,260	1,313	1,575	1,838	2,100	2,205	52
	236	473	709	756	803	851	898	945	992	1,040	1,087	1,134	1,188	1,418	1,654	1,890	1,985	
66,000	275	550	825	880	935	990	1,045	1,100	1,155	1,210	1,265	1,320	1,375	1,650	1,925	2,200	2,310	55
	248	495	743	792	842	891	941	990	1,040	1,089	1,139	1,188	1,238	1,485	1,733	1,980	2,079	
70,000	292	583	875	933	992	1,050	1,108	1,167	1,225	1,283	1,342	1,400	1,458	1,750	2,042	2,333	2,450	58
	263	525	788	840	893	945	998	1,050	1,103	1,155	1,208	1,260	1,313	1,575	1,838	2,100	2,205	
73,000	304	608	913	973	1,034	1,095	1,156	1,217	1,278	1,338	1,399	1,460	1,521	1,825	2,129	2,433	2,555	61
	274	548	821	876	931	986	1,040	1,095	1,150	1,205	1,259	1,314	1,369	1,643	1,916	2,190	2,300	
76,000	317	633	950	1,013	1,077	1,140	1,203	1,267	1,330	1,393	1,457	1,520	1,583	1,900	2,217	2,533	2,660	63
	285	570	855	912	969	1,026	1,083	1,140	1,197	1,254	1,311	1,368	1,425	1,710	1,995	2,280	2,394	
80,000	333	667	1,000	1,067	1,133	1,200	1,267	1,333	1,400	1,467	1,533	1,600	1,667	2,000	2,333	2,667	2,800	66
	300	600	900	960	1,020	1,080	1,140	1,200	1,260	1,320	1,380	1,440	1,500	1,800	2,100	2,400	2,520	
83,000	346	692	1,038	1,107	1,176	1,245	1,314	1,383	1,453	1,522	1,591	1,660	1,729	2,075	2,421	2,767	2,905	69
	311	623	934	996	1,058	1,121	1,183	1,245	1,307	1,370	1,432	1,494	1,556	1,868	2,179	2,490	2,615	
86,000	358	717	1,075	1,147	1,218	1,290	1,362	1,433	1,505	1,577	1,648	1,720	1,792	2,150	2,508	2,867	3,010	71
	323	645	968	1,032	1,097	1,161	1,226	1,290	1,355	1,419	1,484	1,548	1,613	1,935	2,258	2,580	2,709	
90,000	375	750	1,125	1,200	1,275	1,350	1,425	1,500	1,575	1,650	1,725	1,800	1,875	2,250	2,625	3,000	3,150	75
	338	675	1,013	1,080	1,148	1,215	1,283	1,350	1,418	1,485	1,553	1,620	1,688	2,025	2,363	2,700	2,835	
93,000	388	775	1,163	1,240	1,318	1,395	1,473	1,550	1,628	1,705	1,783	1,860	1,938	2,325	2,713	3,100	3,255	77
	349	698	1,046	1,116	1,186	1,256	1,325	1,395	1,465	1,535	1,604	1,674	1,744	2,093	2,441	2,790	2,930	
96,000	400	800	1,200	1,280	1,360	1,440	1,520	1,600	1,680	1,760	1,840	1,920	2,000	2,400	2,800	3,200	3,360	80
	360	720	1,080	1,152	1,224	1,296	1,368	1,440	1,512	1,584	1,656	1,728	1,800	2,160	2,530	2,880	3,024	
100,000	417	833	1,250	1,333	1417	1,500	1,583	1,667	1,750	1,833	1,917	2,000	2,083	2,500	2,917	3,333	,5010	83
	375	750	1,125	1,200	1,275	1,350	1,425	1,500	1,575	1,650	1,725	1,800	1,875	2,250	2,625	3,000	3,150	
110,000	458	917	1,375	1,467	1,558	1,650	1,742	1,833	1,925	2,017	2,108	2,200	2,292	2,750	3,208	3,667	3,850	92
	413	825	1,238	1,320	1,403	1,485	1,568	1,650	1,733	1,815	1,898	1,980	2,063	2,475	2,888	3,300	3,465	

Example illustrating an average annual salary at 24 years of service: 1% of $33,000 = $330, times 24 (years of service) = $7,920 annual annuity or $660 monthly. If the employee opted at retirement to elect a survivor annuity, his monthly annuity would be reduced by 10% to $594. (Employees who continue to serve at age 62 or older with 20 years of service will have their annuity computed at 1.1 percent. For example, the same employee in the example above who retires at age 62 or older would have an annual annuity of $8,712 or $726 monthly. If a survivor annuity is elected, the monthly annuity would be $653.40)

Basic annuity is subject to reduction if (a) deductions are not in the fund for any service since August 1, 1920, (b) retirement—except for disability—is before age 55, (c) a survivor-type anuuity is elected at retirement.

Figure 5-6

- Take early voluntary retirement (at age 50 with 20 years of service, or at any age with 25 years of service) if your agency is undergoing a major reorganization, RIF, or transfer of function. However, the supplement will not begin until you reach the applicable MRA.
- Take an involuntary retirement, but not until you reach the applicable MRA.

Note: If you transferred to FERS from CSRS, you must have at least one full calendar year of FERS-covered service to qualify for the supplement.

If you have earnings from wages or self-employment that exceed the Social Security annual exempt earnings amount, your special retirement supplement will be reduced or stopped. If you earn more than the Social Security exempt amount during a calendar year ($8,640 in 1997), your special retirement supplement will be reduced $1 for every $2 you earn over the limit. This reduction does not apply to law enforcement officers, firefighters, and air traffic controllers.

Special Annuity Systems

Law enforcement, firefighter, and air traffic controller personnel may voluntarily retire if they are age 50 or over and have completed at least 20 years of such service or have 25 years of service at any age. In addition, there are special provisions for computing their annuities.

If you fit into one of these categories, under FERS you are entitled to 1.7 percent times your average "high-3" salary, multiplied by the number of years served in a FERS law enforcement, firefighter, or air traffic control position (not to exceed 20 years). To this, you add 1 percent times your average "high-3" salary for years served in excess of 20 (or in a position that was not in law enforcement, fire fighting, or air traffic control).

If you have a CSRS component, you are entitled to 2.5 percent times your average "high-3" salary, multiplied by the number of years served in a CSRS law enforcement or firefighter position (not to exceed 20 years). To this, you add 2 percent times your average "high-3" salary for years served in excess of 20 (or in a position that was not in law enforcement, fire fighting, or air traffic control), as well as any unused sick leave.

The combination of CSRS and FERS service to which the higher computation rate applies may not exceed 20 years. Thus, an employee who had 19 years of CSRS service before transferring to FERS would be able to use the enhanced rate calculation for only one year of FERS service. All additional FERS service would be computed under the regular formula.

Note: For law enforcement, firefighter, and air traffic controller personnel, there is no annuity reduction for retiring under the MRA.

Potential Reductions in Your Annuity

Once a basic annuity has been computed it may be reduced for several reasons. These include:

- Reduction for Age—If you retire at the MRA with at least 10 years of service but less than 30 years of service, your benefit will be reduced by 5 percent a year for each year you are under age 62, unless you have 20 years of service and your annuity begins at age 60 or later. The reduction will not be eliminated when you become 62.
- Reduction for Unpaid Deposits—The reduction equals 10 percent of the unpaid deposits for service prior to October 1, 1982. No credit can be given for non-deduction service after October 1, 1982, unless a deposit is made to OPM.
- Reduction for Unpaid Redeposits—In most cases, if you received a refund of your CSRS contributions and have not made a redeposit, you must either repay the amount of the refund when you retire or have your annuity reduced by an actuarial formula.
- Reduction for Survivor Annuity—The reduction for a full survivor election (50 percent of the unreduced annuity) is 10 percent of the retiree's basic annuity after it has been reduced for age and unpaid deposits. For a 25 percent survivor election, the reduction is 5 percent. A court-ordered survivor annuity results in a deduction of 10 percent of the court-ordered base.
- Reduction for Post-1956 Military Service—To receive credit for post-1956 military service before you were covered by FERS, you must deposit 3 percent of your military base pay. Interest begins two years after you are hired, or January 1, 1989, whichever is later. (See Figure 5-3 for the addresses you may use to get information about your post-1956 military service earnings.)
- Reduction for Alternative Annuity—If you are eligible for retirement and suffer from an illness or condition that generally would limit your life to two years, you can choose a lump-sum payment equal to the amount of your contributions to the retirement system and a reduced monthly annuity (the amount is determined by an actuarial formula).

Interest Charges

To capture non-deposit service, the full amount must be paid with interest. The amount of interest charged varies depending on the time and circumstances of the contribution. Similarly, amounts of CSRS service for which a refund of contributions has been made can be recredited if a redeposit (with interest) is made. Otherwise, the annuity will be reduced actuarially.

Note: By law, refunds of FERS contributions cannot be repaid. Thus, the service covered by those contributions is lost; it cannot be recaptured.

Interest rate charges are the same as those applicable for CSRS redeposits (see Figure 5-5).

Maximum Annuity Amounts

Unlike CSRS, there is no annuity limit for a FERS retiree — probably because you would have to work for more than 70 years to reach the 80 percent limit placed on CSRS employees. However, if you had a considerable number of years of CSRS-covered service (plus a lot of sick leave) before you switched to FERS, you might be in a position to receive a combined CSRS/FERS annuity of more than 80 percent.

CHAPTER SIX

SURVIVOR BENEFITS UNDER FEDERAL RETIREMENT PROGRAMS — CSRS

The two basic federal retirement systems—CSRS and FERS—both provide survivor benefits for active and retired employees. For most federal employees, these survivor benefits are one of the most valuable and significant components of their retirement coverage.

However, the rules for calculating survivor benefits under the Civil Service Retirement System are different from the survivor benefit rules established under the Federal Employees' Retirement System. Moreover, the survivor benefits of active employees are calculated somewhat differently than the benefits paid to survivors of a retired employee who dies.

This chapter outlines the general rules and procedures governing CSRS survivor benefit payments. It's also important to keep in mind that there are different survivor benefit-calculation rules applicable to the two different employment statuses — active and retired. We will point out the distinctions as we go along. Remember, after you retire, you may need to change a plan for your survivors that you made while you were an active employee.

Current Employees: CSRS Survivor Benefits

Currently employed workers with CSRS coverage who die before retirement are assured their survivors will receive benefits after they are gone. This means that if you die after having met certain minimum CSRS service requirements, your survivors will receive important benefits that can help them to live a more financially secure life. Survivors also have special benefit rights under the Thrift Savings Plan (see Chapter 11). In addition, your survivors may be eligible for Social Security benefits, which generally provides wage-replacement income to the families of deceased workers covered by that general government insurance program (see Chapter 8).

Of all the survivor benefits available to a spouse, a CSRS annuity is usually the most significant financially because it entitles the recipient to a monthly payment as long as he or she remains eligible. For most widow(er)s, this will be for the rest of their lives. For children, the benefit generally ends at age 18.

Your widow(er) and children may qualify for a civil service survivor annuity if your death occurs:

- While you are employed and covered by CSRS; and
- After you have completed at least 18 months of creditable civilian service.

These annuities are increased by annual cost-of-living adjustments (COLAs), which will help your survivors to keep up with inflation.

Eligibility Requirements

The general eligibility rules for CSRS survivor benefits differ, depending on whether the survivor is a spouse or dependent child. Following is a look at these separate sets of eligibility rules.

Surviving Spouse — To qualify for a survivor annuity, your widow(er) must:

- Have been married to you for at least nine months in total before your death; or
- Be the natural parent of your child.

Note: These requirements do not apply if your death is accidental.

A survivor annuity terminates upon a spouse's remarriage, but only if the remarriage occurs while the spouse is still under age 55. If he or she does remarry while under the applicable age, the survivor annuity may be restored if the remarriage is dissolved by death, annulment, or divorce.

Children — Your child, to qualify for a survivor annuity, must be:

- Under age 18; and
- Unmarried.

A stepchild may qualify for a survivor annuity if he or she meets the requirements above and, in addition, has lived with you in a regular parent-child relationship. While there is no specific time requirement, you must be able to demonstrate that the stepchild is a dependent (for example, through your tax records).

Illegitimate children whom you acknowledge may qualify for a survivor annuity if they meet the requirements above and, in addition, can show dependency on you.

Your Financial Guide

A child over 18 may qualify for a survivor annuity if incapable of self-support because of a disability which began before he or she reached age 18. OPM makes this determination based on medical and other relevant factors.

Also, a child over 18 may be eligible for a survivor annuity up to age 22 if he or she is a student in full-time attendance at a high school, college, or other recognized educational institution. The annuity will continue during non-school intervals of not over five months between school years or terms, if the individual can show a clear intention to remain a full-time student. Statements from the student and the school will help to show that intent.

Guaranteed Minimum Benefit

If your surviving spouse qualifies, she or he will receive a guaranteed minimum yearly survivor annuity. The amount of that annuity will be 55 percent of the smaller of the following two figures:

- 40 percent of your highest three consecutive years of average pay, commonly referred to as your "high-3;" or
- The amount your annuity would have been if you had continued working until you were 60 years old at the same "high-3" pay level.

However, the guaranteed minimum does not apply if the widow(er)'s annuity based on the employee's actual service is more than the guaranteed minimum. In that event, the widow(er)'s annuity is 55 percent of the annuity earned by the employee at time of death. (An explanation of possible reductions in an earned survivor annuity is provided late in the chapter.)

The spousal annuity begins on the day after your death and ends on the last day of the month before the one in which your survivor dies or remarries. It is increased annually by cost-of-living adjustments.

Current Employees: Annuity Calculations for Surviving Spouse

The survivor annuity for the spouse of an active CSRS (or CSRS-Offset) employee is based on the disability annuity that would have been payable if the employee had retired on his or her date of death. (The disability annuity formula provides an enhanced benefit for those who retired with fewer years of service.) In the example below (and in any such calculation), the survivor annuity is "A" if it provides the largest benefit. Otherwise, the benefit is the lesser of "B" or "C."

Example
  Deceased Employee Statistics:
  Entered Service at Age 20
  Service = 18 Years
  Average Salary = $30,000 (based on "high-3" years)

A. Earned Annuity:
1.5% x $30,000 x 5 years of service = $2,250
1.75% x $30,000 x 5 years of service = $2,625
2% x $30,000 x remaining 8 years of service = $4,800
Total Annual Annuity = $9,675
55 Percent Limitation = $5,321 (rounded down)

Monthly Annuity = $443.42 ($5,321÷12)

B. Annuity Projected to Age 60 (40 years of service):
1.5% x $30,000 x 5 years of service = $ 2,250
1.75% x $30,000 x 5 years of service = $ 2,625
2% x $30,000 x 30 years of service = $18,000
Total Annual Annuity = $22,875
55 Percent Limitation = $12,581 (rounded down)

Monthly Annuity = $1,048.44 ($12,581÷12)

C. 40 Percent of "High-3" Average Pay:
40% x $30,000 = $12,000

Monthly Annuity = $1,000 ($12,000÷12)

Because Option C is smaller than B, it represents the amount of the survivor benefit in this example. (Benefit amount A—the guaranteed minimum—is smaller than either B or C, and therefore would not be used.)

Surviving Children With a Surviving Parent

If you die as an active employee and are survived by a spouse and/or a former spouse who is the parent of your child or children, these dependents are eligible for a survivor annuity that is increased annually by COLAs. The amount of the survivor annuity is equal to the lowest payment produced by the following formulas:

A. 60% of your "high-3" average pay, divided by the number of your children;
B. $1,011 per month, divided by the number of children; or
C. $337 per month per child.

Note: The dollar amounts in B and C are in effect through December 1, 1997.

Following are two examples of how children's survivor benefits are calculated. The first example involves an active employee with one dependent child; the second involves a deceased employee with four dependent children. In both examples, the employee's average "high-3" pay is $30,000.

Example 1
Calculation of Child's Survivor Annuity — One Dependent of Surviving Spouse

The lowest of:

---

36   *Your Financial Guide*

A. 60% x $30,000 ÷ 1 = $18,000 ÷ 12 = $1,500/month
B. $1,011 per month ÷ 1 = $1,011
C. $337 per month per child

In this example, the annuity will be C because it results in the least payment of the three formulas.

Example 2
Calculation of Children's Survivor Annuity — Four Dependents of Surviving Spouse

The lowest of:

A. 60% x $30,000 ÷ 4 = $4,500 ÷ 12 = $375 per month
B. $1,011 per month ÷ 4 = $252.75 per month
C. $337 per month per child

In this example, the annuity will be B for each child because it results in the least payment of the three formulas.

Surviving Children Without a Surviving Parent

For currently employed workers who die, each qualified child, except an illegitimate child, who has no surviving parent will be paid the lesser of:

A. 75% of your "high-3" average pay, divided by the number of children;
B. $1,212 per month, divided by the number of children; or
C. $404.

Note: The dollar amounts in B & C are those in effect through December 1, 1997.

Following are two examples of how children's survivor benefits are calculated. The first example involves an active employee with one dependent child; the second involves a deceased employee with four dependent children. In both examples, the employee's average "high-3" pay is $30,000.

Example 1
Calculation of Child's Survivor Annuity — One Child Without a Surviving Parent

The lowest of:

A. 75% x $30,000 ÷ 1 = $22,500 ÷ 12 = $1,875/month
B. $1,212 per month ÷ 1 = $1,212
C. $404 per month

In this example, the annuity will be C because it is the least of the three amounts.

Example 2
Calculation of Child's Survivor Annuity — Four Children Without a Surviving Parent

The lowest of:

A. 75% x $30,000 ÷ 4 = $5,625 ÷ 12 = $468.75/month
B. $1,212 per month ÷ 4 = $303
C. $404 per month per child

In this example, the annuity will be B for each child because it is the least of the three amounts.

Note: These benefits are available to qualified dependent children whether your spouse or former spouse died before or after you did.

The survivor annuity for each qualified child begins the day after your death and ends on the last day of the month before the one in which the child dies, marries, reaches age 18, or, if over 18, becomes capable of self-support. This latter category only applies to a child who was incapable of earning a living because of a physical or mental disability incurred before age 18.

Exception: The annuity of a child who is a student will end on the last day of the month before he or she: (1) marries, (2) dies, (3) ceases to be a student, or (4) attains the age of 22. If a student-child drops out of school or his or her annuity is terminated, it can be restored if he or she later returns to school and is still under 22 and unmarried.

A child's annuity will be paid to his or her guardian if one has been appointed by a court. If no guardian is appointed, payment will be made, at the discretion of the Office of Personnel Management, to the person who has the care and custody of the child.

In general, a child's annuity is considered a contribution for the care of the child, and therefore the money normally is controlled by the parent or guardian. If a child continues receiving an annuity after age 18 — for example, as a full-time student — the child may receive the annuity directly. This is a family decision.

Note for CSRS-Offset Employees: *CSRS annuity benefits are offset by the amount of Social Security benefits payable to your children based on your CSRS-Offset service. Generally there is no difference in the total amount of benefits they will receive.*

Potential Reductions in an Earned Survivor Annuity

An earned survivor annuity is one based on your "high-3" salary and the years of service you had completed when you died. Your survivor will receive it if it is greater than the guaranteed minimum survivor annuity. However, if you performed any creditable service for which no retirement deductions were made and did not make a deposit to cover that service, it will adversely affect the annuity payable to your survivors. The specific impact of not paying a deposit depends on when the service was performed. Here are the basic rules:

Your Financial Guide

- *Service performed before October 1, 1982* – The period of non-deduction service counts toward eligibility for retirement and is used to compute the annual annuity. However, the annual annuity is reduced by 10 percent of the total deposit owed, including interest.
- *Service performed after September 30, 1982* – The period of non-deduction service counts toward eligibility for retirement and may be used for computing a "high-3" average salary. However, it cannot be used for determining total creditable service for annuity-computation purposes.

In addition, if you die before making or completing a deposit for post-1956 military service (or if you received a refund of CSRS contributions and had not made a redeposit), those years will not be creditable for retirement purposes. However, your survivor will be given an opportunity to make the necessary payment. Whether this would be worth doing would depend on how much was owed, including interest, and how much the repayment would increase the survivor's annuity. The Office of Personnel Management will send information that will assist your survivor in making an informed decision.

Note: If you die in service, reductions that normally would have been made in your own annuity under age 55 will not be made in your survivor's annuity.

Retired Employees: Survivor Annuities

There are three kinds of annuities a retiring employee may elect under CSRS. All three guarantee that annuities will be paid to any eligible children. The amount of these annuities will be the same as those provided to the children of employees who die in service.

Basic Life Annuity — This is an annuity without a survivor benefit, such as the kind you would provide to your spouse.

Reduced Annuity With Benefit to Widow(er) or Former Spouse — You may agree to take a reduction in your basic annuity and name your spouse or former spouse as the person who will receive your survivor annuity. The amount of a full survivor annuity will be 55 percent of your annuity before the reduction is made to provide survivor benefits. If you have a current spouse, the law requires that you choose this option unless you and your spouse agree in writing to either a partial spousal annuity or to waive that right entirely.

Note: You are required to provide a survivor annuity to a former spouse if this is stipulated in a divorce agreement or annulment that ended your marriage after May 6, 1985. By law, the stipulated amount cannot exceed 55 percent of your unreduced annuity entitlement amount.

Reduced Annuity With Benefit to a Specific Individual — If you are in good health and there is no court-order in force for a former spouse annuity, you may name a specific individual who has a continuing financial interest in you to receive your survivor annuity. Such an "insurable interest" election may be made in addition to or instead of a spousal annuity. If made instead of a spousal annuity, you must obtain your spouse's consent in writing. By law, you may not elect both a regular annuity and an "insurable interest" annuity for your spouse. However, an insurable interest election can be made for your current spouse if a court order is in effect.

An insurable interest is presumed to exist with:

- A current spouse (where a court order for a former spouse has prevented you from providing him or her with a regular survivor annuity);
- A blood or adoptive relative closer than first cousins;
- A former spouse;
- A person to whom the employee is engaged to be married; or
- A person living in a common-law marriage relationship with the employee that is not recognized by the state in which they are domiciled. If the state recognizes common-law marriages, a regular survivor annuity, which is much less expensive, may be elected.

However, there are others who may be eligible to receive an insurable interest annuity. OPM's only requirement is that the individual named have a clear financial interest in you and might reasonably expect to continue to benefit from your continued life.

To prove good health, you must arrange and pay for a medical examination and provide a dated report signed by a licensed physician along with your retirement application.

Note: While the insurable interest election is a convenient way to provide for someone near and dear to you, you should still consider other options that may be more cost effective, such as a term insurance policy naming that person as the beneficiary.

Should You Elect a Survivor Annuity?

Nearly all retiring employees who are married elect a survivor annuity for their spouses. They do this for a variety of good reasons, but the most compelling one is that it's hard to beat the government's deal. Not only are the terms of the annuity significant, but providing one allows your widow(er) to continue federal employee health benefits insurance (FEHB) coverage after your death.

Although a retiree—with the agreement of his or her spouse—could elect a full annuity without a survivor benefit and instead purchase an insurance policy to make up the difference, it is very difficult for a private insurer to match the value you get from a government survivor annuity. That's because private insurers load investment costs, agent commissions, and other overhead onto their premiums. None of these are added to the amount paid for a federal survivor annuity. If a financial planner claims you can do better, make sure you get a detailed explanation before you buy the alternative.

While there may be instances where not electing a survivor annuity may seem like the right thing to do, you must remember that this is not a decision you can make on your own. An annuity election for your spouse is automatic at the time of your retirement unless you and your spouse ask in writing for an annuity without any (or reduced) survivor benefits.

Retired Employees: Calculating Annuity for Surviving Spouse

Normally, the decision to elect a survivor annuity is made at the time you retire. However, under certain circumstances that decision may be made after retirement.

Choosing a survivor benefit not only will provide an income to your spouse but also will have an immediate effect on your annuity. Simply stated, the normal annuity benefits you would have received will be reduced during your lifetime in order to provide a survivor benefit.

The standard survivor annuity under CSRS is 55 percent of your annuity before the reduction to provide survivor benefits. However, with your spouse's concurrence it can be based on a smaller amount. There are a number of reasons why a couple may agree to a reduced spousal annuity. The most common are these:

- Where each partner has earned a retirement income that is adequate to meet each's individual needs; or
- Where their financial situation is such that receiving a higher monthly income now is more important than receiving it later in the form of a higher survivor annuity.
- Where it is highly unlikely that the person who would be designated for the survivor benefit will outlive the primary beneficiary.

If you elect an Annuity With Survivor Benefit to Widow, Widower or Former Spouse, your annuity will be reduced by:

- 2.5 percent of the first $3,600 used as a base for the survivor annuity; plus

- 10 percent of any amount over $3,600 used as a base for the survivor annuity.

Note: *If the retiree and spouse definitely do not want to elect the full reduction, the retiree should still consider a $3,600 base. This provides a minimum survivor benefit of $165 per month, with COLAs added after retirement, for only $90 per year.*

Example of Annuity Reduced for Full Survivor Benefit
Annual Annuity: $26,000
Reductions:
  A. 2.5% x $3,600 = $90
  B. 10% of any amount over $3,600 ($26,000 - $3,600 = $22,400 x 10 percent) = $2,240
Total reductions (A+B) = $2,330
Your reduced annuity = $23,670÷12 = $1972.50/month
Survivor benefit = 55 percent of the unreduced annuity:
$26,000 x 55 percent = $14,300÷12 = $1,191.66/mo.
For most retirees, electing a full survivor annuity amounts to about a 9 percent net reduction in their own annuity.

Example of an Annuity Reduced for a Partial Survivor Benefit
Annual annuity: $26,000
Amount jointly selected for the survivor annuity base: $10,000
Reductions:
  A. 2.5% x $3,600 = $90
  B. 10% of amount over $3,600 ($10,000 - 3,600 = $6,400 x 10 percent) = $640
Total reductions (A+B) = $730
Reduced annuity = $25,270 ÷12 = $2,105.83/month
Survivor benefit = 55 percent of the chosen annuity base:
$10,000 x 55 percent = $5,500 ÷ 12 = $458.33 per month

Even if the partial survivor benefit is reduced to as little as $1 a month, your widow(er) will receive annual COLA increases on that amount. More importantly, if your widow(er) was covered under your Federal Employees Health Benefits plan, he or she will continue to be eligible for health benefits coverage. The same would be true of a former spouse who has been granted a court-ordered annuity.

If the spouse you named at time of retirement dies before you do (or the marriage is otherwise dissolved), you are entitled to have your full annuity restored as of the first of the month following your spouse's death. The amount deducted from your annuity while your spouse was still alive won't be refunded to you.

If you remarry, the person you married after retirement will be eligible to receive a survivor benefit if your written request is received by the OPM no later than two years after date of remarriage.

Your Financial Guide

If you are unmarried at the time of retirement and later marry, you may, within two years after marriage, elect a reduced annuity with survivor benefits to your spouse. Your request for such a change must be received by the Office of Personnel Management no later than two years after you marry. Once a change in election is accepted by OPM, it cannot be changed again.

Note: *A retiree who marries on or after October 1, 1993, and elects a survivor annuity for that spouse has his or her annuity permanently reduced based on actuarial tables. This actuarial reduction is in addition to the regular survivor annuity reduction. The dollar amount of the survivor annuity will be the same as if the election had been made at retirement.*

To be eligible for a survivor benefit in the above circumstances, the spouse must be married to you for at least nine months before your death, or, if married less than nine months, be the natural parent of your child, or your death must be accidental.

Note: *The term "accidental" does not include death as a result of intentional self-destruction, while sane or insane, or as a result of the self-administration of illegal or illegally obtained drugs.*

Dependent Children

If upon your death after retirement you are survived by children, they could, regardless of the type of annuity you had elected, qualify for a survivor annuity under the standard rules governing dependent children's benefits.

Specific Individual (Insurable Interest)

If you elect an insurable interest annuity, a survivor annuity will, upon your death after retirement, be paid to the person you named when you retired. The benefit will be based on 55 percent of your basic annuity after it has been reduced to account for the difference in age between you and the person you designate. (See Figure 6-1.)

Example
Annual annuity of $26,000.
Reduction of 30 percent for beneficiary 22 years or younger = $7,800.
Reduced annuity = $18,200
Insurable interest annuity of 55 percent of the reduced annuity = $10,010, or $385 per month

If the person you named dies before you do, you must notify OPM so that your annuity can be restored to the higher, unreduced rate. The amount deducted from your annuity while the designated individual was still alive won't be refunded to you.

Insurable Interest Annuity Reductions

Age of Person Named in Relation to That of Retiring Employee	Reduction in Annuity of Retiring Employee
Older, same age, or less than 5 years younger	10%
5 but less than 10 years younger	15%
10 but less than 15 years younger	20%
15 but less than 20 years younger	25%
20 but less than 25 years younger	30%
25 but less than 30 years younger	35%
30 or more years younger	40%

Figure 6-1

An insurable interest election may be changed to a reduced annuity with a survivor benefit to a spouse, if you marry after retirement. Your written request for such a change must be received by OPM no later than one year after you marry. Once a change in election is accepted by OPM, it cannot be changed.

Disability Retirement

If you are totally disabled for useful and efficient service in your current position (or any other vacant position at the same grade and pay for which you are qualified) and have at least five years of creditable civilian service, you may be eligible for a disability retirement.

Your agency personnel office can help you to fill out the necessary form (SF-2801, Application for Immediate Retirement) and forward it to OPM, along with necessary statements from you, your supervisor, and your physician. OPM is solely responsible for making the final determination as to whether you are disabled and its standards are strict.

OPM considers disability retirement to be a last resort, appropriate only when you can no longer do the job because of injury or disease (including mental illness), and after every reasonable effort has been made to keep you on the job. The disability must be expected to continue for at least one year to qualify for a disability retirement.

If your application is approved, you are guaranteed a minimum retirement benefit if it is greater than the basic annuity you would be eligible for under the standard computation. This guarantee helps employees who are under 60 years of age at retirement and have less than 22 years of creditable service. The guarantee is based on two formulas that give credit for more service than the annuitant actually has:

- 40 percent computation. The annuity is computed as though the employee had served 21 years and 11 months; or

- Projected service through age 60. The annuity is computed as though the employee had worked to age 60 by adding projected service to actual service.

The annuity payable is the lesser of the two formulas above. For example, an employee who entered service at age 26 and retires on disability with 14 years of actual service would have a projected service of 20 more years, bringing him or her to age 60. This would give the employee an annuity based on that service or on 40 percent of actual salary, whichever is lower.

Example
Entered Service at Age 26
Service = 14 years
$35,000 "high-3" average salary

A. Basic Annuity Computation Formula
1.5% x $35,000 x 5 years = $2,625
1.75% x $35,000 x 5 years = $3,062.50
2.0% x $35,000 x 4 years = $2,800
Basic Annuity = $8,487 (rounded down)÷12 = $707.25 per month

B. 40 Percent Formula
40% x $35,000 = $14,000

Basic Annuity = $14,000÷12 = $1166.66 per month

C. Service Projected to Age 60 Formula (34 years of service)
1.5% x $35,000 x 5 years = $2,625
1.75% x $35,000 x 5 years = $2,800
2.0% x $35,000 x 24 years (50 + 10 = 60) = $16,800
Basic Annuity = $22,225/12 = $1,852.08 per month

In this example, the employee would receive annuity B ($14,000). This benefit, while it is more than A ($8,487), is less than an annuity based on service projected to age 60 ($22,225).

Note: The guaranteed minimum computation will never exceed 40 percent. It may, however, be less than that, if you are receiving military retired pay or VA benefits in lieu of military retirement pay.

A disability annuity is not reduced if you are under age 55. However, if you qualify for an annuity based on service projected to age 60, your annuity will be reduced for non-deduction service and any survivor annuity election you make. If you qualify for an annuity based on 40 percent of your average salary, your annuity will only be reduced for the survivor annuity.

If a disability retiree recovers or is restored to earning capacity before reaching age 60, the annuity will be continued temporarily to afford an opportunity to seek reemployment. The annuity payments will be discontinued from the earliest of the following dates:

- Reemployment by the government.
- One year from the date of a medical exam showing recovery.
- Six months from the end of the calendar year in which earning capacity is restored.

Restoration to earning capacity means that the retiree has income from wages or self-employment (or both), that equals at least 80 percent of the current salary for the position he or she occupied immediately before going on disability retirement.

Survivor annuities for disability retirees are calculated in the same way they are for any other retiree. Using the example above, a full survivor annuity election would reduce the employee's $14,000 annual annuity by $1,130 per year to $12,870. However, the survivor's annuity would be 55 percent of the higher figure, or $7,078 per year (rounded down).

Cost-of-Living Adjustments (COLAs)

All CSRS retirees and survivors receive an annual annuity increase based on a cost-of-living adjustment formula approved by Congress. That formula calls for the increase to become effective each December and payable in the January checks. However, in recent years, COLA payments frequently have been delayed by Congress from January to April.

Retiree COLAs of Recent Years
Table of CSRS COLAs

Effective Date	Year	Rate
12/1	1997	2.9
3/1	1996	2.6*
3/1	1995	2.8*
3/1	1994	2.6*
12/1	1992	3.0
12/1	1991	3.7
12/1	1990	5.4
12/1	1989	4.7
12/1	1988	4.0
12/1	1987	4.2
12/1	1986	1.3
12/1	1985	0.0
12/1	1984	3.5
4/1	1983	3.9
3/1	1982	8.7
3/1	1981	4.4
9/1	1980	7.7
3/1	1980	6.0
9/1	1979	6.9
3/1	1979	3.9
9/1	1978	4.9
3/1	1978	2.2
9/1	1977	4.3
3/1	1977	4.8
3/1	1976	5.4

Note: COLAs are actually paid in the month following their effective date.
*The COLA was delayed three months, under PL 103-66.

Figure 6-2

The percentage increase of these COLAs is determined by the average increase of the third-quarter Consumer Price Index for Urban Wage Earners and Clerical Workers (CPI/W) over the same period during the previous year.

The number of months for which a retiree or survivor receives the COLA is prorated over the number of months during the year the employee was retired. For example, a person retiring in May would receive 7/12 of the COLA, if retiring in October, 2/12 of the COLA, etc.

In recent years, COLA payments ranged from a high of 8.7 percent in 1983 to a low of 0 in 1986 (when Congress repealed an indicated 3.1 percent COLA).

Death Benefits

In certain circumstances, the survivors of current employees and retirees may be eligible for a death benefit, which is payable in a lump sum. This lump-sum payment generally represents a refund of the undistributed portion of your retirement-fund contributions. If you have not designated a beneficiary on a form SF-2808, lump-sum payments will be made according to the Order of Precedence (see below) mandated by law.

The rules governing this type of lum sum death benefit differ, depending on whether the deceased employee is an active or retired worker:

If Death Occurs Before Retirement — If you have less than 18 months of service, or leave no one who can qualify for a survivor annuity, your contributions to the retirement fund (but not your agency's contributions), with interest, will be paid as a lump-sum death benefit following the Order of Precedence outlined below.

If you leave someone who qualifies for a survivor annuity, no lump-sum death benefit is payable immediately. A lump-sum death benefit may be payable later if the annuities to your survivors end and they have received less than your contributions to the retirement fund, plus interest. This situation might occur if your spouse dies shortly after you do and you have no children who are young enough to be eligible for a survivor annuity.

The amount payable as a lump-sum death benefit will be the difference between your contributions, plus interest, and the total paid out in survivor annuities. That amount will be paid to the next eligible person on the Order of Precedence.

Note: Only the interest received in a lump-sum payment is taxable. The remainder represents a return of money that has already been taxed.

If Death Occurs After Retirement — If you leave no one who can qualify for a survivor annuity, a lump-sum death benefit consisting of the annuity accrued to date of death generally is payable immediately. Also, if the total annuity already paid to you is less than what you have contributed to the retirement fund, the difference will represent a balance payable as an immediate lump-sum death benefit to the next eligible person on the Order of Precedence (see below). No interest is included in this payment.

If you leave someone who qualifies for a survivor annuity, no lump-sum death benefit (other than unpaid annuity accrued to date of death) is payable immediately. A lump-sum death benefit may be payable later if the annuities to your survivors end (for example, if your spouse dies shortly after you did and you have no children who are young enough for a survivor annuity). The amount paid will be the amount you contributed to the retirement fund minus the amount of annuity already paid to you and your survivors. No interest is included. The lump-sum death benefit will be paid to the next eligible person on the Order of Precedence.

Note: These lump-sum payments represent a return of contributions you made while employed and have already been taxed. Therefore, they will not be taxed again.

If you have children who survive you and are under age 18, or who are full-time students aged 18 through 21 (or a child who is incapable of self-support because of a disability incurred before age 18), they are entitled to the same benefits received by the children of employees who die during active service. Such benefits are subject to cost-of-living adjustments and currently amount to approximately $300 per month.

Order of Precedence

The Order of Precedence is a legally mandated list indicating the order in which property passes to beneficiaries, usually in the absence of a binding or enforceable will. The Order of Preference is the prescribed order in which your undistributed retirement contributions will be paid, as a lump sum death benefit, if you have not designated a beneficiary on Form SF-3102.

Under the Order of Preference, any lump-sum death benefit payable after your death will be paid to the following person or persons in the order indicated:

(1) to the beneficiary designated by you on a Standard Form 3102, Designation of Beneficiary;
(2) if you did not designate a beneficiary, to your widow(er);
(3) if you leave no widow(er), to your child or children in equal shares, with the share of any deceased child

Your Financial Guide

distributed among the descendants of the child;
(4) if none of the above, to your parents (or parent);
(5) if none of the above, to the executor or administrator of your estate;
(6) if none of the above, to your next of kin who may be entitled under the laws of the state in which you are living at the time of your death.

Designation of Beneficiary

A designation of beneficiary must be in writing—Form SF 2808—and must be received by the Office of Personnel Management before your death. Employees wishing to make a designation should fill out the form and give it to their personnel office, which will forward it to OPM. Retirees may send it directly to OPM.

You do not need to designate a beneficiary to receive the lump-sum death benefit unless you wish to name a person or persons not mentioned in the order of precedence shown above, or unless you wish to name a person who is mentioned but in a different order or for a different share. A designation of beneficiary is for lump-sum death benefit purposes only and does not affect the right of any person who can qualify for a survivor annuity.

If you designate a beneficiary, remember to keep your designation current. Changes in your family or employment status without a corresponding change in your designation may result in a settlement other than you intended.

How Your Survivors Collect Benefits After You Die

Current Employees

One of the first things your survivors or a family friend should do is call the office you worked for and notify them of your death. That office will call the servicing personnel office in your agency.

As a current employee, your agency is responsible for helping your survivors to receive benefits. Your agency's personnel office will answer any questions, supply the necessary forms and, on their completion, forward them to OPM. OPM will, in turn, get in touch with your survivors by mail. From that time forward, OPM will be their point of contact. For your convenience, we have included a copy of the SF-2800, Application for Death Benefits (see Appendix).

Retirees

Your survivor, another family member or a friend may call or write OPM to report your death and begin the process of securing benefits. Whether the notification is made by phone or in writing, the following information must be provided:

- Your full name,
- Your annuity claim number (CSA number),
- Your date of birth,
- The date of your death, and
- The name and address of the person(s) who may be entitled to death benefits.

A sample notification letter that your survivors can use appears in the Appendix. OPM's phone number is (202) 606-0500 (TDD 202-606-0551). A recorded message can be left 24 hours a day, 7 days a week. To speak to a customer service representative, call Monday through Friday (except federal holidays) from 7:30 a.m. to 6 p.m. Eastern time.

When it receives notification, OPM will stop your annuity payments and send an Application for Death Benefits (SF-2800) to the person(s) who appear to be entitled to benefits. If your deceased spouse was covered by the FEHB, OPM will provide the form needed to authorize a change of health insurance coverage (if you do not have dependent children) to the "Self-Only" option. If Federal Employees' Group Life Insurance (FEGLI) is payable, OPM will also send an application for those benefits.

Your death certificate must be included with the completed SF-2800 returned to OPM. The funeral director or a third party who is helping to settle your estate will help your survivor obtain certified copies of the death certificate for this and other required notification purposes. For example, an additional copy of the death certificate will be needed if you were covered by FEGLI.

Note: Having the death certificate certified, that is, stamped or embossed, will expedite the processing of your case by OPM and the Office of Federal Employees' Group Life Insurance.

In some cases, OPM may ask for additional documentation. To make sure that your survivor can respond quickly to such a request, it's a good idea to take a moment now and obtain certified copies of your marriage certificate and the birth certificates of your dependent child(ren) and keep them on file. Similarly, if you have a child who was disabled before age 18, obtain documentation from your physician to support his/her eligibility.

Note: To further assist your survivor(s), in the Appendix we have provided a list of situations that might cause your survivor(s) to want to get in touch with OPM, plus the addresses and phone numbers.

Annuity Amounts Received After Your Death

Most retirees have their monthly annuity payments transferred to a financial institution electronically. If the final month's payment was sent this way, your survivor must have the financial institution return the funds in question to the Treasury Department without delay. If you have been receiving your annuity payments through the mail, any checks dated after your death should be returned to:

> Director, Regional Finance Center
> PO Box 7367
> Chicago, IL 60680-7367

A statement that you died and the date of your death should be included or written across the face of any returned check(s).

Since annuity payments are made retroactively—for example, on June 1 for the month that ended on May 31—any money due for the part of the month when you were alive will be paid in a lump-sum. Annuity benefits eligibility for your survivors begins on the day following your death.

What to Do If Your Spouse Dies Before You Do

As soon as possible, notify OPM of your spouse's death. You may either phone or write OPM. In either case you will be asked to provide OPM with a copy of the death certificate (a certified copy is best). For your convenience, a sample notification letter is provided in the Appendix.

If you elected a reduction in annuity in order to provide your spouse with a survivor's benefit, you now are entitled to have your full annuity restored as of the first of the month following your spouse's death. The money deducted from your annuity while your spouse was alive will not be refunded to you.

If you did not elect a survivor annuity, you need only notify OPM if your deceased spouse was covered by your government health benefits (FEHB) plan or life insurance (FEGLI).

What to Do If You Get Divorced

If you get divorced after retirement, and had elected a reduced annuity in order to give your spouse a survivor annuity, then OPM will be obligated to honor a divorce-related court order that stipulates a survivor annuity payment. If the court does not order a survivor annuity payment, your annuity reduction will be eliminated and you will begin receiving an unreduced annuity. The same is true if a court order stipulated a survivor annuity and your ex-spouse predeceases you. In neither case will you receive a refund of the amount withheld from your annuity for this benefit.

Note: To have your full annuity restored, you should notify OPM immediately so that it can implement the change. OPM's address and phone number are provided in the Appendix.

Taxability of Annuities

All CSRS annuities, whether paid to you or your survivors, are taxable. However, under the General Rule or the Simplified General Rule (which apply to annuities that started after July 1, 1986), a percentage of your annuity is tax-free, while the rest is taxable. That's because part of it represents a return of your contributions to the retirement fund, which were taxed at the time they were made.

The formulas used to determine how much of your annuity is tax-free are based either on actuarial tables (the General Rule) or on your age when the annuity starts and how much you contributed to the retirement fund before you retired (the Simplified General Rule). According to the Internal Revenue Service, the Simplified General Rule "will usually be more beneficial than the General Rule in terms of tax result and ease of computation."

Note: If you die before recovering all the money you contributed to the retirement fund, that unexpended balance will either (1) transfer over to your survivor and result in part of his or her annuity being non-taxable or (2) be paid out in a tax-free lump sum to your survivor(s), where no one is eligible for an annuity.

For further information, see IRS Publication 721 — Tax Guide to U.S. Civil Service Retirement Benefits. You can order a copy by calling 1-800-TAX-FORM (1-800-829-3676).

Note: A disability annuity is treated as regular income and is taxed as such until you reach the age at which you could have first retired on a non-disability annuity. At that point it will be taxed under the General Rule or the Simplified General Rule as described above.

OPM will withhold federal income tax from your first annuity payment and send you information about your right to change the amount of federal income tax withholding—or have it stopped—and how to do this.

OPM has established a toll-free "Annuitant Express" Service that allows federal retirees and annuitants to call in changes to their federal and state income tax withholdings and also arrange for certain U.S. Savings Bond transactions. Using a touch-tone phone, retirees can reach OPM's toll-free Annuitant Express by dialing 1-800-409-6528. Before dialing this number, be sure that you have certain information available, including your CSA or CSF retirement claim number and Social Security number. If you need to talk with an OPM customer service specialist, call (202) 606-0500, Monday through Friday between 7:30 a.m. and 5:30 p.m. (EST).

Making changes or elections for state tax withholding requires the caller to identify the state by a two-letter abbreviation and corresponding two-digit dial pad code. Only states that have reached a tax withholding agreement with OPM are included in the Annuitant Express options.

Where to Go for More Information

If you currently are employed by the federal government, your best source of information about retirement benefits and options is the benefits officer in your own personnel office. If you're planning your retirement, you need our best-selling guide *Your CSRS Retirement*.

Another useful pamphlet that should be available in your personnel office is IRS Publication 1798, "Retiring Qs & As: Answers to Many Common Questions for the Federal Retiree."

If you are retired, OPM provides two avenues for answering your questions and getting copies of forms and publications. General questions can be answered by phone at (202) 606-0500 (TDD 202-606-0551). But be prepared to wait. This is a very popular phone number and is often busy. When you call, have your retirement claim number handy.

You may also write to OPM. For your convenience, we have compiled a list of typical retiree concerns and the address you should write to, and a few situations where a phone call would be in order (see Appendix).

Survivor Questions & Answers

Q. May a retiree drawing a civil service annuity also draw a civil service survivor annuity?
A. Yes.

Q. Is a child's survivor annuity payable in addition to the widow's or widower's annuity?
A. Yes. For example, if a deceased employee is survived by a widow and three children, all of whom are eligible to receive survivor annuities, a benefit would be paid to all four survivors.

Q. If a widow or widower dies, will the children's annuity be increased?
A. Yes. If the children are still drawing annuities, their payments will be increased as though the employee had not been survived by a spouse, unless a living former spouse is the parent of any of the eligible children.

Q. If the annuity to one child stops for any reason will the annuity to any remaining children be increased?
A. When the annuity to any one child stops, the other children's annuities are recomputed as if the one child had never been eligible. In some cases this will increase the annuities to the other eligible children.

Q. When a child's annuity stops, is the widow's or widower's annuity affected?
A. No.

Q. Under what conditions would a lump-sum benefit be payable immediately after the death of an employee?
A. A lump-sum benefit is payable immediately if the deceased employee had less than 18 months of civilian service, or if the employee had completed 18 months but leaves no widow, widower, former spouse or children who are eligible for a survivor annuity.

Q. Of what does the immediate lump-sum benefit consist?
A. The amount paid into the Civil Service Retirement Fund by the employee, plus any accrued interest.

Q. May a lump-sum benefit be paid if the employee leaves a surviving spouse, former spouse or children who are eligible for a survivor annuity?
A. No lump-sum benefit may be paid while the surviving spouse, former spouse or children are eligible for a survivor annuity. If when all the survivors' annuities have ended they have received less than the employee paid into the Civil Service Retirement Fund, plus any accrued interest, the difference would be payable as a lump-sum benefit.

Q. May an employee or annuitant change or cancel a designation of beneficiary?
A. Yes. Change or cancellation may be made by executing a new SF-2808 (see Appendix).

Q. Must the husband name his wife as beneficiary on SF 2808 in order that she may be awarded an annuity upon his death?
A. No. The designation or beneficiary is for the lump-sum benefit only. It has no effect on the widow's right to a survivor annuity.

Q. If an employee leaves the government before becoming eligible for an immediate annuity and opts for a deferred annuity at age 62 and dies before reaching that age, will his or her spouse be eligible for a survivor annuity?
A. No. The spouse, however, would be entitled to receive the lump-sum of the employee's contribution to the retirement fund, including interest.

Q. Is an annuity, after reductions to provide for survivor benefits, eligible for cost-of-living increases?
A. Yes. Annual COLAs are applied to the annuity paid to the retiree.

Q. Do survivors of deceased federal employees receive the balance of their retirement contributions?
A. The general answer is yes. However, the formula for determining the amount of refund, if any, the interest, the options for type of refund, and the eligibility criteria for both the deceased federal employee and

survivor(s) can vary depending upon several factors, including length of service and whether the federal employee was under CSRS or FERS.

Q. Can a federal retiree who elected the survivor benefit have his or her annuity restored to full value upon the death of his or her spouse?

A. Yes. The annuity amount can be adjusted to eliminate the survivor reduction, but only if there is no former spouse who is entitled to survivor benefits by court order or by election of the employee. To start the process, call OPM at (202) 606-0500. A death certificate (preferably certified) must be provided as evidence of death.

Q. As a retiree or survivor, can I change the amount of federal income tax being withheld from my annuity?

A. Yes. Using a touch-tone phone, you can call OPM's toll-free number (1-800-409-6528). By following the menu prompts, you can change the amount of federal income tax withheld from your annuity check (along with state tax withholding for a number of states). All you need is your CSA or CSF claim number and your Personal Identification Number, which is the last four digits of your Social Security number. Or, you can request a personalized tax election form (W-4P-A) by writing OPM at the following address:

OPM
P.O. Box 961
Washington, D.C. 20044-0001

Be sure to include your claim number. OPM will provide the form and instructions, then make the changes you request as soon as they receive your completed form.

CSRS Survivor Annuity Options at a Glance
Choices if you are Single at Time of Election

Your Choices:	Requirements:	What Will Happen:
Survivor benefit for person having insurable interest	Must be in good health (OPM requires proof of a physical exam before approving this election). Must elect the benefit for a person who has a reasonable expectancy of financial benefit in the continuance of your life.	Your yearly annuity (after reduction for unpaid deposit for non deduction service) will be reduced by 10%, plus 5% for each 5 years the person is younger than you are up to a maximum 40% reduction. Your insurable interest survivors' annuity will be 55% of the annuity remaining after the above reduction. After your death, your insurable interest survivor will receive annuity for life.
No survivor benefit		You will receive full annuity with no reduction for survivor benefit.
Survivor benefit to former spouse	Marriage must have dissolved on or after May 7, 1985. Marriage must have lasted at least 9 months. If you die in service, you must have performed at least 18 months of service covered by Civil Service Retirement contributions. You must choose what percentage (up to 55%) of your annuity you want your former spouse to receive.	Your annuity will be reduced by 2 ½% of the first $3,600 of the survivor base and 10% of the remainder. Former spouse's benefit will continue until death, or remarriage before age 55.

Figure 6-3

Your Financial Guide

CSRS Survivor Annuity Options at a Glance
Choices if you are Married at Time of Election

Your Choices:	Requirements:	What Will Happen:
Maximum survivor benefit to current spouse	At time of your death, your spouse must have been married to you for at least 9 months unless a child was born of the marriage or the death was accidental.	Your annuity will be reduced by 2 1/2% of the first $3,600, and by 10% of any portion of your annuity which exceeds $3,600. Your spouse's survivor benefit will equal 55% of your full annuity before the above reduction. Your spouse's benefit will continue until death, or until any remarriage occurring before age 55.
Less than maximum survivor benefit to current spouse	At time of your death, your spouse must have been married to you for at least 9 months, unless a child was born of the marriage or the death was accidental. Current spouse's consent	Your annuity will be reduced by 2 1/2% of whatever base you elected up to and including $3,600 and by 10% of any portion of the base you elected which exceeds $3,600. Your spouse's survivor benefit will equal only 55% of the base you elected for the survivor benefit. Your spouse's benefit will continue until death, or until any remarriage before age 55.
No survivor benefit	Current spouse's consent	You will receive full annuity, with no reduction for survivor benefit. Surviving spouse will receive no annuity if you predecease him or her.
Survivor benefit to person having insurable interest	Must be in good health. OPM requires proof of a physical exam before approving this election. Must elect the benefit for a person who has a reasonable expectancy of financial benefit in the continuance of your life.	Your yearly annuity will be reduced by 10%, plus 5% for each 5 years the person is younger than you are up to a maximum 40% reduction Your insurable interest survivor's annuity will be 55% of the annuity remaining after the above reduction. After your death, your insurable interest survivor will receive annuity for life.

Figure 6-3

CSRS Survivor Annuity Options at a Glance
Choices if you are Married at Time of Election

Your Choices:	Requirements:	What Will Happen:
Maximum survivor benefit for former spouse Less than maximum benefit to current spouse	Marriage dissolved on or after May 7, 1985 Marriage lasted at 9 months If you die in service, you have performed at least 18 months of service covered by the Civil Service Retirement Act. Current spouse's consent Your election must be a percentage age not to exceed 55%.	Your annuity will be reduced by the same amount as if the election had been made for a current spouse. The former spouse's benefit will equal the percentage you elected of your survivor base. The former spouse's benefit will continue until death or remarriage prior to age 55.
Survivor benefit to both current and former spouse	Former spouse must meet requirements listed above. Current spouse must meet requirements listed above. Current spouse must consent. Total election cannot exceed 55%.	Your annuity will be reduced using the same formula as for current spouse election. Current and former spouse(s) elected will receive a percentage of your basic annuity as per your election. All current and former spouses' benefits will continue until death, or remarriage prior to age 55.

Figure 6-3

Your Financial Guide

Effect of Court Orders on Survivor Elections if You are Single at Time of Election

Type of Benefit You Elected	What Will Happen If a Court Order Is Involved
Survivor benefit to a person	Your basic annuity will be reduced twice to provide any court ordered survivor having insurable interest benefit to a former spouse, not to exceed 55% of your basic annuity, and the benefit to the person having insurable interest. The court-ordered former spouse's survivor benefit will continue until: • death, or • remarriage prior to age 55, or • a court order is ruled invalid by another court order, or • special circumstances stipulated in the court order take place which require the benefit to end. The insurable interest will continue to receive annuity for life.
No survivor benefit	Your basic annuity will be reduced twice to provide any court ordered survivor benefit to a former spouse, not to exceed 55% of your basic annuity. The court-ordered former spouse's survivor benefit will continue until: • death, or • remarriage prior to age 55, or • a court order is ruled invalid by another court order, or • special circumstances stipulated in the court order take place which require the benefit to end.
Survivor benefit to a former spouse	If a court order involves a different former spouse than the former spouse for whom a survivor benefit was elected: Your basic annuity will be reduced to provide a survivor benefit to the former spouse with the court order, not to exceed 55% of your basic annuity. If any of the 55% full benefit is remaining after the court order is honored, the former spouse for whom a survivor benefit was elected will be eligible to receive the balance. The court order also has priority over any smaller election for the same former spouse. The court-ordered former spouse's survivor benefit will continue until: • death, or • remarriage prior to age 55, or • a court order is ruled invalid by another court order, or • special circumstances stipulated in the court order take place which require the benefit to end.

Figure 6-3

Effect of Court Orders on Survivor Elections if You are Married at Time of Election

Type of Benefit You Elected	What Will Happen If a Court Order Is Involved

Maximum survivor benefit to current spouse.	Count-ordered benefit generally supersedes a benefit you elect for a current spouse. Your basic annuity will be reduced to provide a survivor benefit to a former spouse not to exceed 55% of your basic annuity.
	If court orders the full 55% benefit:
	• You make a "contingency" election for your current spouse which would go into effect when and if the former spouse loses entitlement.
	• No extra reduction to your basic annuity for a "contingency" election.
	• If court orders less than the full benefit:
	• You may insure that your current souse also gets a partial survivor benefit by electing full survivor coverage for your current spouse.
	• Former spouse will get the countordered benefit. Current spouse will get the balance of the full current spouse benefit that remains after subtracting the former spouse's benefit
	• Such a contingency election will mean an additional reduction in the annuity to the extent that the benefit elected for the current spouse exceeds the court-ordered benefit for the former spouse.
	• If the former spouse loses entitlement, current spouse will receive whatever benefit (55% or a partial one) you elected.
	• The court-ordered former spouse's survivor benefit will continue until:
	   - death, or
	   - remarriage prior to age 55, or
	   - a count order is ruled invalid by another court order, or
	   - special circumstances stipulated in the court order take place which require the benefit to end.

Partial (25%) survivor benefit to current spouse	Count ordered benefit generally supersedes a benefit you elect for a current spouse if total benefits exceed 55%.
	Your basic annuity will be reduced to provide a survivor benefit to a former spouse not to exceed 55% of your basic annuity.
	You may still elect a partial survivor benefit (contingency election) for a current spouse, if court orders the full 55% benefit:
	• Former spouse will get the court ordered benefit.
	• If former spouse loses entitlement, the current spouse will only receive the partial benefit you elected.
	The court-ordered former spouse's survivor benefit will continue until:
	   - death, or
	   - remarriage prior to age 55, or
	   - a court order is ruled invalid by another court order, or
	   - special circumstances stipulated in the court order take place which require the benefit to end.

No survivor benefit	Same rules apply as for (2), assuming current spouse's consent obtained
Survivor benefit to a person having insurable Interest	Same rules apply as for (1), assuming current spouse's consent obtained
Survivor benefit to a former spouse	Same rules apply as for (3), assuming current spouse's consent obtained
Survivor benefit to both a current and former spouse	If court order involves a different former spouse than the former spouse for whom a survivor benefit was elected: • Your basic annuity will be reduced to provide a survivor benefit to the former spouse with the court order, not to exceed 55% of your basic annuity. • If any of the 55% full benefit is remaining after the court order is honored, the current and former spouses for whom a survivor benefit was elected will be eligible to receive the balance. The court order also has priority over any election for same former spouse.

Figure 6-3

How Survivor Benefit Might Change After Retirement

Type of Survivor Elected	Post Retirement Possibilities
1. Single person elects no benefit of entitlement.	If you later marry, you may elect a new spouse within 2 years of marriage, or within 2 years of any former spouse's loss Survivor benefit goes into effect after 9 months of marriage unless your death is accidental or spouse is the natural parent of your child. Your annuity will be reduced retroactive to the commencing date of your annuity, plus 6% interest, compounded annually. This deposit is paid by a permanent acturarial reduction.
2. Married person elects no benefit	You may change a current spouse survivor annuity election no later than 18 months after your annuity started if you are: • changing your election so as to provide a survivor annuity; or • increasing a less than maximum survivor annuity election. In either case, you would have to pay a retroactive adjustment, a charge of 24.5% of the amount of the increase from the original base to the new survivor base, *plus* applicable interest (see Figure 6-5). This is the same rate that is used for deposits and redeposits (and VC accounts). If you later divorce, you may not elect a benefit for the ex-spouse. If you marry a different person, the rules in (1) apply. In the case of a post-retirement divorce, OPM will not honor a court-ordered survivor benefit for a person who, at the time of retirement, had consented to having no survivor coverage. *NOTE:* An election during this 18-month period is void if it is received by OPM after the retiree dies.
3. Married person elects full (55%) benefit for current spouse only	If your marriage ends by death or divorce, annuity reduction ends. If divorced, you may elect benefit for ex-spouse within 2 years of divorce if: • person was married to you a total of at least 9 months, • former spouse does not remarry prior to age 55, • you had 18 months of creditable service, and • any new spouse to whom you are married at the time of election consents to it. In the case of post-retirement divorce, OPM will honor an acceptable court order providing continued survivor coverage for the spouse who had survivor coverage at time of retirement. If you later remarry the same or a different spouse, you may elect as in (1).
4. Married person elects partial benefit for current spouse only.	Rules in (2) and (3) apply except that you may elect a benefit for an ex-spouse to whom married at retirement, but not one that exceeds the benefit consented to at time of retirement. In the case of a post-retirement divorce, OPM will not honor a court-ordered survivor coverage larger than the one elected at the time of retirement.

Figure 6-3

How Survivor Benefit Might Change After Retirement

Type of Survivor Elected	Post Retirement Possibilities
5. Retiree elects benefit for former spouse only	If you later marry or remarry, you may not change the election of an eligible former spouse. If former spouse loses eligibility (by death or remarriage under age 55), reduction in annuity ends.
6. Retiree elects combination benefit for current & former spouse.	If either the current or former spouse loses eligibility (by death, etc.) the portion of the benefit reduction in annuity for that person (but not the other) ends. Rules in (4) apply if marriage ends. If former spouse loses eligibility, the elected benefit may not be increased for current spouse.
7. Retiree elects an insurable interest benefit only.	If person elected as insurable interest dies, reduction for insurable interest ends. If you later marry someone other than the insurable interest designee, you may elect a benefit for a spouse as in (1) above, and (if desired) end the insurable interest election. If you later marry the insurable interest designee and, within 2 years, elect a regular survivor annuity for that person, the insurable interest benefit will be automatically canceled. If a former spouse with a court-ordered benefit loses entitlement, you may change (if within 2 years) an insurable interest benefit for a current spouse to a regular survivor benefit for a current spouse. If you have already died, widow(er) can elect (within 2 years of former spouse losing entitlement) to change the insurable interest annuity to a regular survivor annuity.
8. Retiree elects both a full survivor interest benefit for another person.	If marriage ends, or the person with insurable interest dies, the annuity reduction for the benefit for spouse and an insurable relevant election ends. If marriage ends, rules in (3) or (4) apply.

Figure 6-3

Survivor Benefits for Children

Type/Eligibility Requirements:	*Amount of Benefits:*	*Commencement/Termination:*
Child can be: • legitimate • recognized natural (born out of wedlock) • adopted • stepchild (if living with employee) Must be unmarried. Must be under age 18, or between age 18 and 22 and a full-time student, or disabled before age 18 and incapable of self support as determined by the Social Security Administration. You must have contributed to child's support. Benefit is automatic for eligible dependents; no election required.	1-3 children payable: each child will received the maximum rate. 4 or more children payable: the rate is reduced proportionately for each so that total for all children equals the total 3 children would get. If no former or current spouse survives who is a parent of any eligible children — higher rate is payable.	Annuity commences the day after your death. Annuity terminates end of the month preceding the terminating event: 1. Marriage 2. Death 3. Attainment of age 18 (if not a full-time student) 4. Attainment of age 22 (if a full-time student; however, if this occurs during the school year, annuity continues until end of the school year). 5. Ceases to attend school as a full-time student. 6. Becomes capable of self support (disabled child).

Figure 6-3

How COLAs are Added to Survivor Annuities

Survivor Type:	When Eligible:	How Amount of COLA is Determined
Current Spouse	Commencing date of Survivor annuity.	Based on increases in the Consumer Price Index.
Former Spouse	Effective December 1 of each year and reflected in the payment dated January 2, unless changed by Congress.	If a deceased annuitant has been on rolls less than 11 months at time of death, survivor gets 1/12 of the COLA percentage for each month during which either s/he or the retiree was on the rolls prior to the effective date of the COLA.
Children	Commencing date of child's annuity.	Includes all CSRS COLAs authorized with the percentage increase applying to the child's entire monthly benefit.
	Effective December 1 of each year and reflected in the payment dated January 2, unless changed by Congress.	Includes full CSRS COLA, regardless of how long the deceased annuitant was on the rolls.

Lump Sum Benefits Following Death of Annuitant

Type Available:	Conditions of Payment:	Amount Payable:	Eligible Beneficiaries:
Unexpended Balance	If no monthly survivor annuity is payable, and no Alternative Annuity lump sum was elected at retirement.	Amount by which your contributions to the Retirement Fund, plus any interest due, exceeds the total amount of the annuity you and all your eligible survivors receive.	Based upon Order of Precedence: 1. Designated Beneficiary (listed on valid SF2808) 2. Widow(er) 3. Child(ren) in equal shares, with the share of any deceased child distributed to descendants of that child. 4. Parent(s) 5. Executor of Administrator of your estate. 6. Next of kin entitled under the laws of the state in which you are domiciled at the time of your death.
Accrued Annuity	If deceased had annuity at time of death. Paid whether or not there is a survivor eligible for a recurring monthly annuity.	Prorated amount of the last monthly retirement check you were entitled to.	

Figure 6-3

Your Financial Guide

CHAPTER SEVEN

SURVIVOR BENEFITS UNDER FEDERAL RETIREMENT PROGRAMS — FERS

If you are covered by the Federal Employees' Retirement System, FERS is designed to be the first element in your basic retirement and survivor benefits package. The other two are Social Security and the Thrift Savings Plan.

One of the most important features of FERS is that it provides survivor benefits for both active and retired employees. These benefits are purchased by the contributions that you and your agency make to the Civil Service Retirement Fund, which is administered by OPM.

While the benefits of active and retired employees and their survivors are generally based on age, years of service and earnings, they are calculated in different ways as explained below. When calculating these benefits, you should bear in mind that there are differences between the status of an active worker and a retired employee. We will point out the distinctions as we go along. Remember, after you retire, you may need to arrange for changes in a plan that you made while you were an active employee.

Current Employees: FERS Survivor Benefits

If you are a currently employed worker who dies after having met certain minimum service requirements, your survivors will receive important benefits that can help them to live a more financially secure life after you are gone. In addition, Social Security's wage insurance provisions will provide benefits to the families of deceased workers covered by that program (see Chapter 8). Your survivors also may have special rights under the Thrift Savings Plan (see Chapter 11).

Among the survivor benefits available to a spouse, a FERS annuity is among the most significant financially because it entitles the recipient to a monthly payment as long as he or she remains eligible. For most widow(er)s, this will be for the rest of their lives. For children, the benefit generally ends at age 18.

Your widow(er) and children may qualify for a survivor benefit if your death occurs:

- While you are employed and covered by FERS; and
- After you have completed at least 18 months of creditable civilian service.

These annuities are increased by annual cost-of-living adjustments (COLAs), which can help your survivors to keep up with inflation.

Specific Eligibility Requirements

Active employees who die are assured that their survivors, including spouses and dependent children, will be eligible for FERS survivor benefits. Here's a closer look at the eligibility criteria.

Surviving Spouse — To qualify for a survivor benefit, your widow(er) must:

- Have been married to you for at least nine months in total before your death; or
- Be the natural parent of your child.

Note: These requirements do not apply if your death is accidental.

Children — To qualify for a survivor annuity, your child must be:

- Under age 18; and
- Unmarried.

A stepchild may qualify for a survivor annuity if he or she meets the requirements above and, in addition, has lived with you in a regular parent-child relationship. Similarly, an illegitimate child that you acknowledge may qualify for a survivor annuity if he or she meets the requirements above and, in addition, can show dependency on you.

A child over 18 may qualify for a survivor annuity if incapable of self-support because of a disability that began before he or she reached age 18.

Also, a child over 18 may be eligible for a survivor annuity up to age 22 if he or she is a student in full-time attendance at a high school, college, or other recognized educational institution. The annuity will continue during non-school intervals of not over five months between school years or terms, if a clear intention to remain a full-time student is shown. Statements from both the student and the school will help prove this intent.

Your Financial Guide

Current Employees: Survivor Annuity Calculations

Survivors of a deceased, actively employed federal worker are generally entitled to FERS benefit payments. They are calculated as described below.

Surviving Spouse

The surviving spouse of a deceased, active employee generally is entitled to two kinds of benefits: a death benefit and annuity benefits.

Death Benefit— If you die as an active employee and your surviving spouse qualifies, she or he will be paid a death benefit, which usually is paid as a lump-sum amount. The amount of the benefit changes annually (reflecting changes in the CPI), and is based in part on your years of service:

More than 18 months but less than 10 years	1. A lump sum payment (in 1997-- $21,335.30) *Plus* 2. A lump sum equal to the higher of: a. 1/2 of annual basic pay at time of death *or* b. 1/2 of the "high-3" average salary
10 or more years of FERS service	A combination of 1 and 2 above *Plus* 3. A survivor annuity equal to 50% of the employee's basic annuity under FERS*

* For employees with prior CSRS service, the spouse receives 50 percent of the combined CSRS and FERS benefit.

Note: The basic employee death benefit is not payable if Office of Workers' Compensation Programs (OWCP) benefits are elected.

This lump-sum benefit may be taken in one payment or in 36 monthly installments. Your spouse will be able to make that decision on a Standard Form 3104B, "Documentation and Elections in Support of Application for Death Benefits When Deceased Was an Employee at the Time of Death." Your employing agency will provide that form after inserting the amounts payable. An election to receive the lump sum in installments may be canceled at any time, and the undistributed balance provided in one check.

Note: The amount your spouse receives under the installment plan will be slightly higher because it includes interest earned on the unexpended balance.

Annuity Benefits— If you are an active employee and die with 10 or more years of service, your surviving spouse also is entitled to an annual annuity under FERS. The amount of this annual survivor annuity is based on a simple formula:

$$1\% \times \text{"high-3" average salary} \times \text{years of service} \div 2$$

Example

If your "high-3" average salary was $35,000 and you had 14 years of service, your spouse would be eligible to receive $204.71 per month in addition to the lump-sum payout. That monthly amount is computed as follows:

$$1\% \times \$35{,}000 = \$350 \times 14 \text{ years} = \$4{,}900$$
$$\div 2 = \$2{,}450 \div 12 = \$204.71$$

The spousal annuity begins on the day after your death and ends on the last day of the month before the one in which your widow(er) dies or remarries. It will be increased annually by COLAs.

A spousal annuity will terminate upon the spouse's remarriage only if the remarriage occurs while the individual is under age 55. If he or she does remarry while under the applicable age, the annuity may be restored if the remarriage is dissolved by death, annulment, or divorce.

Note: Annuity benefits may be reduced if your survivors are eligible for Social Security benefits based on your FERS service. Generally, there is no difference in the total amount of benefits your spouse will receive.

Surviving Children With a Surviving Parent

If you are survived by a spouse or former spouse who is the parent of your child or children, these dependents are eligible for a survivor annuity. The survivor annuity rate is determined as follows:

- Compute the total amount payable to all children;
- Subtract the total amount payable to all children by Social Security; and
- Divide that amount by the number of children.

The total amount payable to all children is the lesser of:

- $337 per month per child; or
- $1,011 per month divided by the number of eligible children.

Note: These dollar amounts are in effect through December 1, 1997.

Following are two examples of how survivor benefit amounts are calculated. The first example involves an active employee with one dependent child; the second, an employee with four children.

Example 1

Calculation of Child's Survivor Annuity — One Dependent of Surviving Spouse

The lesser of:
A. $337 per month
B. $1,011 per month ÷ 1 = $1,011

In this example, the annuity will be A because it is the lesser of the two amounts.

Example 2
Calculation of Children's Survivor Annuity—Four Dependents of Surviving Spouse

The lesser of:
A. $337 per month per child
B. $1,011 per month ÷ 4 = $252.75 per month

In this example, the annuity will be B for each child because it is the lesser of the two amounts.

Surviving Children Without a Surviving Parent

Each qualified child, except an illegitimate child, who has no surviving parent will be paid the lesser of:

A. $404 per month per child; or
B. $1,212 per month, divided by the number of children.
Note: The dollar amounts above are in effect through December 1, 1997.

Following are two examples of how survivor benefit amounts are calculated. The first example involves an active employee with one dependent child; the second, an employee with four children.

Example 1
Calculation of Child's Survivor Annuity—One Child Without a Surviving Parent

A. $404 per month
B. $1,212 per month ÷ 1 = $1,212
In this example, the annuity will be A because it is the lesser of the two amounts.

Example 2
Calculation of Child's Survivor Annuity — Four Children Without a Surviving Parent
A. $404 per month per child
B. $1,212 per month ÷ 4 = $303

In this example, the annuity will be B for each child because it is the lesser of the two amounts.

Note: These benefits are available to qualified dependent children whether your spouse or former spouse died before or after you did.

The survivor annuity for each qualified child begins the day after your death and ends on the last day of the month before the one in which the child dies, marries, reaches age 18, or, if over 18, becomes capable of self-support. This latter category only applies to a child who was incapable of earning a living because of a physical or mental disability incurred before age 18.

Exception: The annuity of a child who is a student will end on the last day of the month before he or she: (1) marries, (2) dies, (3) ceases to be a student, or (4) attains the age of 22. If a student-child drops out of school and his or her annuity is terminated, it can be restored if he or she later returns to school and is still under 22 and unmarried.

A child's annuity will be paid to his or her guardian if one has been appointed by a court. If no guardian is appointed, payment will be made, at the discretion of the Office of Personnel Management, to the person who has the care and custody of the child. In general, a child's annuity is considered a contribution for the care of the child, and therefore the money normally is controlled by a parent or guardian. If a child continues receiving an annuity after age 18—for example, as a full-time student—the child may receive the money directly. This is a family decision.

Note: FERS annuity benefits are offset by the amount of Social Security benefits payable to your children based on your FERS service. Generally, there is no difference in the total amount of benefits they will receive.

Potential Reductions in a Survivor Annuity

Generally, a survivor annuity must be reduced if you performed any creditable government service before January 1, 1989, for which no retirement contributions were made, unless you made a deposit to cover that service. That's because those years can't be included in the annuity computation. The annuity reduction is equal to 1 percent for each year of non-deduction service.

In addition, if you died before making or completing a deposit for post-1956 military service performed before you were covered by FERS (or have received a refund of CSRS contributions and have not made a redeposit), those years of service will not be creditable for retirement purposes. However, your survivor will be given the opportunity to make the necessary payment. If made, the deposit would be credited to the CSRS component of your FERS benefit. Whether making this payment would be worth doing will depend on how much was owed, including interest, and how much the repayment would increase your survivor's annuity. The Office of Personnel Management will send information that will assist your survivor in making an informed decision.

Note: Reductions that would normally be made in your own annuity if you were under age 55 or in a leave-without-pay status for six months or less in the calendar year that you retired will not be made in your survivor's annuity.

Retired Employees: Survivor Annuities

There are three kinds of annuities a retiring employee may elect under FERS. All three guarantee that annuities will be paid to any eligible children. The amount of these annuities will be the same as those provided to the children of employees who die.

Basic Life Annuity — This is an annuity without a survivor benefit, such as the kind you would provide to your spouse.

Reduced Annuity With Benefit to Widow(er) or Former Spouse — You may agree to take a reduction in your basic annuity and name your wife, husband, or former spouse as the person who will receive your survivor annuity. If you have a current spouse, the law requires that you choose this option, unless you and your spouse agree in writing to waive that right.

Note: You are required to provide a survivor annuity to a former spouse if this is stipulated in a divorce agreement or annulment that ended your marriage after May 6, 1985. By law, the stipulated amount cannot exceed 50 percent of your unreduced annuity entitlement amount.

Reduced Annuity With Benefit to Specific Individual — If you are in good health and there is no court order in force for a former spouse annuity when you retire, you may name a specific individual who has a continuing financial interest in you to receive a survivor annuity. Such an "insurable interest" election may be made in addition to or instead of a spousal annuity. If made instead of a spousal annuity, you must obtain your spouse's consent in writing. The amount of your annuity is reduced by 10 to 40 percent based on the difference between your ages.

An insurable interest is presumed to exist with:

- A current spouse (where a court order for a former spouse has prevented you from providing him or her with a regular survivor annuity);
- A blood or adoptive relative closer than first cousins;
- A former spouse;
- A person to whom the employee is engaged to be married; or
- A person living in a common-law marriage relationship with the employee that is recognized by the state in which they are domiciled.

However, you may be able to designate others to receive an insurable interest annuity. The individual named must have a clear financial interest in you and be reasonably expected to benefit from your continued life.

To prove good health, you must arrange and pay for a medical examination and provide a dated report signed by a licensed physician along with your retirement application.

Note: While the insurable interest election is a convenient way to provide for someone near and dear to you, you should still consider other options that may be more cost effective, such as a term insurance policy naming that person as the beneficiary.

Should You Elect a Survivor Annuity?

Nearly all retiring employees who are married elect a survivor annuity for their spouses. They do this for a variety of good reasons, but the most compelling is that it's hard to beat the government's deal. Not only are the terms of the annuity significant, but providing one allows your widow(er) to continue federal employee health benefits insurance (FEHB) coverage after your death.

Although a retiree—with the agreement of his or her spouse—could elect a full annuity without a survivor benefit and instead purchase an insurance policy to make up the difference, it is very difficult for a private insurer to match the value you get from a government survivor annuity. That's because private insurers load investment costs, agent commissions, and other overhead onto their premiums. None of these are added to the amount paid for a civil service survivor annuity. If a financial planner claims you can do better, make sure you get a detailed explanation before you buy the alternative.

While there may be instances where not electing a survivor annuity may seem like the right thing to do, you must remember that this is not a decision you can make on your own. An annuity for your spouse is automatic at the time of your retirement unless you and your spouse ask in writing for an annuity without any (or reduced) survivor benefits.

Calculating Annuity Payments for Retiree's Survivors

Widow(er) or Former Spouse

Normally, the decision to elect a survivor annuity is made at the time you retire. However, under certain circumstances that decision may be made after retirement.

Choosing a survivor benefit will not only provide an income to your spouse, but also will have an immediate effect on your annuity. Simply stated, the normal annuity benefits you would have received will be reduced during your lifetime in order to pay for a survivor benefit. The standard survivor annuity under FERS is 50 percent of your unreduced annuity. However, with your spouse's concurrence it can be based on 25 percent.

There are a number of reasons why a couple may agree to a reduced spousal annuity. Most common are:

- Where both parties have earned their own retirement and it is adequate to meet their individual needs; or
- Where their financial situation is such that receiving a higher monthly income now is more important than receiving it later in the form of a higher survivor annuity.
- When it is highly unlikely that the person who would be designated for the survivor benefit would outlive the primary beneficiary.

If you elect an Annuity With Survivor Benefit to Widow, Widower, or Former Spouse, your annuity will be reduced by 10 percent. For this, your surviving spouse will receive an annuity of 50 percent of your unreduced FERS benefit plus a special supplementary annuity payable until age 60, if your spouse will not be eligible for Social Security benefits until age 60.

The amount of this supplement is equal to the lesser result of two formulas:

- The amount of the survivor benefit payable under CSRS minus the amount payable under FERS.
- The amount of Social Security survivor benefit attributable to FERS service based on the annuity formula payable when the spouse attains age 60.

If you and your spouse choose a survivor annuity of 25 percent of your unreduced benefit, your annuity will be reduced by 5 percent. The same rules for the supplementary annuity apply.

Note: Separate provisions apply to spouses of disabled retirees.

Examples of Annuity Reduced for a Full Survivor Benefit

Example 1: FERS Service Only
Your Annual Annuity: $10,000
Reduction: 10%
Your Reduced Annuity = $9,000
  ($10,000 - $1,000) ÷ 12 = $750 per month

Survivor Annuity = 50% of the unreduced annuity:
  $10,000 × 50% = $5,000 ÷ 12 = $416.66 per month

Example 2: Combined CSRS and FERS Service
Your Annual Annuity: $26,000

CSRS Component
CSRS Annuity: $20,600
Reduction: 10%
Your Reduced CSRS Annuity = $18,540
($20,600 - $1,790) ÷ 12 = $1,545/month

FERS Component
Your FERS Annuity: $5,400
Reduction: 10%
Your Reduced FERS Annuity = $4,860
  ($5,400 - $540) ÷ 12 = $405/month

Total Reduced Annuity = $23,400
($26,000 - $2,600 ($2,060 + $540) ÷ 12 = $1,950/ month

Total Survivor Annuity = 50 percent of your total unreduced annuity:

$26,000 × 50% = $13,000 ÷ 12 = $1,083.33/month

Examples of Annuity Reduced for a 25 Percent Survivor Annuity

Example 1: FERS Service Only
Your Annual Annuity: $10,000
Reduction: 5%
Your Reduced Annuity =
$9,500 ($10,000 - $500) ÷ 12 = $791.66/month

Survivor Annuity = 25% of the unreduced annuity:
$10,000 × 25% = $2,500 ÷ 12 = $208.33/ month

Example 2: Combined CSRS and FERS Service
Your Annual Annuity: $26,000

CSRS Component
CSRS Annuity: $20,600
Reduction: 5%

Your Reduced CSRS Annuity =
$19,570 ($20,600 - $1,030) ÷ 12 = $1,630.83/ month

FERS Component
Your FERS Annuity: $5,400
Reduction: 5%

Your Reduced FERS Annuity =
$5,130 ($5,400 - $270) ÷ 12 = $427.50/month

Your Total Reduced Annuity = $24,700 (26,000 - $1,300
($1,030 + $270) ÷ 12 = $2,058.33/month

Total Survivor Annuity = 25 percent of your total unreduced annuity: $26,000 × 25% = $6,500 ÷ 12 = $541.66/month

Effect of Marital Changes
If the spouse you named at the time you retired dies before you do (or the marriage is otherwise dissolved), you are entitled to have your full annuity restored as of the first of the month following your spouse's death. The amount deducted from your annuity while your spouse was still alive won't be refunded to you.

If you remarry, the person you married after retirement will be eligible to receive a survivor benefit if your written request is received by the OPM no later than two years after the date of remarriage.

Your Financial Guide

If you are unmarried at the time of retirement and later marry, you may, within two years after marriage, elect a reduced annuity with survivor benefits to your spouse. Your request for such a change must be received by OPM no later than two years after you marry. Once a change in election is accepted by OPM it cannot be changed again.

Note: A retiree who marries on or after October 1, 1993, and elects a survivor annuity for that spouse has his or her annuity permanently reduced based on actuarial tables. This actuarial reduction is in addition to the regular survivor annuity reduction. The dollar amount of the survivor annuity will be the same as if the election had been made at retirement.

To be eligible for a survivor benefit in the above circumstances, the spouse must be married to you for at least nine months before your death, or, if married less than nine months, be the natural parent of your child (or your death must be accidental).

Note: The term "accidental" does not include death as a result of intentional self-destruction, while sane or insane, or as a result of the self-administration of illegal or illegally obtained drugs.

Dependent Children

If, upon your death after retirement, you are survived by children, they could, regardless of the type of annuity you had elected, qualify for a survivor annuity under the same conditions and in the same amounts as generally applicable for dependent children.

Specific Individual

If you elect an "insurable interest" annuity, a survivor annuity will, upon your death after retirement, be paid to the person you named when you retired. The benefit will be based on 50 percent of your basic annuity after it has been reduced to account for the difference in age between you and the designated person. (Figure 7-1)

Example
Annual annuity of $28,000
Reduction of 30 percent for beneficiary 22 years younger = $8,400
Reduced annuity = $19,600

Insurable interest annuity of 50 percent of the reduced annuity = $9,800 ÷ 12 = $816.66 per month

If the person you named dies before you do, you must notify OPM so that your annuity can be restored to the higher unreduced rate. The reduction made to your annuity while your designee was still alive won't be refunded to you, however.

An insurable interest election may be changed to a "reduced annuity with a survivor benefit to a spouse," if you marry after retirement. Your written request for such a change must be received by OPM no later than one year after you marry. Once a change in election is accepted by OPM, it cannot be changed.

Disability Retirement

If you are totally disabled for useful and efficient service in your current position (or any other vacant position at the same grade and pay for which you are qualified) and have at least 18 months of creditable service, you may be eligible for a disability retirement.

Your personnel office will provide and can help you fill out the necessary form, SF-3107, "Application for Immediate Retirement," and forward it to OPM, along with the necessary statements from you, your boss, and your physician. OPM is solely responsible for making the final determination as to whether you are disabled and its standards are strict.

OPM considers disability retirement to be a last resort, appropriate only when you can no longer do your job because of injury or disease (including mental illness), and after every reasonable effort has been made to keep you on the job. The disability must be expected to continue for at least one year to qualify for a disability retirement.

If your application is approved, you will qualify for disability retired pay. For the first year of eligibility, you get 60 percent of your "high-3" average salary, minus 100 percent of any Social Security benefit payable.

After the first year and until age 62, if you do not qualify for Social Security disability benefits, your benefit drops to 40 percent of your "high-3." If you do qualify for Social Security benefits, your benefit will be reduced by 60 percent of the initial Social Security benefit to which you are entitled. The resulting total will be equal to at least 40 percent of your "high-3" plus 40 percent of your Social Security benefits. Both your FERS and Social Security benefits will be increased by COLAs annually.

Insurable Interest Annuity Reductions

Age of Person Named in Relation to that of Retiring Employee	Reduction in Annuity of Retiring Employee
Older, same age, or less than 5 years younger	10%
5 but less than 10 years younger	15%
10 but less than 15 years younger	20%
15 but less than 20 years younger	25%
20 but less than 25 years younger	30%
25 but less than 30 years younger	35%
30 or more years younger	40%

Figure 7-1

Note: If your earned annuity rate (1 percent x "high-3" average pay x years of service) is higher than the above rates with the reduction for Social Security, you will receive the higher benefit.

When you reach age 62, your disability benefit will be recomputed. An artificial retirement benefit is calculated for you, based on the assumption that you had worked until age 62. Thus, actual service is added to the time spent on the disability rolls to age 62. The total time is then multiplied by 1 percent (or by 1.1 percent if you have at least 20 years of service). The amount produced by this calculation is then multiplied by your "high-3" average salary at the onset of your disability retirement and increased by COLAs payable from that time to age 62.

Because FERS and Social Security are intertwined, if you apply for disability benefits under FERS you also must apply for Social Security disability benefits. The government cannot pay any benefits—even interim payments pending final adjudication of your claim—until the Office of Personnel Management confirms that you have filed a Social Security disability application.

Note: If a disability retiree recovers or is restored to earning capacity before reaching age 60, the annuity will be continued temporarily to afford an opportunity to seek reemployment. The annuity payments will be discontinued from the earliest of the following dates:

- Reemployment by the government.
- One year from the date of a medical examination showing recovery.
- Six months from the end of the calendar year in which earning capacity is restored.

Restoration to earning capacity means that the retiree has income from wages or self-employment, or both, that equals at least 80 percent of the current salary for the position occupied immediately before going on disability retirement.

The amount of a survivor annuity depends on the age of the disability retiree when he or she died. If the retiree died after reaching age 62, then the annuity is computed the same as it would be for the survivor of any other retiree. If the retiree died before age 62, a special computation is used.

- Nondisability Retirement Survivor Computation—The full FERS survivor annuity is 50 percent of the retiree's annuity before it was reduced by the cost of the survivor benefit. If the retiree (with spousal consent) chose a reduced annuity, the survivor will receive 25 percent of the unreduced annuity.
- Special Computation—If the disability retiree died before age 62, the retiree's earned annuity is increased by the amount of time between retirement and age 62 and the average salary is increased by the annual COLAs the annuitant received. The survivor then receives an annuity of 50 percent (or 25 percent if the couple elected a partial survivor benefit) of that amount as an annuity.

Note: Regardless of which annuity computation is used, all survivor annuities are increased annually by COLAs.

Cost of Living Adjustments (COLAs)

The following FERS benefits are increased annually by COLAs.

- Retirement benefits payable to retirees age 62 and older.
- Retirement benefits payable to law enforcement officers, firefighters, air traffic controllers, military reserve technicians who lost their military status due to medical reasons and who were age 50 with at least 25 years of service, and CIA employees.
- Survivor benefits
- Disability retirement benefits

The amount of the increase depends on the annual change in the Consumer Price Index for Urban Wage Earners and Clerical Workers (CPI/W). If the CPI increases by 3 percent or more in any year, then the above benefits are increased by the CPI/W minus one percentage point. If the CPI/W increases by 2 to 3 percent, the adjustment will be 2 percent. If the CPI/W increase is 2 percent or less, then the adjustment will equal the CPI/W.

There are no limitations placed on the CSRS component of a combined FERS-CSRS annuity. It will be increased annually by the unreduced CPI/W, regardless of age or circumstance of retirement.

Retiree COLAs of Recent Years

Table of FERS COLAs

Effective Date	Year	Rate
12/1	1997	2.0*
3/1	1996	2.0*
3/1	1995	2.0*
3/1	1994	2.0*
12/1	1992	2.0
12/1	1991	2.7
12/1	1990	4.4
12/1	1989	3.7
12/1	1988	3.0
12/1	1987	3.2

Note: COLAs are actually paid in the month following their effective date.
* The COLA was delayed three months, under PL 103-66.

Figure 7-2

Your Financial Guide

These congressionally-approved COLA formulas call for increases to become effective each December and payable in the January checks. However, in recent years COLA payments frequently have been delayed by Congress from January to April.

Initially, the number of months for which an retiree or survivor receives the COLA is prorated over the number of months during the year the employee retired. For example, a person eligible in May would receive 7/12 of the COLA, compared with 2/12 of the COLA for a person retiring in October, etc. Over the last decade, FERS COLA increases have ranged from a high of 4.4 percent to a low of 2 percent. For CSRS they have ranged between 2.6 and 5.4 percent.

Death Benefits

In certain circumstances, the survivors of current employees and retirees may be eligible for a death benefit, which is payable in a lump sum. This lump-sum payment generally represents a refund of the undistributed portion of your retirement-fund contributions. If you have not designated a beneficiary on a form SF-3102, lump-sum payments will be made according to the Order of Precedence (see below) mandated by law.

The rules governing this type of lum sum death benefit differ, depending on whether the deceased employee is an active or retired worker:

If Death Occurs Before Retirement — If you have less than 18 months of service, or leave no one who can qualify for a survivor annuity, your contributions to the retirement fund (but not your agency's contributions), with interest, will be paid as a lump-sum death benefit following the Order of Precedence outlined below.

If you leave someone who qualifies for a survivor annuity, no lump-sum death benefit is payable immediately. A lump-sum death benefit may be payable later if the annuities to your survivors end and they have received less than your contributions to the retirement fund, plus interest. This situation might occur if your spouse dies shortly after you do and you have no children who are young enough to be eligible for a survivor annuity.

The amount payable as a lump-sum death benefit will be the difference between your contributions, plus interest, and the total paid out in survivor annuities. That amount will be paid to the next eligible person on the Order of Precedence.

Note: Only the interest received in a lump-sum payment is taxable. The remainder represents a return of money that has already been taxed.

If Death Occurs After Retirement — If you leave no one who can qualify for a survivor annuity, a lump-sum death benefit consisting of the annuity accrued to date of death generally is payable immediately. Also, if the total annuity already paid to you is less than what you have contributed to the retirement fund, the difference will represent a balance payable as an immediate lump-sum death benefit to the next eligible person on the Order of Precedence (see below). No interest is included in this payment.

If you leave someone who qualifies for a survivor annuity, no lump-sum death benefit (other than unpaid annuity accrued to date of death) is payable immediately. A lump-sum death benefit may be payable later if the annuities to your survivors end (for example, if your spouse dies shortly after you did and you have no children who are young enough for a survivor annuity). The amount paid will be the amount you contributed to the retirement fund minus the amount of annuity already paid to you and your survivors. No interest is included. The lump-sum death benefit will be paid to the next eligible person on the Order of Precedence.

Note: These lump-sum payments represent a return of contributions you made while employed and have already been taxed. Therefore, they will not be taxed again.

If you have children who survive you and are under age 18, or who are full-time students aged 18 through 21 (or a child who is incapable of self-support because of a disability incurred before age 18), they are entitled to the same benefits received by the children of employees who die during active service. Such benefits are subject to cost-of-living adjustments and currently amount to approximately $300 per month.

Order of Precedence

The Order of Precedence is a legally mandated list indicating the order in which property passes to beneficiaries, usually in the absence of a binding or enforceable will. The Order of Preference is the prescribed order in which your undistributed retirement contributions will be paid, as a lump sum death benefit, if you have not designated a beneficiary on Form SF-3102.

Under the Order of Preference, any lump-sum death benefit payable after your death will be paid to the following person or persons in the order indicated:

(1) to the beneficiary designated by you on a Standard Form 3102, Designation of Beneficiary;
(2) if you did not designate a beneficiary, to your widow(er);
(3) if you leave no widow(er), to your child or children in equal shares, with the share of any deceased child distributed among the descendants of the child;
(4) if none of the above, to your parents (or parent);

(5) if none of the above, to the executor or administrator of your estate;
(6) if none of the above, to your next of kin who may be entitled under the laws of the state in which you are living at the time of your death.

Designation of Beneficiary

A designation of beneficiary must be in writing—Form SF 3102 is specified for this purpose—and must be received by the Office of Personnel Management before your death. Employees wishing to make a designation should fill out the form and give it to their personnel office, which will forward it to OPM. Retirees may send it directly to OPM.

You do not need to designate a beneficiary to receive the lump-sum death benefit unless you wish to name a person or persons not mentioned in the order of precedence shown above, or unless you wish to name a person who is mentioned but in a different order or for a different share. A designation of beneficiary is for lump-sum death benefit purposes only and does not affect the right of any person who can qualify for a survivor annuity.

If you designate a beneficiary, remember to keep your designation current. Changes in your family or employment status without a corresponding change in your designation may result in a settlement other than you intended.

How Your Survivors Collect Benefits After You Die

Current Employees

One of the first things your survivors or a family friend should do is call the office you worked for and notify them of your death. That office will call the servicing personnel office in your agency.

If you die while currently employed, your agency is responsible for helping your survivors to receive benefits. Your agency's personnel office will answer any questions and supply the necessary forms and, on their completion, forward them to OPM. OPM will, in turn, get in touch with your survivors by mail. From that time forward, OPM will be their point of contact. For your convenience, we have enclosed a copy of the SF-3104, Application for Death Benefits in the Appendix.

Retirees

Your survivor, another family member, or a friend may call OPM or write OPM to report your death and begin the process of securing benefits. Whether the notification is made by phone or in writing, the following information must be provided:

- Your full name,
- Your annuity claim number (CSA number),
- Your date of birth,
- The date of your death, and
- The name and address of the person(s) who may be entitled to death benefits.

A sample notification letter for your survivor's use is in the Appendix. However, the best way to expedite a case is to call OPM. OPM's phone number is 202-606-0500; TDD 202-606-0551. A recorded message can be left 24 hours a day, 7 days a week. To speak to a customer service representative, call Monday through Friday (except federal holidays) from 7:30 a.m. to 5 p.m. (EST).

When it receives notification, OPM will stop your annuity payments and send an Application for Death Benefits — Survivor Supplement (SF-3104A) to the person(s) who appear to be entitled to benefits. If your deceased spouse was covered by the FEHB, OPM will provide the form needed to authorize a change of health insurance coverage (if you do not have dependent children) to the "self-only" option. If Federal Employees' Group Life Insurance (FEGLI) is payable, OPM will also send an application for those benefits.

Your death certificate must be included with the completed SF 3104 that your survivor returns to OPM. The funeral director or a third party who is helping to settle your estate will help your survivor obtain certified copies of the death certificate for this and other required notification purposes. For example, an additional copy of the death certificate will be needed if you were covered by FEGLI.

Note: Having the death certificate certified, (i.e., oficially stamped or embossed) will expedite the processing of your case by OPM and the Office of Federal Employees' Group Life Insurance.

In some cases, OPM may ask for additional documentation. To help your survivor respond quickly to a request, take a moment now to obtain certified copies of your marriage certificate and the birth certificates of your dependent child(ren) and place them in a secure file. Similarly, if you have a child who was disabled before age 18, obtain documentation from your physician to support his/her eligibility.

Note: To further assist your survivor(s), in the Appendix we have provided a list of situations that might cause your survivor(s) to get in touch with OPM, plus the addresses and phone numbers.

Annuity Amounts Received After Your Death

Most retirees have their monthly annuity payments electronically transferred to a financial institution. If the final month's payment was sent this way, your survivor must have the financial institution return the funds in question to the Treasury Department without delay. If you have been receiving your annuity checks through the mail, any checks dated after your death should be returned to:

Director, Regional Finance Center
PO Box 7367
Chicago, IL 60680-7367

A statement that you died and the date of your death should be included or written across the face of any returned check(s).

Since annuity payments are made retroactively (for example, on June 1 for the month ending May 31), any money due for the part of the month when you were alive will be paid in a lump sum. Any survivor annuity will begin on the day following your death.

What to Do If Your Spouse Dies Before You Do

As soon as possible, notify OPM of your spouse's death. You may either phone or write OPM. In either case, you will be asked to provide OPM with a certified copy of the death certificate. A sample notification letter is provided in the Appendix.

If you elected a reduction in annuity in order to provide your spouse with a survivor's benefit, you now are entitled to have your full annuity restored as of the first of the month following your spouse's death. The amount deducted from your annuity while your spouse was alive will not be refunded to you, however.

If you did not elect a survivor annuity, you need only notify OPM if your spouse was covered by your health benefits plan (FEHB) or life insurance (FEGLI).

If You Get Divorced

If you get divorced after retirement, and had elected a reduced annuity in order to give your spouse a survivor annuity, then OPM will be obligated to honor a divorce-related court order that stipulates a survivor annuity payment. If the court does not order a survivor annuity payment, your annuity reduction will be eliminated and you will begin receiving an unreduced annuity. The same is true if a court stipulated a survivor annuity and your ex-spouse predeceases you. In neither case will you receive a refund of the amount withheld from your annuity for this benefit.

Note: To have your full annuity restored, you should notify OPM immediately so that it can implement the change.

Taxability of Annuities

All annuities, whether paid to you or your survivors, are taxable. However, under the IRS's General Rule or the Simplified General Rule (which applies to annuities that started after July 1, 1986), a percentage of your annuity is tax-free, while the rest is taxable. That's because part of it represents a return of your contributions to the retirement fund, which were taxed at the time they were made.

The formulas used to determine how much of your annuity is tax-free are based either on actuarial tables (the General Rule) or on your age when the annuity starts and how much you contributed to the retirement fund before you retired (the Simplified General Rule). According to the Internal Revenue Service, the simplified Rule "will usually be more beneficial than the General Rule in terms of tax result and ease of computation."

Note: *If you die before recovering all the money you contributed to the retirement fund, that undistributed balance will either: (1) transfer over to your survivor and result in part of his her annuity being non-taxable, or (2) be paid out in a tax-free lump sum to your survivors, where no one is eligible for an annuity.*

A disability annuity is treated as regular income and is taxed as such until you reach the age at which you could have first retired on a non-disability annuity. At that point it will be taxed under the General Rule or the Simplified General Rule as described above.

For further information, see IRS Publication 721—Tax Guide to U.S. Civil Service Retirement Benefits. You can get a copy by calling 1-800-TAX-FORM (1-800-829-3676).

OPM will withhold federal income tax from your first annuity payment and send you information about your right to change the amount of federal income tax withholding—or have it stopped—and how to do this.

OPM has established a toll-free "Annuitant Express" Service that allows federal retirees and annuitants to call in changes to their federal and state income tax withholdings and also arrange for certain U.S. Savings Bond transactions. Using a touch-tone phone, retirees can reach OPM's toll-free Annuitant Express by dialing 1-800-409-6528. Before dialing this number, be sure that you have certain information available, including your CSA or CSF retirement claim number and Social Security number. If you need to talk with an OPM customer service specialist, call (202) 606-0500, Monday through Friday between 7:30 a.m. and 5:30 p.m. (EST).

Making changes or elections for state tax withholding requires the caller to identify the state by a two-letter abbreviation and corresponding two-digit dial pad code. Only states that have reached a tax withholding agreement with OPM are included in the Annuitant Express options.

Where to Go for More Information

If you are currently employed by the federal government, a good source of information about retirement benefits and options is the benefits officer in your own personnel office. Along with answering your questions, he or she should have a supply of forms and publications on hand. Additionally, you might wish to obtain *Your FERS Retirement: How to Prepare for It, How to Enjoy It*, published by the Federal Employees News Digest. This is a thorough guide to the FERS retirement process.

If you are retired, OPM provides two avenues for answering your questions and getting copies of forms and publications. General questions can be answered by phone. Call OPM's Retirement Information Office at (202) 606-0500 to talk to a retirement representative. But be prepared to wait. This is a very popular phone number and is often busy. If you call, have your retirement claim number handy. You may also write to OPM.

Survivor Questions & Answers

Q. May a retiree drawing a civil service annuity also draw a civil service survivor annuity?
A. Yes.

Q. Is a child's survivor annuity payable in addition to the widow's or widower's annuity?
A. Yes. For example, if a deceased employee is survived by a widow and three children, all of whom are eligible to receive survivor annuities, a benefit would be paid to all four survivors.

Q. If a widow or widower dies, will the children's annuity be increased?
A. Yes. If the children are still drawing annuities, their payments will be increased as though the employee had not been survived by a spouse, unless a living former spouse is the parent of any of the eligible children.

Q. If the annuity to one child stops for any reason will the annuity to any remaining children be increased?
A. When the annuity to any one child stops, the other children's annuities are recomputed as though the one child had never been eligible. In some cases this will increase the annuities to the other eligible children.

Q. When a child's annuity stops, is the widow's or widower's annuity affected?
A. No.

Q. Under what conditions would a lump-sum benefit be payable immediately after the death of an employee?
A. A lump-sum benefit is payable immediately if the deceased employee had less than 18 months of civilian service, or if the employee had completed 18 months but leaves no widow, widower, former spouse or children who are eligible for a survivor annuity.

Q. Of what does the immediate lump-sum benefit consist?
A. The amount paid into the Civil Service Retirement Fund by the employee, plus any accrued interest.

Q. May a lump-sum benefit be paid if the employee leaves a surviving spouse, former spouse or children who are eligible for a survivor annuity?
A. No lump-sum benefit may be paid while the surviving spouse, former spouse or children are eligible for a survivor annuity. When all the survivors' annuities have ended, if the deceased employee's beneficiaries have received less than the employee paid into the Civil Service Retirement Fund, plus any accrued interest, the difference would be payable as a lump-sum benefit.

Q. May an employee or annuitant change or cancel a designation of beneficiary?
A. Yes. Changes or cancellations may be made by executing a new SF-3102.

Q. Must the husband name his wife as beneficiary on the SF 3102 in order that she may be awarded an annuity upon his death?
A. No. The designation or beneficiary is for the lump-sum benefit only. It has no effect on the widow's right to a survivor annuity.

Q. If an employee leaves the government before becoming eligible for an immediate annuity and opts for a deferred annuity at age 62 and dies before reaching that age, will his or her spouse be eligible for a survivor annuity?
A. No. The spouse, however, would be entitled to receive the lump sum of the employee's contribution to the retirement fund, including interest.

Q. Is an annuity, after reductions to provide for survivor benefits, eligible for cost-of-living increases?
A. Yes. Annual COLAs are applied to the annuity paid to the retiree.

Q. Are benefits payable to my surviving spouse from FERS affected by Social Security survivor benefits?
A. A spouse may collect both FERS and Social Security survivor benefits. In cases where the Social Security survivor benefit is not payable because the spouse is

Your Financial Guide

under age 60, FERS provides special benefits to create spouse benefits approximate to the benefits payable to similar spouses of deceased workers under the Civil Service Retirement System (CSRS).

Q. Do survivors of deceased federal employees receive the balance of their retirement contributions?

A. The general answer is yes. However, the formula for determining the amount of refund, if any, the interest, the options for type of refund, and the eligibility criteria for both the deceased federal employee and survivor(s) can vary depending upon several factors, including length of service and whether the federal employee was under CSRS or FERS.

Q. Can a federal retiree who elected the survivor benefit have his or her annuity restored to full value upon the death of his or her spouse?

A. Yes. The annuity amount can be adjusted to eliminate the survivor reduction, but only if there is no former spouse who is entitled to survivor benefits by court order or by election of the employee. To start the change process call OPM at (202) 606-0500. A death certificate (preferably certified) must be provided as evidence of death.

Q. As a retiree or survivor, can I change the amount of federal income tax being withheld from my annuity?

A. Yes. Using a touch-tone phone, you can call OPM's toll-free number (1-800-409-6528). By following the menu prompts, you can change the amount of federal income tax withheld from your annuity check (along with state tax withholding for a number of states). All you need is your CSA or CSF claim number and your Personal Identification Number, which is the last four digits of your Social Security number. Or, you can request a personalized tax election form (W-4P-A) by writing OPM at the following address:

OPM
P.O. Box 961
Washington, D.C. 20044-0001

Be sure to include your claim number. OPM will provide the form and instructions, then make the changes you request as soon as they receive your completed form.

FERS Survivor Annuity Options at a Glance
Choices if you are Single at Time of Election

Your Choices:	Requirements:	What Will Happen:
Survivor benefit for person having insurable interest	Must be in good health (OPM requires proof of a physical exam before approving this election). Must elect the benefit for a person who has a reasonable expectancy of financial benefit in the continuance of your life. May elect an insurable interest benefit and a former spouse benefit at the same time if for different persons (annuity will be reduced twice for the 2 benefits). Must return election letter to OPM, since the election will not go into effect without written confirmation from you, along with the results of your physical exam.	Your yearly annuity will be reduced by 10%, plus 5% for each 5 years the person is younger than you are up to a maximum 40% reduction. Your insurable interest survivors' annuity will be 55% of the annuity remaining after the above reduction, plus the total percent by which your annuity was increased by COLAs since retirement. After your death, your insurable interest survivor will receive annuity for life.
No survivor benefit		You will receive full annuity with no reduction for survivor benefit (unless OPM must honor a court order for a former spouse).
Survivor benefit to former spouse - maximum - partial	Must have been married to you for a total of at least 9 months. You must have performed at least 18 months of creditable service (includes both military and civil service. You must choose what percentage (50% or 25%) of your annuity you want your former spouse(s) to receive. If electing benefits for more than one former spouse, total percentages elected for the former spouses must equal either 50% or 25%. (For example: 20% and 30%, or 15% and 10%) OPM will send a confirmation letter providing annuity figures with and without this election. Benefit is automatic 30 days after date of confirmation letter unless you change it in writing within that time.	Your basic annuity will be reduced by 10% or 5% depending on whether you elected full or partial survivor benefits. If you are a disability retiree age 62 or over at death: Total survivor annuities = 50% or 25% of basic disability annuity. under age 62 at death: Total survivor annuities = 50% or 25% of what you would have received at age 62, but Hi3 aver age salary is adjusted only through date of death. Former spouse's benefit will continue until remarriage before age 55, or until death.

You may elect an insurable interest benefit at the same time you elect a former spouse benefit, if for two different individuals. The insurable interest election reduction will take place in addition to the reduction for the former spouse benefit.

Figure 7-3

Your Financial Guide

FERS Survivor Annuity Options at a Glance
Choices if you are Married at Time of Election

Your Choices:	Requirements:	What Will Happen:
1. Maximum survivor benefit to current spouse	At time of your death, your spouse must have been married to you for at least 9 months (or less: if your spouse is a parent of your child, or your death is accidental. Earlier marriages to the same spouse count toward the 9-month total, as well as the marriage at time of death. Benefit automatic unless you and your spouse change election in writing within 30 days of date of annuity statement sent by OPM.	Your annuity will be reduced by 10%. Your spouse's survivor benefit will equal 50% of your full annuity before the above reduction, plus total percent by which your annuity was increased by COLAs since retirement. If your spouse will, at age 60, become eligible for SSA survivor benefits (based on your eligibility for SSA benefits) s/he will also receive a "supplementary benefit" from OPM until age 60. This supplementary benefit will equal the lesser of: a. The benefit the spouse would have received if you had been a CSRS retiree with the 50% benefit you elected minus an amount equal to the regular FERS survivor benefit; or b. Any estimated SSA spouse survivor benefit the spouse would receive if s/he were age 60 (with earnings for nonFERS years adjusted to level of FERS years). If you are a disability retiree age 62 or over at death: Survivor annuity = **50%** of basic disability annuity. If you are a disability retiree under age 62 at death: Survivor annuity = 500/0 of what you would have received at age 62 but High-3 averge salary is adjusted only through date of death. Your spouse's benefit will continue until his or her death, or until any remarriage occurring before age 55.

Figure 7-3

FERS Survivor Annuity Options at a Glance
Choices if you are Married at Time of Election

Your Choices:	Requirements:	What Will Happen:
2. Partial survivor benefit to current spouse	At the time of your death, your spouse must have been married to you for a total of at least 9 months (or less: if your spouse is a parent of your child or your death is accidental). Current spouse's consent. OPM will send a confirmation letter after retirement providing annuity figures with and without the full benefit. Benefit is automatic 30 days after the date of election notice, unless you change it in writing within that time.	Your yearly annuity will be reduced by 5%. Your survivor's benefit will equal only 25% of your full annuity before the above reduction, plus total percent by which your annuity was increased by COLAs since retirement. Same "supplementary benefit" applies to the 25% partial survivor benefit as in (5). Same disability computation applies to the 25% partial survivor benefit as in (5). Your spouse's benefit will continue until his or her death, or until any remarriage occurring before age 55.
3. No survivor benefit	Current spouse's consent OPM will send a confirmation letter after retirement providing annuity figures with and without the full benefit. Benefit is automatic 30 days after the date of election notice, unless you change it in writing within that time.	You will receive full annuity with no reduction for survivor benefit (unless OPM honors a court order for a former spouse). Surviving spouse will receive no annuity if you predecease him or her.
4. Survivor benefit to person having insurable interest	Must be in good health. OPM requires proof of a physical exam before approving this election. Must elect the benefit for a person who has a reasonable expectancy of financial benefit in the continuance of your life. Must return election letter to OPM, since the election will not go into effect without written confirmation from you, along with the results of your physical exam. If electing insurable interest for current spouse, s/he must consent to having no regular current spouse benefit (you cannot elect both benefits for the same person).	Your yearly annuity will be reduced by 10%, plus 5% for each 5 years the person is younger than you are - up to a maximum 40% reduction. Your insurable interest survivor's annuity will be 50% of the annuity remaining after the above reduction, plus total percent by which your annuity was increased by COLAs. After your death, your insurable interest survivor will receive annuity for life.

Figure 7-3

FERS Survivor Annuity Options at a Glance
Choices if you are Married at Time of Election

Your Choices:	Requirements:	What Will Happen:

5. Survivor benefit for former spouse
  - maximum
  - partial
	Must have been married to you for a total of at least 9 months. You must have performed at least 18 months of creditable service (including military and civilian service).
	
	Current spouse's consent.
	
	You must choose what percentage (50% or 25%) of you annuity you want your former spouse(s) to receive.
	
	In electing benefits for more than one former spouse, total percentages elected for the former spouses must equal either 50% or 25%. (For example: 20% and 30%, or 15% and 10%)
	
	OPM will send confirmation letter providing annuity figures with and without this election. Benefit is automatic 30 days after date of confirmation letter, unless you change it in writing within that time.
		Your annuity will be reduced by 10% or 5% depending on whether you elect full or partial survivor benefits.
		
		The former spouse's benefit will equal the percentage you elected.
		
		Same disability computation for survivor benefit to former spouse as in (3). The former spouse's benefit will continue until his or her remarriage occurring prior to age 55, or until death.

6. Survivor benefit to both current and former spouse	Former spouse must meet requirements listed above (in item 8). Current spouse must meet requirements listed above (in item 5). You must have performed at least 18 months of creditable service including military and civilian service. Current spouse must consent to less than the full survivor benefit. Total election cannot exceed 50% of your basic annuity - 25% for current spouse, a total of 25% for former spouse(s). OPM will send confirmation letter providing annuity figures with and without this election. Benefit is automatic 30 days after date of confirmation letter, unless you change it in writing within that time.	Your basic annuity will be reduced by 10%. All current and former spouses elected will together receive a percentage of your basic annuity equaling 50%. Same "supplementary benefit" for (6) applies only to the benefit elected for current spouse. Same disability computation for (3), (5) or (6) applies based on percentage of each election. Each current and former spouse's benefit will continue until his or her remarriage prior to age 55, or until death.

7. You may also elect an insurable interest benefit at the same time as you elect current and/or former spouse benefits if for different individuals. The reduction for the insurable interest election will take place in addition to the reductions for the other benefits elected.

Figure 7-3

Your Financial Guide

Effect of Court Orders on Survivor Elections if You are Single at Time of Election

Type of Benefit You Elected	What Will Happen If a Court Order Is Involved
1. Survivor benefit to a person having insurable interest	Your basic annuity will be reduced twice to provide any court ordered survivor benefit to a former spouse, not to exceed 55% of your basic annuity, and the benefit to the person having insurable interest. The court-ordered former spouse's survivor benefit will continue until: • death, or • remarriage prior to age 55, or • a court order is ruled invalid by another court order, or • special circumstances stipulated in the court order take place which require the benefit to end. The insurable interest will continue to receive annuity for life.
2. No survivor benefit	Your basic annuity will be reduced twice to provide any court ordered survivor benefit to a former spouse, not to exceed 55% of your basic annuity. The court-ordered former spouse's survivor benefit will continue until: • death, or • remarriage prior to age 55, or • a court order is ruled invalid by another court order, or • special circumstances stipulated in the court order take place which require the benefit to end.
3. Survivor benefit to a former spouse	If court order involves a different former spouse than the former spouse for whom a survivor benefit was elected: Your basic annuity will be reduced to provide a survivor benefit to the former spouse with the court order, not to exceed 55% of your basic annuity. If any of the 55% full benefit is remaining after the court order is honored, the former spouse for whom a survivor benefit was elected will be eligible to receive the balance. The court order also has priority over any smaller election for the same former spouse. The court-ordered former spouse's survivor benefit will continue until: • death, or • remarriage prior to age 55, or • a court order is ruled invalid by another court order, or • special circumstances stipulated in the court order take place which require the benefit to end.

Figure 7-3

Your Financial Guide

Effect of Court Orders on Survivor Elections if You are Married at Time of Election

Type of Benefit You Elected	What Will Happen If a Court Order Is Involved
1. Maximum survivor benefit to current spouse	Count-ordered benefit generally supersedes a benefit you elect for a current spouse. Your basic annuity will be reduced to provide a survivor benefit to a former spouse not to exceed 55% of your basic annuity. If court orders the full 55% benefit: • You make a "contingency" election for your current spouse which would go into effect when and if the former spouse loses entitlement. • No extra reduction to your basic annuity for a "contingency" election. If court orders less than the full benefit: • You may insure that your current souse also gets a partial survivor benefit by electing full survivor coverage for your current spouse. • Former spouse will get the countordered benefit. Current spouse will get the balance of the full current spouse benefit that remains after subtracting the former spouse's benefit • Such a contingency election will mean an additional reduction in the annuity to the extent that the benefit elected for the current spouse exceeds the court-ordered benefit for the former spouse. • If the former spouse loses entitlement, current spouse will receive whatever benefit (55% or a partial one) you elected. The court-ordered former spouse's survivor benefit will continue until: • death, or • remarriage prior to age 55, or • a count order is ruled invalid by another court order, or • special circumstances stipulated in the court order take place which require the benefit to end.
2. Partial (25%) survivor benefit to current spouse	Count ordered benefit generally supersedes a benefit you elect for a current spouse if total benefits exceed 55%. Your basic annuity will be reduced to provide a survivor benefit to a former spouse not to exceed 55% of your basic annuity. You may still elect a partial survivor benefit (contingency election) for a current spouse, if court orders the full 55% benefit: • Former spouse will get the court ordered benefit. • If former spouse loses entitlement, the current souse will only receive the partial benefit you elected. The court-ordered former spouse's survivor benefit will continue until death, or: • remarriage prior to age 55, or • a court order is ruled invalid by another court order, or • special circumstances stipulated in the court order take place which require the benefit to end.
3. No survivor benefit	Same rules apply as for (2), assuming current spouse's consent obtained
4. Survivor benefit to a person having insurable Interest	Same rules apply as for (1), assuming current spouse's consent obtained
5. Survivor benefit to a former spouse	Same rules apply as for (3), assuming current spouse's consent obtained
6. Survivor benefit to both a current and former spouse	If court order involves a different former spouse than the former spouse for whom a survivor benefit was elected: • Your basic annuity will be reduced to provide a survivor benefit to the former spouse with the court order, not to exceed 55% of your basic annuity. • If any of the 55% full benefit is remaining after the court order is honored, the current and former spouses for whom a survivor benefit was elected will be eligible to receive the balance. The court order also has priority over any election for same former spouse.

Figure 7-3

How Survivor Benefit Might Change After Retirement

Type of Survivor Elected	Post Retirement Possibilities
1. Single person elects no benefit	If you later marry, you may elect a new spouse within 2 years of marriage, or within 2 years of any former spouse's loss of entitlement. Survivor benefit goes into effect after 9 months of marriage unless your death is accidental or spouse is the natural parent of your child. Your annuity will be reduced retroactive to the commencing date of your annuity, plus 6% interest, compounded annually. This deposit is paid by a permanent actuarial reduction.
2. Married person elects no benefit	You may change a current spouse survivor annuity election no later than 18 months after your annuity started if you are: • changing your election so as to provide a survivor annuity; or • increasing a less than maximum survivor annuity election. In either case, you would have to pay a retroactive adjustment, a charge of 24.5% of the amount of the increase from the original base to the new survivor base, *plus* applicable interest (see Figure 6-5). This is the same rate that is used for deposits and redeposits (and VC accounts). If you later divorce, you may not elect a benefit for the ex-spouse. If you marry a different person, the rules in (1) apply. In the case of a post-retirement divorce, OPM will not honor a court-ordered survivor benefit for a person who, at the time of retirement, had consented to having no survivor coverage. *NOTE:* An election during this 18-month period is void if it is received by OPM after the retiree dies.
3. Married person elects full (55%) benefit for current spouse only	If your marrige ends by death or divorce, annuity reduction ends. If divorced, you may elect benefit for ex-spouse within 2 years of divorce if: • person was married to you a total of at least 9 months, • former spouse does not remarry prior to age 55, • you had 18 months of creditable service, and • any new spouse to whom you are married at the time of election consents to it. In the case of post-retirement divorce, OPM will honor an acceptable court order providing continued survivor coverage for the spouse who had survivor coverage at time of retirement. If you late remarry the same or a different spouse, you may elect as in (1).
4. Married person elects partial benefit for current spouse only.	Rules in (2) and (3) apply except that you may elect a benefit for an ex-spouse to whom married at retirement, but not one that exceeds the benefit consented to at time of retirement. In the case of a post-retirement divorce, OPM will not honor a court-ordered survivor coverage larger than the one elected at the time of retirement.

Figure 7-3

Your Financial Guide

How Survivor Benefit Might Change After Retirement

Type of Survivor Elected	Post Retirement Possibilities
5. Retiree elects benefit for former spouse only	If you later marry or remarry, you may not change the election of an eligible former spouse. If former spouse loses eligibility (by death or remarriage under age 55), reduction in annuity ends.
6. Retiree elects combination benefit for current & former spouse.	If either the current or former spouse loses eligibility (by death, etc.) the portion of the reduction in annuity for that person (but not the other) ends. Rules in (4) apply if marriage ends. If former spouse loses eligibility, the elected benefit may not be increased for current spouse.
7. Retiree elects an insurable interest benefit only.	If person elected as insurable interest dies, reduction for insurable interest ends. If you later marry someone other than the insurable interest designee, you may elect a benefit for a spouse as in (1) above, and (if desired) end the insurable interest election. If you later marry the insurable interest designee and, within 2 years, elect a regular survivor annuity for that person, the insurable interest benefit will be automatically canceled. If a former spouse with a court-ordered benefit loses entitlement, you may change (if within 2 years) an insurable interest benefit for a current spouse to a regular survivor benefit for a current spouse. If you have already died, widow(er) can elect (within 2 years of former spouse losing entitlement) to change the insurable interest annuity to a regular survivor annuity.
8. Retiree elects both a full survivor benefit for spouse and an insurable interest benefit for another person.	If marriage ends, or the person with insurable interest dies, the annuity reduction for the relevant election ends. If marriage ends, rules in (3) or (4) apply.

Figure 7-3

Survivor Benefits for Children

Type/Eligibility Requirements:	Amount of Benefits:	Commencement/Termination:
Child can be: • legitimate • recognized natural (born out of wedlock) • adopted • stepchild (if living with employee) Must be unmarried. Must be under age 18, or between age 18 and 22 and a full-time student, or disabled before age 18 and incapable of self support as determined by the Social Security Administration. You must have contributed to child's support. Benefit is automatic for eligible dependents; no election required.	1-3 children payable: each child will received the maximum rate. 4 or more children payable: the rate is reduced proportionately for each so that total for all children equals the total 3 children would get. If no former or current spouse survives who is a parent of any eligible children — higher rate is payable.	Annuity commences the day after your death. Annuity terminates end of the month preceding the terminating event: 1. Marriage 2. Death 3. Attainment of age 18 (if not a full-time student) 4. Attainment of age 22 (if a full-time student; however, if this occurs during the school year, annuity continues until end of the school year). 5. Ceases to attend school as a full-time student. 6. Becomes capable of self support (disabled child).

Figure 7-3

Your Financial Guide

How COLAs are Added to Survivor Annuities

Survivor Type:	When Eligible:	How Amount of COLA is Determined
Current Spouse: Former Spouse Insurable Interest	• Commencing date of Survivor annuity. • Effective December 1 of each year and reflected in the payment dated January 2, unless changed by Congress.	Based on increases in the Consumer Price Index. If a deceased annuitant has been on roll less than 11 months at time of death, survivor gets 1/12 of the COLA percentage for each month during which either s/he or the retiree was on the rolls prior to the effective date of the COLA.
Children	• Commencing date of child's annuity. • Effective December 1 of each year and reflected in the payment dated January 2, unless changed by Congress.	Includes all CSRS COLAs authorized with the percentage increase applying to the child's entire monthly benefit. Includes full CSRS COLA, regardless of how long the deceased annuitant was on the rolls.

Lump Sum Benefits Following Death of Annuitant

Type Available:	Conditions of Payment:	Amount Payable:	Eligible Beneficiaries:
Unexpended Balance	If no monthly survivor annuity is payable, and no Alternative Annuity lump sum was elected at retirement.	Amount by which your contributions to the Retirement Fund, plus any interest due, exceeds the total amount of the annuity you and all your eligible survivors receive.	Based upon Order of Precedence: 1. Designated Beneficiary (listed on valid SF2808) 2. Widow(er) 3. Child(ren) in equal shares, with the share of any deceased child distributed to descendants of that child.
Accrued Annuity	If deceased had annuity at time of death. Paid whether or not there is a survivor eligible for a recurring monthly annuity.	Prorated amount of the last monthly retirement check you were entitled to. Eligible Beneficiaries:	4. Parent(s) 5. Executor or Administrator of your estate. 6. Next of kin entitled under the laws of the state in which you are domiciled at the time of your death.

Figure 7-3

CHAPTER EIGHT

SOCIAL SECURITY SURVIVOR BENEFITS

If you are a FERS employee, you already are covered by Social Security. It is the second main element in your retirement and survivor benefit package. On the other hand, many federal and postal employees covered by CSRS will have spent some time in jobs covered by the Social Security system. Heading into retirement, these CSRS-covered employees may end up accruing Social Security credit in a variety of ways, including:

- Work under Social Security before entering the civil service retirement system;
- Working evenings and weekends under Social Security while employed full time under civil service;
- Operating a small business in addition to their full-time permanent job under civil service; or
- Performing military service after 1956.

Beginning in 1984, all former employees returning to the government with at least a one-year break in service are automatically covered by Social Security. However, those whose prior employment spanned at least five years of creditable service under CSRS are eligible to reenter that system. Those who do are called CSRS-Offset employees. They are covered by CSRS and Social Security.

If you are one of those who have accrued some Social Security credit, you may be entitled to benefits because of this covered employment. If so, you should include them as you calculate your retirement and survivor benefits.

What Social Security Provides

Social Security is a package of protections covering retirement, survivors, and disability insurance. It protects you and your family while you work, after you retire, and when you die. CSRS employees can qualify by working in the private sector or by having a spouse who has done sufficient covered work.

If you are fully insured when you reach retirement age, you and certain members of your family can receive monthly benefits. Monthly Social Security benefits also are paid to eligible spouses and children of workers who have retired. The same is true of ex-spouses. Benefits are also payable to the survivors and ex-spouses of deceased employees and retirees.

Eligibility Requirements

To qualify to receive benefits you must first have credit for a certain amount of work in jobs covered by the Social Security system. You can earn a maximum of four credits (sometimes called "quarters") per year. These credits may have been earned at any time since the Social Security system was created in 1936. In no case are more than 40 credits needed.

If you work for a while and then leave the covered occupation, the credits you have earned will be kept on your Social Security Administration (SSA) records. You can add to them later if you return to work in a covered occupation.

How Social Security Figures Your Benefits

In general, a Social Security benefit is based on your earnings averaged over your working lifetime. This is different from your retirement benefit under CSRS, which is based on a "high-3" year average salary. In the simplest terms, here's how the Social Security Administration figures your Social Security benefit:

Step 1 — They determine the number of years of earnings to use as a base.
Retirement benefits: For everybody born after 1928 and retiring in 1991 or later, that number is 35 years.
Disability benefits: Most of the years of earnings posted to your record.

Step 2 — These earnings are adjusted for inflation.

Step 3 — Your average adjusted monthly earnings is computed based on the years determined in Step 1.

Step 4 — Your average adjusted earnings in multiplied by percentages in a formula set by law.

The Social Security formula results in benefits that replace about 42 percent of a person's earnings. This applies to those who had average earnings during their working years. The percentage is lower for employees in the upper income brackets and higher for those with low incomes. That's because the Social Security formula is weighted in favor of low-income workers who have less opportunity to save and invest during their working years.

Your Financial Guide

Note: For employees who receive a civil service pension based in whole or part on CSRS service, a modified benefit formula will be used in computing the Social Security retirement or disability benefit, if they have less than 30 years of "substantial" Social Security earnings. (See "Windfall Elimination Provision," Figure 8-4.)

An employee's primary insurance amount (PIA) is the monthly benefit amount payable at disability or at the full-benefit retirement age. All other monthly benefit amounts are derived from the PIA.

Full-benefit retirement age is 65 if you were born before 1938. However, if you were born in 1938 or later, your retirement age will be higher. Beginning in the year 2000, the age at which full benefits become payable will increase in gradual steps from 65 to 67. For example, if you were born in 1940, your full retirement age is 65 and 6 months. If you were born in 1950, your full retirement age is 66. Anybody born in 1960 or later will be eligible for full retirement at 67.

Note: Social Security benefits are increased automatically each year whenever the cost of living rises, as measured by the Consumer Price Index for Urban Wage Earners and Clerical Workers (CPI/W).

When You Start Receiving Benefits

No matter what your full-benefit retirement age is, you may start receiving benefits as early as age 62. However, if you start receiving your benefits early, they are reduced five-tenths of one percent for each month before your full retirement age. For example, if your full retirement age is 65 and you sign up for Social Security when you're 62, you would only get 80 percent. At age 64 it would be 93 1/3 percent. Of course, the reduction will be greater in future years as the full retirement age increases.

Should you start receiving reduced benefits early, or wait until you are eligible for full benefits? While some may resolve the issue by flipping a coin, it is better to consider the advantages and disadvantages of each option. The advantage of taking your benefits early is that you receive them for a longer period of time. The disadvantage is that they are permanently reduced. Since each person's situation is different, it's a good idea to check with the Social Security Administration before making a decision. They can show you the difference in benefits to which you will be entitled at each age.

Approximate Monthly Retirement Benefits if the Worker Retires at Normal Retirement Age and Had Steady Lifetime Earnings
RETIRED WORKER'S EARNINGS IN 1995

WORKER'S AGE	WORKER'S FAMILY	$10,000	$20,000	$30,000	$40,000	$50,000	MAXIMUM WAGE BASE OR MORE[1]
25	Retired worker only	$532	$786	$1,053	$1,201	$1,326	$1,485
	Worker and spouse[2]	798	1,179	1,579	1,801	1,989	2,227
	Replacement rate[3]	64%	47%	42%	36%	32%	29%
35	Retired worker only	532	786	1,053	1,201	1,326	1,482
	Worker and spouse[2]	798	1,179	1,579	1,801	1,989	2,223
	Replacement rate[3]	64%	47%	42%	36%	32%	29%
45	Retired worker only	532	786	1,053	1,201	1,326	1,457
	Worker and spouse[2]	798	1,179	1,579	1,801	1,989	2,185
	Replacement rate[3]	64%	47%	42%	36%	32%	29%
55	Retired worker only	532	786	1,053	1,192	1,287	1,369
	Worker and spouse[2]	798	1,179	1,579	1,788	1,930	2,053
	Replacement rate[3]	64%	47%	42%	36%	31%	27%
65	Retired worker only	532	785	1,047	1,151	1,211	1,248
	Worker and spouse[2]	798	1,177	1,570	1,726	1,816	1,872
	Replacement rate[3]	64%	47%	42%	35%	29%	25%

Source: Social Security Administration

[1] Earnings equal to or greater than the OASDI wage base from age 22 through the year before retirement.
[2] Spouse is assumed to be the same age as the worker. Spouse may qualify for a higher retirement benefit based on his or her own work record.
[3] Replacement rates are shown for retired worker only.

Note: The accuracy of these estimates depends on the pattern of the worker's actual past earnings, and on his or her earnings in the future. Estimates for future retirees are calculated on the same basis used for the Personal Earnings and Benefit Estimate Statement (PEBES).

The above table shows benefits payable to the worker and spouse. To use the table, find the age which is closest to your age and the earnings closest to your earnings in 1995. These figures will give you an estimate of the amount of your retirement benefits at various ages.

Figure 8-1

Approximate Monthly Disability Benefits if the Worker Becomes Disabled in 1996 and Had Steady Earnings

To use the table, find the age and earnings closest to your age and earnings in 1995

DISABLED WORKER'S EARNINGS IN 1995

WORKER'S AGE	WORKER'S FAMILY	$10,000	$20,000	$30,000	$40,000	$50,000	MAXIMUM WAGE BASE OR MORE[1]
25	Disabled worker only	$520	$786	$1,053	$1,201	$1,326	$1,455
	Disabled worker, spouse, and child[2]	708	1,179	1,580	1,801	1,989	2,182
35	Disabled worker only	520	786	1,053	1,201	1,326	1,425
	Disabled worker, spouse, and child[2]	708	1,179	1,580	1,801	1,989	2,137
45	Disabled worker only	520	786	1,053	1,201	1,310	1,377
	Disabled worker, spouse, and child[2]	708	1,179	1,580	1,801	1,966	2,066
55	Disabled worker only	520	786	1,053	1,177	1,252	1,297
	Disabled worker, spouse, and child[2]	708	1,179	1,579	1,766	1,878	1,946
64	Disabled worker only	532	802	1,068	1,177	1,238	1,275
	Disabled worker, spouse, and child[2]	722	1,203	1,603	1,766	1,857	1,913

Source: Social Security Administration

[1] Earnings equal to or greater than the OASDI wage base from age 22 through 1995. [2] Equals the maximum family benefit.
Note: The accuracy of these estimates depends on the pattern of the worker's earnings in prior years.

Figure 8-2

Benefits to Family Members

Who Is Eligible
When you begin collecting Social Security retirement or disability benefits, benefits can also be paid to certain members of your family. These include:

- Your spouse if he or she is 62 or older (unless he or she collects a higher Social Security benefit on his or her own record);
- Your spouse at any age if he or she is caring for your child (the child must be under 16 or disabled and receiving Social Security benefits);
- Your children, if they are unmarried and under age 18, under 19 but in elementary or secondary school as a full-time student, or are 18 or older and severely disabled (the disability must have been incurred before age 22).

Note: Unless your death is accidental, your spouse must have been married to you for at least nine months or be the natural parent of your child.

Amount of Benefits
Usually each family member will be eligible for a monthly benefit that is up to 50 percent of your retirement or disability rate. However, there is a limit to the total amount of money that can be paid to a family (including yourself) on your Social Security record. The limit varies, but generally is equal to about 150 percent to 180 percent of your PIA in retirement and survivor cases. In disability cases, it ranges from 100 percent of the PIA to 150 percent of the PIA. If the sum of the benefits payable is greater than the family limit, the benefits to family members will be reduced proportionately. Your benefit will not be affected.

Benefits for Your Ex-Spouse
If you are divorced (even if you have remarried), your ex-spouse can be eligible for benefits on your record. In some cases, he or she may get benefits even if you are not receiving them. In order to qualify, your ex-spouse must:

- Have been married to you for at least 10 years;
- Be at least 62 years old;
- Be unmarried;
- Not be eligible for an equal or higher benefit on his or her own Social Security record, or on someone else's record.

Note: If your ex-spouse receives benefits on your account, it does not reduce the amount of any benefits payable to you or other family members.

Your Financial Guide

Approximate Monthly Survivors Benefits if the Worker Dies in 1996 and Had Steady Earnings

DECEASED WORKER'S EARNINGS IN 1995

WORKER'S AGE	WORKER'S FAMILY	$10,000	$20,000	$30,000	$40,000	$50,000	MAXIMUM WAGE BASE OR MORE[1]
25	Spouse and 1 child[2]	$780	$1,179	$1,580	$1,801	$1,989	$2,193
	Spouse and 2 children[3]	780	1,457	1,842	2,101	2,320	2,558
	1 child only	390	589	790	900	994	1,096
	Spouse at age 60[4]	371	562	753	858	948	1,045
35	Spouse and 1 child[2]	780	1,179	1,580	1,801	1,989	2,150
	Spouse and 2 chidren[3]	780	1,457	1,842	2,101	2,320	2,508
	1 child only	390	589	790	900	994	1,075
	Spouse at age 60[4]	371	562	753	858	948	1,025
45	Spouse and 1 child[2]	780	1,179	1,580	1,801	1,975	2,081
	Spouse and 2 children[3]	780	1,457	1,842	2,101	2,303	2,427
	1 child only	390	589	790	900	987	1,040
	Spouse at age 60[4]	371	562	753	858	941	992
55	Spouse and 1 child[2]	780	1,179	1,579	1,766	1,878	1,946
	Spouse and 2 children[3]	780	1,457	1,841	2,060	2,190	2,270
	1 child only	390	589	789	883	939	973
	Spouse at age 60[4]	371	562	752	842	895	927
65	Spouse and 1 child[2]	799	1,178	1,570	1,727	1,817	1,873
	Spouse and 2 children[3]	799	1,460	1,832	2,014	2,119	2,184
	1 child only	399	589	785	863	908	936
	Spouse at age 60[4]	381	561	748	823	866	892

Source: Social Security Administcation

[1] Earnings equal to or greater than the OASDI wage base from age 22 through 1995.
[2] Amounts shown also equal the benefits paid to two children, if no parent survives or surviving parent has substantial earnings.
[3] Equals the maximum family benefit.
[4] Amounts payable in 1996. Spouses turning 60 in the future would receive higher benefits.

Note: The accuracy of these estimates depends on the pattern of the worker's earnings in prior years.
[1] Earnings equal to or greater than the OASDI wage bare from age 22 through 1995.
[2] Equals the maximum family benefit.

Figure 8-3

Survivor Annuity Benefits

Who Is Eligible
When you die, certain members of your family may be eligible for benefits on your Social Security record, including:

- A widow(er) who is: 60 or older; 50 or older and disabled; or any age if he or she is caring for a child under 16 or a disabled child who is receiving Social Security benefits.
- Children if they are unmarried and under 18, under 19 but in elementary or secondary school as a full-time student, or 18 or older and severely disabled (the disability must have started before age 22).
- Your parents, if they were dependent on you for at least half of their support.

Payment Amounts
The amount payable to your survivors is a percentage of your PIA—usually in the range of 75 to 100 percent each. However, there is a limit to the amount of money that can be paid each month to a family. The limit varies, but generally is equal to about 150 to 180 percent of your PIA. If the sum of the benefits payable to your surviving family members is greater than this limit, then the benefits to your family will be reduced proportionately.

Benefits for Divorced Widow(er)s
If you are divorced (even if you have remarried), your ex-spouse may be eligible for benefits on your record when you die. In order to qualify, your ex-spouse must:

- Be at least 60 years old (or 50 if disabled) and have been married to you for at least 10 years;
- Be any age if caring for a child who is eligible for benefits on your record;
- Not be eligible for an equal of higher benefit on his or her own record;
- Not be currently married, unless the marriage occurred after age 60 (or 50 for disabled widow(er)s). In case of remarriage after age 60, your ex-spouse will be eligible for a widow(er)'s benefit based on

Your Financial Guide

your record or a dependent's benefit based on the record of his or her new spouse, whichever is higher. *Note: If your ex-spouse receives benefits on your account, it does not come at the cost of benefits payable to other survivors on your record.*

Dual-Entitlement Provision

A person who qualifies for benefits based on the earnings of more than one employee (for example, a benefit as an employee and a benefit as a spouse of another employee) cannot receive both benefits in full. The amount of the spouse's or surviving spouse's benefit is offset dollar for dollar against the person's own employee benefit, resulting in the individual receiving the larger of the two benefits.

Lump-Sum Death Payment

On the death of an employee, a one-time payment of $255 is payable either to a spouse with whom the employee was living at the time of death or to any minor children who are eligible for monthly survivor benefits in the month of the employee's death.

Reductions in Retirement Benefits

Two of the most misunderstood provisions of the retirement system are the "Public Pension Offset" and the "Windfall Elimination Provision." They both have a negative impact on the amount of Social Security benefits available to CSRS employees. The Social Security benefits of FERS and CSRS employees are affected only by the Windfall elimination provision.

Public Pension Offset

The Public Pension Offset (PPO) provision is similar to the dual entitlement provision. Under the PPO, the Social Security benefits a person receives as a spouse or surviving spouse will be reduced if that person also receives a pension based on government service that was not covered by Social Security. As a result, all federal and postal employees under CSRS are subject to this offset. CSRS-Offset employees are exempt.

Here's how the offset works. If you retire from federal or postal service and are also eligible for Social Security benefits as a spouse or survivor, your Social Security benefit will be reduced. For every $3 you receive from your CSRS pension, your Social Security spousal benefit will be reduced by $2.

Example: Let's assume you are eligible for a $500 Social Security spousal benefit. Suppose you were also receiving a CSRS benefit amounting to $900 a month. The Public Pension Offset would be two-thirds of your monthly CSRS benefit or $600. Since the offset amount is larger than your Social Security benefit, your Social Security benefit would be eliminated.

Windfall Elimination Provision (WEP)

The WEP reduces Social Security benefits for those who have less than 30 years of substantial coverage under Social Security and have earned a retirement benefit working in a job not covered by Social Security. This provision is designed to eliminate the "windfall" that would result if an employee receiving a pension based on government service not covered by Social Security also qualified for a full Social Security benefit, even though he or she only had a few years of covered employment.

Are You Affected? —The modified formula affects all CSRS-covered workers or FERS workers with a CSRS component who reach age 62 or become disabled after 1985 and first become eligible after 1985 for a monthly pension. You are considered eligible to receive a pension if you meet the requirements of the pension, even if you continue to work.

The modified formula will be used in figuring your Social Security benefit beginning with the first month you get both a Social Security benefit and your CSRS or FERS/CSRS pension.

How Does It Work? — Social Security benefits are based on your average monthly earnings adjusted for inflation. When Social Security figures your benefits, it separates your average earnings into three amounts and multiplies the figures using three factors. For example, if you had only worked under Social Security and turned 62 in 1996, the first $455 of average monthly earnings was multiplied by 90 percent; the next $2,741 multiplied by 32 percent; and the remainder by 15 percent.

In the modified formula, the 90 percent factor is reduced. The reduction was phased in for workers covered by CSRS (or with a CSRS component) who reached age 62 or became disabled between 1986 and 1989. For those who reach 62 or become disabled in 1990 or later, the 90 percent factor is reduced to 40 percent.

However, if you have 30 or more years of "substantial" Social Security earnings (see Figure 8-4), Social Security uses the regular formula to figure your benefit.

If you have 21-29 years of "substantial" Social Security earnings, the Social Security Administration will still use the modified formula, but it will affect you less than if you have fewer years of covered earnings. The first factor in the formula is reduced as follows:

To protect workers with relatively low pensions, the reduction in the Social Security benefit under the modified formula cannot be more than half of that part of the pension attributable to earnings after 1956 not covered by Social Security.

Your Financial Guide

If you don't expect to be eligible for Social Security benefits and have family members who are dependent on you, it might still be worth your while to take a job covered by Social Security—even if it's only part time—in order to gain eligibility. Despite the fact that your own benefits will be reduced by the Windfall Elimination Provision and your spouse's by the Public Pension Offset (unless you are covered by CSRS-Offset), if you die first your spouse and/or other dependents would be eligible for full, unreduced benefits.

Note: The WEP has no effect on Social Security credits earned under FERS or in the private sector, nor will it affect survivor benefits. They will not be reduced.

The Earnings Test

Anyone receiving Social Security benefits, whether based on personal earnings or as the spouse, ex-spouse, or survivor of someone else, may have their benefits reduced based on outside earnings. SSA withholds $1 in benefits for each $2 in earnings above $8,640 for those under 65 and $1 for every $3 in earnings above $13,500 for those aged 65 through 69. There is no earnings test for those age 70 and above. Different rules apply to people receiving disability or Supplemental Security Income benefits. They should check with their local Social Security office for details.

Applying for Social Security Benefits

You must apply at any Social Security office before you can receive any Social Security benefits. Check your phone book for the nearest address and give them a call to get things started. If you plan to retire before you reach age 65 (and are eligible), it is important to apply for monthly benefits no later than the last day of the month you want benefits to begin.

When you apply for benefits you will have to furnish certain documents. They include:

- Your Social Security card or a record of the number,
- Your birth certificate (other proofs of age may be substituted if your birth was not recorded),
- Children's birth certificates and Social Security numbers if they are applying for benefits,
- Evidence showing your recent earnings (last year's W-2 forms or a copy of last year's self-employment tax return),
- Proof of the worker's death if you are applying for survivor's benefits.

The Social Security Administration recommends that you apply promptly, even if you lack one or more of the documents required because it will save you time in trying to find what is missing. The people at Social Security can tell you of other documents that can be substituted.

The Windfall Elimination Provision

Years of Social Security Earnings	First Factor
30 or more	90 percent
28	80 percent
27	75 percent
26	70 percent
25	65 percent
24	60 percent
23	55 percent
22	50 percent
21	45 percent
20 or less	40 percent

For the modified formula, you are considered to have a year of substantial earnings if your earnings equal or exceed the figures shown for each year in the chart below.

Year	Earnings
1937-50	$900[1]
1951-54	900
1955-58	1,050
1959-65	1,200
1966-67	1,650
1968-71	1,950
1972	2,250
1973	2,700
1974	3,300
1975	3,525
1976	3,825
1977	4,125
1978	4,425
1979	4,725
1980	5,100
1981	5,550
1982	6,075
1983	6,675
1984	7,050
1985	7,425
1986	7,875
1987	8,175
1988	8,400
1989	8,925
1990	9,525
1991	9,900
1992	10,350
1993	10,725
1994	11,250
1995	11,325
1996	11,625
1997	12,150

[1] Total credited earnings from 1937-50 are divided by $900 to get the number of years of coverage (maximum of 14 years)

Figure 8-4

Taxability of Social Security Payments

Whether you have to pay federal taxes on your Social Security benefits depends on your marital status and income level.

If you file a federal tax return as an individual and your combined income is between $25,000 and $34,000, you may have to pay taxes on 50 percent of your Social Security benefits. If your combined income is above $34,000, 85 percent of your Social Security benefits is subject to income tax.

If you file a joint return, you may have to pay taxes on 50 percent of your benefits if you and your spouse have a combined income that is between $32,000 and $44,000. If your combined income is more than $44,000, 85 percent of your Social Security benefits is subject to income tax.

Note: Combined income means your and your spouse's adjusted gross income (as reported on your Form 1040) plus nontaxable interest plus one-half of your Social Security benefits.

Where to Go for More Information

You can get a Personal Earnings and Benefit Estimate Statement by calling Social Security at 1-800-772-1213. This statement will provide you with a measurement of potential benefits due you and your survivors. However, when you review the benefit dollar amounts, remember that they have been computed for someone whose benefits will not be reduced or wiped out by the Windfall Elimination Provision. The same goes for the Public Pension Offset.

Using that same toll free number — 1-800-772-1213 — you can get more information 24 hours a day. Service representatives are available between the hours of 7 a.m. and 7 p.m. Eastern time Monday through Friday (except federal holidays). If you have a touch-tone phone, recorded information is available after hours, on weekends and holidays. There is also a TTY number for those who are hard of hearing. Call 1-800-325-0778.

For more information about the taxation of Social Security benefits, call the IRS and ask for Publication 554, Tax Information for Older Americans, and Publication 915, Social Security Benefits and Equivalent Railroad Retirement Benefits. Their phone number is 1-800-TAX-FORM (1-800-829-3676).

Social Security Survivor Benefits Questions & Answers

Q. What are the qualifications for receiving Old-Age, Survivors, and Disability Insurance (OASDI) Benefits?

A. A qualified surviving spouse generally receives a monthly insurance benefit equal to the amount that the deceased employee spouse would have received. However, the surviving spouse is not entitled to this benefit if he/she already is entitled to a retirement insurance benefit that is equal to or more than the deceased employee's primary insurance amount. A qualified widow or widower must have been married to the employee for at least nine months and have attained age 60 (50 if disabled) or be caring for children younger than age 19. Such children include biological sons and daughters born to the worker and the claimant, as well as children who were legally adopted before age 18. Figure 8-3 shows the approximate amount your qualified survivor would receive based on your Social Security-covered earnings, if any, if you died in 1996.

Q. Are there any exceptions to the nine-month duration-of-marriage requirement?

A. The nine-month duration-of-marriage requirement is waived if the employee died due to an accident.

Q. What provisions allow continued benefits after remarriage?

A. The remarriage of a widow or widower after age 60, or a disabled widow or widower after age 50 does not prevent the individual from receiving benefits based on his or her prior spouse's Social Security earnings record.

Q. What is the widow or widower's insurance benefit rate?

A. The rate is equal to 100 percent of the deceased employee's primary insurance amount (PIA), subject to possible deductions such as:
- When the "Family Maximum" benefit is exceeded for all covered beneficiaries.
- When the widow or widower also is entitled to a smaller retirement insurance benefit, only the difference between this smaller retirement benefit and the larger survivor benefit is payable as a survivor's benefit.
- A reduction applies if the widow or widower is not yet age 65 and elects to receive a reduced benefit at that time. The reduced benefit rate will then remain in effect for as long as he or she receives these benefits. However, if the widow or widower has responsibility for the care of the deceased spouse's child who is under age 16 or disabled, the reduction will not be below 75 percent of the deceased spouse's primary insurance amount.

Q. Under what circumstances are payments to widows or widowers delayed?

A. Under the following circumstances:
- If the individual is under age 70, working, and earning more than the annual exempt amount, or
- Is entitled, based on his or her own employment, to a federal, state, or other government pension which requires an offset (reduction) for the Social Security payment.

Q. When do widow or widower insurance benefits end?

A. They end:
- When the widow or widower dies,
- When the widow or widower becomes entitled to a retirement benefit that is equal to or greater than the deceased spouse's primary insurance amount, or

- The widow or widower's disability ceases during the period between age 50 and age 60 when benefits are normally provided. Benefits end the second month after the month that the disability ceases.

Q. When is a surviving child entitled to insurance benefits?
A. An unmarried dependent child is entitled to benefits:
- If the child is under age 18 or under 19 and a full-time elementary or secondary school student, or
- If the child is age 18 or over and disabled.

Q. What are the surviving child's benefits?
A. The surviving child receives 75 percent of the deceased parent's primary insurance amount. However, this amount may be less if the "Family Maximum" applies.

Q. Under what circumstances are payments to surviving children delayed?
A. Payments are delayed:
- If the child works and earns more than the prescribed maximum,
- If a disabled child age 18 or over refuses to accept vocational rehabilitation services without good cause. However, the child's insurance benefits may be payable for all months while still under age 19 if a full-time student.

Q. When do surviving child insurance benefits end?
A. Insurance benefits end when:
- The surviving child dies,
- The surviving child reaches age 18 and is not disabled or attending elementary or high school on a full-time basis,
- The disabled child ceases to be disabled unless under age 19 and still attending school full-time, or
- The child marries.

Q. When is a lump-sum payment authorized?
A. A lump-sum death payment may be made in addition to any monthly survivors benefits that are due. The full amount is paid to the widow or widower. If there is no surviving spouse, the lump-sum is payable to a child or the children of the deceased employee in equal shares. An application for this benefit must be filed within two years.

CHAPTER NINE

OTHER SURVIVOR BENEFITS

Voluntary Contributions Program (VCP)

The VCP is a little-known benefit that can help CSRS employees and survivors receive higher annuities by making voluntary contributions to the Civil Service Retirement Fund. This can provide an additional source of revenue to your survivors. The money in a VCP account may be cashed out at any time, the interest rolled over into an IRA, or the entire amount may be used to purchase an additional annuity (with a survivor option) on your retirement. The VCP program is not available to employees covered by FERS.

Overview

As a CSRS or CSRS-Offset employee, you are entitled to make voluntary contributions to the CSRS Fund over and above the retirement contribution required by law and the 5 percent limit placed on your contributions to the TSP. These voluntary contributions—with interest—may be withdrawn at any time and for any reason. However, if you withdraw your money, you must take it all out and close the account.

You may make voluntary contributions of up to 10 percent of the total basic salary paid to you since you were first employed in the federal civil service. In a VCP account, your contributions earn a fixed rate of interest, which is set in January of each year (for 1997, the rate is 6.875 percent). Each contribution is required to be a multiple of $25; however, payments do not have to be made on a regular basis. You may elect to make a number of contributions throughout the course of each year.

You are entitled to make the contributions unless you are a former voluntary contributor who withdrew your funds. The rules generally prohibit those who withdraw funds from further participation in the program.

To participate, you must complete an SF-2804, Application to Make Voluntary Contributions. Your agency will file the SF-2804 with OPM. After OPM approves your participation, you will make your payments directly to OPM. The instructions for doing so are on the form.

Voluntary contributions and interest can translate into additional annuity dollars. For example, every $100 in your account provides another $7 plus 20 cents for each year you are over age 55 at retirement. This can add to your retirement income and provide further protection for your loved ones. As indicated above, your contributions earn interest, which is not taxed until you begin withdrawing the funds. That makes the voluntary contribution program a tax shelter, as well. Keep in mind that since your contributions to the fund are made with after-tax dollars, that portion of your account is not taxed when withdrawn.

Withdrawing Your Money

You may withdraw your voluntary contributions with accrued interest before you separate from the service or after, unless you have begun receiving an annuity based on this amount. Such a withdrawal, however, may have negative tax consequences unless you roll the interest over into an IRA. Think twice or consult with a tax adviser before making such a move.

Note: Because your account stops earning interest as of the day following your retirement, you will want to decide then whether to take the money as a cash refund or as an annuity.

Survivor Benefits

If you use the money in your account to purchase additional annuity coverage when you retire and elect to provide a survivor benefit for someone, your VC annuity will be reduced to account for the difference in age between you and your survivor. At the time of your death during your retirement, your survivor will be paid an additional annuity equal to 50 percent of your reduced VC annuity.

Lump-Sum Death Benefit

Should your death occur before retirement, your voluntary contributions, including interest, will be paid as a lump-sum death benefit either to the person(s) you named on an SF-2808, Designation of Beneficiary, or according to the standard Order of Precedence. Your contributions cannot be used to provide an additional annuity for your survivors until you retire.

Your Financial Guide

Things to Consider
Before Investing in the VCP
Many financial advisors agree that you should maximize your contributions to the TSP before considering contributing to a VC account. The reason is that TSP contributions are tax-advantaged, while VCP contributions aren't — only the interest earned is sheltered.

Although a VC annuity, unlike your regular annuity, will be included in your regular monthly annuity payments, it will not be increased by COLAs.

A married employee does not need the consent of his or her spouse when deciding not to provide a VC survivor annuity, or when naming another person to receive the benefit.

The reduction to provide a VC survivor annuity is permanent and will not stop even if the person to receive the benefit dies. The survivor benefit cannot be transferred to another person.

Where to Go for More Information
Your personnel office should be able to provide you with a copy of an OPM publication called "Retirement Facts 10: Voluntary Contributions Under the Civil Service Retirement System." If they don't have it, ask the benefits officer to get in touch with your agency's headquarters-level Retirement Counselor, who will supply one.

Increase Your CSRS Retirement, the only comprehensive guide in or out of government to the Voluntary Contributions Program, is published by the Federal Employees News Digest Inc. For ordering information, see the back of this book.

Federal Employees' Compensation Act (FECA) Death Benefits
Two additional protections for you and your survivors are made available through the Federal Employees' Compensation Act. In certain circumstances, you may be eligible for disability and death benefits administered by the Department of Labor's Office of Workers' Compensation Programs (OWCP).

Disability Benefits
As a federal employee you are covered in the event of injury or illness related to your employment. If you sustain a disabling traumatic injury, you are entitled to continuation of regular pay for a period not to exceed 45 calendar days. This is considered salary for all intents and purposes (including tax deductions) and not compensation. Compensation benefits for wage loss begin at the conclusion of the period of continuation of pay, if you are disabled. The amount of monetary compensation generally is based on your monthly pay at the time of the injury.

Basic compensation for total disability is two-thirds of your monthly pay. This is increased to three-fourths of the monthly pay if you have a spouse, minor child or wholly dependent parent.

In general, compensation for disability cannot be paid concurrently with a government annuity (including a lump-sum payment). If you are entitled to both benefits, you must make an election; however, you may make a new election whenever it is to your advantage to do so.

Note: *You may receive compensation concurrently with military retirement or retainer pay, subject to the reduction of such pay in accordance with law (5 U.S.C. 5532(b)).*

Death Benefits
If you die as a result of an on-the-job injury, your eligible survivors will receive income benefits, and certain funeral and burial expenses will be reimbursed. If the death resulted from a person or party other than the federal government, and a third party action lawsuit may be indicated, the Department of Labor will provide instructions.

Just as with disability benefits, an election of benefits may also be required where there is dual entitlement. An election is also required where a beneficiary is also eligible to receive benefits (other than the proceeds of an insurance policy) from the United States for the same injury or death.

Survivors Who Are Eligible For Benefits
Your survivors who are eligible for death compensation include the widow(er) who was living with you or was separated from you for reasonable cause prior to your death, children under 18 (unmarried natural, adopted, and stepchildren, as well as children over 18 whose mental or physical disabilities make them incapable of self-support), and other specified family members who were dependents of the deceased employee, including grandparents, parents, minor brothers and sisters, and grandchildren.

Compensation for your children may be paid up to age 23 while they are completing their college education full-time. Benefits are discontinued if a dependent child completes four years of high school and does not attend college. This also is the case for children who marry.

Monthly Wage Loss Allowance Payments For Survivors
The maximum allowance for all beneficiaries may not exceed three-fourths of the monthly wage on which

Labor Department District Offices
Office of Workers' Compensation Programs

DISTRICT OFFICE ADDRESS	JURISDICTION
District No. 1 One Congress Street, 11th Floor Boston, Massachusetts 02114	Connecticut, Maine, Massachusetts, New Hampshire, Rhode Island, and Vermont
District No. 2 201 Varick Street, Room 750 New York, New York 10014	New Jersey, New York, Puerto Rico, and the Virgin Islands
District No. 3 Gateway Building, Room 15200 3535 Market Street Philadelphia, Pennsylvania 19104	Pennsylvania, Delaware, and West Virginia
District No. 6 214 North Hogan Street, Suite 1006 Jacksonville, Florida 32202	Alabama, Florida, Georgia, Kentucky, Mississippi, North Carolina, South Carolina, and Tennessee
District No. 9 Room 851 1240 East 9th Street Cleveland, Ohio 44199	Indiana, Michigan, and Ohio
District No. 10 8th Floor 230 South Dearborn Street Chicago, Illinois 60604	Illinois, Minnesota, and Wisconsin
District No. 11 City Center Square 1100 Main Street, Suite 750 Kansas City, Missouri 64106	Iowa, Kansas, Missouri, and Nebraska
District No. 12 1801 California Street Suite 915 Denver, Colorado 80202	Colorado, Montana, North Dakota, South Dakota, Utah, and Wyoming
District No. 13 71 Stevenson Street, 2nd Floor San Francisco, California 94105	Arizona, California, Nevada, Hawaii and all U.S. citizens and residents injured in U.S. territories and trust territories and possessions in the Pacific
District No. 14 Suite 615 1111 Third Avenue Seattle, Washington 98101-3212	Alaska, Idaho, Oregon, and Washington
District No. 16 525 South Griffin Street Room 100 Dallas, Texas 75202	New Mexico, Oklahoma, Texas, Louisiana, and Arkansas
District No. 25 800 North Capitol Street, N.W., Room 800 Washington, D.C. 20211	District of Columbia, Maryland, Virginia, and all claims originating outside the U.S., its possessions, territories and trust territories, including claims by U.S. citizens and residents, as well as foreign nationals, wherever employed.

Figure 9-1

compensation is computed. In no case may the monthly pay rate exceed three-fourths of the highest monthly pay level for GS-15, step 10. The minimum monthly pay rate used for computing death benefits is GS-2, step 1. In no case may the monthly benefits exceed the decedent's monthly pay, except for increases resulting from COLAs.

Your widow(er) is eligible for compensation equal to 50 percent of your pay. If your survivors include dependent children, your spouse would receive 45 percent of your former pay and an additional allowance of 15 percent for each child. The initial maximum monthly payment cannot exceed 75 percent of your final pay. However, your survivors will receive cost-of-living increases.

If you don't have a qualified spouse, an eligible child may receive 40 percent of your monthly salary. If you have more than one eligible child, each would receive 15 percent, plus an equal share in the 40 percent allowance up to the stipulated maximum monthly payment.

Widow(er)s receive benefits until death or remarriage (if under age 55).

Funeral Expense Payments
A funeral expense allowance of up to $800 is paid. Should you die away from home, payment will be made for the full cost of transporting your remains to the place of burial (in the area of your last place of residence.) A $200 allowance also can be paid to anyone hired as a representative for the costs of terminating your status as an employee of the United States.

Filing a Claim for Death Benefits
To file a claim for death benefits, your survivor(s) must complete Form CA-5, Claim for Compensation. To ensure that OWCP requirements are met, the claim should be filed within 30 days of your death. In order to speed up death claim benefits payments, your survivor(s) should attach the required supporting documentation, all copies of which must be certified:

- Marriage certificate
- Death certificate
- Birth certificate/adoption document for each child.
- Legal documents proving dissolution of the marriage(s), if either you or your surviving spouse was married previously.
- Original itemized funeral and burial bills. If these bills have been paid, so indicate and give the name and address of the individual who made payment.

- If an executor or administrator has been appointed, give the name and address of this individual and include a copy of the appointment document.

In completing the claim form, any item that is not applicable should be indicated by entering "N/A."

The Attending Physician's Report, to be entered on the reverse side of the form, also must be completed before the form is submitted to the OWCP district office that provides service to your geographic area.

If the employee died as a result of an injury incurred while performing his/her duties, or because of an employment-related disease, the deceased employee's supervisor or other official must complete Form CA-6. This is the Official Superior's Report of Employee's Death. The person who fills out this form must attach a certified copy of your death certificate, and submit it to OWCP.

Payment of Claims
The adjudication and payment of OWCP claims takes place at the district office level. Inquiries concerning specific cases should be directed to your district office.

Where to Go For More Information
For more information about OWCP's programs, you may write to:

> Office of Workers' Compensation Programs
> U.S. Department of Labor
> Washington, D.C. 20210

The OWCP district offices may also be able to help you. You may either write to them or look up their phone number in the federal government section of your phone book and call.

Veterans Life Insurance
If you are a veteran of U.S. military service, you already may have insurance supervised by the Department of Veterans Affairs. If not, you may be eligible for it. Such insurance can be a valuable asset for your survivors and should not be overlooked in your estate planning.

Types of VA Insurance
Veterans who are granted a service-connected disability but are otherwise in good health may apply for up to $10,000 of life insurance coverage at standard insurance rates within two years of being disabled. This insurance is limited to veterans who left service after April 24, 1951. Veterans who are totally disabled may apply for a waiver of premiums. For those veterans who are eligible for this waiver, an additional policy of up to $20,000 is available. Premiums cannot be waived on the additional insurance.

In addition, there are three life insurance programs currently open for new members:

- Veterans Mortgage Life Insurance (VMLI) — The maximum amount of mortgage life insurance available for those approved for a specially adapted housing grant is $90,000. Protection is automatic unless the veteran declines. Premiums are automatically deducted from VA benefit payments or paid direct, if the veteran does not draw compensation. They will continue until the mortgage has been liquidated, the home is sold, or the coverage terminates because the veteran reaches age 70. If a mortgage is paid off, VMLI may be obtained on the mortgage of a subsequent home.
- Servicemen's Group Life Insurance (SGLI) — Members of the uniformed services on active duty, including commissioned officers of the Public Health Service and the National Oceanographic and Atmospheric Administration, Ready Reservists, and Retired Reservists are automatically insured for $100,000. While members can elect to be covered for a lesser amount or not at all, they also may purchase up to an additional $100,000 of insurance.
- Veterans Group Life Insurance (VGLI) — This is available upon separation from service, on or after August 1, 1974, to veterans wishing to convert their SGLI coverage to renewable five-year term insurance. The amount of coverage may not be more than the amount of SGLI that the member had in force at the time of separation, the maximum being $200,000. A VGLI policy holder has the right to convert to an individual commercial policy at the standard premium rates, regardless of health, with any of the participating insurance companies.

Note: The SGLI and VGLI programs are administered by the Office of Servicemen's Group Life Insurance, 213 Washington Street, Newark, N.J. 07102.

Filing Information

If you have an active insurance policy with the VA, make sure that your survivors know where it is located, its value, and how to file for a death benefit payment by contacting the local VA office. The easiest way to do this is to call 1-800-827-1000. Dialing that number will automatically connect you to the nearest VA regional office during normal office hours.

Veterans Survivor Pension

For the survivors of deceased wartime veterans whose deaths are not service-connected, a pension payment is provided as a partial means of support in needy cases. If they have a limited income, the qualifying widow(er) and children of a veteran with at least 90 days of honorable wartime service may be eligible for benefits. Children must be age 18 or younger, and unmarried. Under one exception, that qualifying age goes to 23 if a child is still attending school full-time. Another exception applies to children disabled before age 18; no age limit applies in these cases.

Your local Department of Veterans Affairs office has detailed information on the pension rates, which are adjusted each year for inflation.

CHAPTER TEN

INSURANCE

One of the most significant sources of immediate financial relief for the survivor(s) of federal employees is Federal Employees' Group Life Insurance. More than 90 percent of federal employees carry FEGLI Basic Insurance and most of them carry it into retirement. There are five good reasons for this:

1. Employees are automatically covered for Basic Insurance unless they say in writing that they don't want it.
2. No physical examination is required.
3. The cost of Basic Insurance is shared by the employees and the government. An executive branch employee pays two-thirds of the cost through payroll deduction, the government pays the rest. (The U.S. Postal Service picks up all of the cost of basic insurance for its employees but not for its retirees.)
4. The amount an employee pays for each $1,000 of Basic Insurance coverage is 16.5 cents biweekly per $1,000 of coverage. And it stays the same regardless of age, unlike many private sector term-life insurance policies.
5. Unlike private insurance, FEGLI premiums aren't loaded with cost run-ups, such as commissions to agents, risk charges, investment return, and profit.

Basic Insurance—For Employees

Basic Insurance coverage is equal to:

A. The actual rate of annual basic pay (rounded to the next higher $1,000) plus $2,000; or
B. $10,000 if it is greater than the amount provided by A.

Note: Your Basic Insurance amount will change if your salary rate increases or decreases enough. The new amount of Basic Insurance will be effective on the date the salary rate change occurs.

The benefit paid is double the Basic Insurance amount until you reach age 36. Thereafter, it decreases at the rate of 10 percent per year until age 45 when this extra coverage ends.

There also is an Accidental Death and Dismemberment benefit that is equal to the amount of the employee's Basic Insurance only, not the extra benefit for being under age 45.

To determine your current Basic Insurance coverage, use the worksheet below:

Basic Insurance Worksheet

Your current actual rate of annual basic pay (rounded up to the next Thousand) $ _____

Add $2,000 $ _____

Your Basic Insurance amount $ _____*

* *Remember, this amount will be greater if you are under age 45.*

Basic Insurance—For Retirees

You are eligible to continue your Basic Insurance into retirement as long as you: 1) retire on an immediate annuity and 2) have been enrolled for at least five years (or for the entire time it was available to you).

If you decide to keep your Basic Insurance, you will be given three options, one of which you must choose. Obviously, the one you pick will depend on your survivors' projected needs. For example, if your survivor's annuity would be insufficient for him or her to live comfortably and pay off outstanding debts, you might want to decline a reduction. On the other hand, your family financial obligations may have declined to the point that the maximum reduction makes better sense. The three basic insurance options are:

A. No Reduction in Coverage — Your Basic Insurance amount continues in full for a monthly premium payment of $2.0475 per $1,000 of coverage before age 65, and $1.69 thereafter.
B. 50 Percent Reduction in Coverage — Your Basic Insurance amount at retirement will be reduced by 1 percent per month after age 65, until 50 percent of the amount of your Basic Insurance remains. Until age 65, you will pay $0.8775 per $1,000 of coverage; thereafter you'll pay $0.52 per $1,000.
C. 75 Percent Reduction in Coverage — Your Basic Insurance amount at retirement will be reduced by 2 percent per month after age 65, until 25 percent of the amount of your Basic Insurance remains. This option provides Basic Insurance coverage at no cost after age 65.

Your Financial Guide

Regardless of which option you choose, if you retire before age 65 your premiums will not increase. You will continue to pay the same amount per $1,000 of coverage that you did while you were still working. At age 65 the premiums will only increase for those who elected options A or B above.

Note: *In no case will the Accidental Death and Dismemberment coverage under Basic Insurance continue after your retirement.*

Optional Life Insurance

In addition to Basic Life Insurance, the government offers three other insurance options for employees, any of which you may acquire at your own expense through payroll deductions. However, you must be covered by Basic Insurance to participate in any of them.

Option A—Standard

This option provides an additional $10,000 of life insurance coverage, plus coverage of $10,000 for Accidental Death and Dismemberment while you are an employee.

Option A—Standard Insurance Withholdings			
	Per $10,000 of coverage:		
Age Group	Bi-weekly	Semi-monthly	Monthly
Under age 35	$0.40	$0.43	$ 0.87
Age 35 through 39	0.50	0.54	1.08
Age 40 through 44	0.70	0.76	1.52
Age 45 through 49	1.10	1.19	2.38
Age 50 through 54	1.80	1.95	3.90
Age 55 through 59	3.00	3.25	6.50
Age 60 or over	7.00	7.58	15.17

Figure 10-1

You pay the full cost of Option A—Standard insurance. And the amount you pay depends on your age. As you reach the next age group, your withholdings will increase correspondingly, (see Figure 10-1).

For withholding purposes, you are assumed to have reached the next applicable level in January of the year after your birthday.

Option A—Standard insurance continues automatically after you retire as long as you keep your Basic Insurance coverage.

Deductions will continue to be made from your monthly annuity payment until you reach age 65 or from your paycheck if you retire at a later age. When you reach age 65 (or when you retire, if at a later age), your Option A—Standard coverage will begin to reduce by 2 percent each month until it reaches 25 percent of its initial value, namely, $2,500.

Note: *In no case will the Accidental Death and Dismemberment coverage under Option A—Standard continue after you retire.*

Option B—Additional

This option offers you the opportunity to purchase a substantial amount of additional life insurance—from one to five times the amount of your Basic Insurance (after your basic pay is rounded up to the next $1,000). You decide on the number of multiples you want. An Accidental Death and Dismemberment provision is not included in this option.

To find out how much your Option B—Additional insurance would amount to, fill out the worksheet below:

Option B—Additional Insurance Worksheet

1. Your current actual rate of annual basic pay (rounded up to the next thousand) $ _____
2. Number of multiples you elect (1,2,3,4,5) _____
3. Amount of Option B—Additional insurance (multiply line 2 by line 1) $ _____

Note: *Your Option B—Additional Insurance amount will change if your salary rate increases or decreases enough to change your Basic Insurance amount. The new amount of Option B—Additional insurance will be effective on the date the salary rate change occurs. Your premiums will change accordingly.*

Option B—Additional insurance continues automatically after you retire if you continue your Basic Life coverage, unless you were not insured for:

- The five years immediately preceding the day on which your annuity begins; or
- The entire period of service during which Option B—Additional coverage was available to you (if you were covered for fewer than five years).

Option B—Additional Withholdings			
	Per $10,000 of coverage:		
Age Group	Bi-weekly	Semi-monthly	Monthly
Under age 35	$.04	$.043	$ .087
Age 35 through 39	.05	.054	.108
Age 40 through 44	.07	.076	.152
Age 45 through 49	.11	.119	.238
Age 50 through 54	.18	.195	.390
Age 55 through 59	.30	.325	.650
Age 60 or over	.70	.758	1.517

Figure 10-2

If you have met the criteria above:

- Withholdings will continue to be made from your monthly annuity payment until you reach age 65 or from your paycheck if you retire at a later age.
- When you reach age 65 (or when you retire, if at a later age), your Option B—Additional coverage will begin to reduce by 2 percent each month for 50 months, when coverage will end.

Remember, you pay the full cost of this insurance. And the amount you pay depends on your age. As you reach the next age group, your withholdings will increase correspondingly, (as shown in Figure 10-2).

Note: For withholding purposes, you are assumed to have reached these ages in January of the year after your birthday.

Option C—Family

This option allows you to cover the lives of eligible family members, that is, your spouse and any unmarried dependent children. Coverage for the spouse is $5,000, and for each eligible child, $2,500. Accidental death and dismemberment coverage is not included in this option.

Option C—Family Withholdings

Per $10,000 of coverage:

Age Group	Bi-weekly	Semi-monthly	Monthly
Under age 35	$.30	$.33	$ .65
Age 35 through 39	.31	.34	.67
Age 40 through 44	.52	.56	1.13
Age 45 through 49	.70	.79	1.52
Age 50 through 54	1.00	1.08	2.17
Age 55 through 59	1.50	1.63	3.25
Age 60 or over	2.60	2.82	5.63

Note: For withholding purposes, you are assumed to have reached these ages in January of the year after your birthday.

Figure 10-3

Retirees at age 65 no longer have to pay premiums for additional optional insurance, but the amount of coverage starts to reduce by 2 percent each month for 50 months, at which point coverage ceases.

Remember, you pay the full cost of Option C—Standard insurance. And the amount you pay depends on your age. As you reach the next age group, your withholdings will increase correspondingly. (Figure 10-3)

Estimating FEGLI Benefits

If Death Occurs Before Retirement

To determine how much insurance would be paid to your survivor(s) based on your current FEGLI coverage, use the worksheet provided in Figure 10-4.

If Death Occurs After Retirement

To determine how much insurance would be paid to your survivor(s) after retirement, you use the same approach as shown in Figure 10-4. The only difference is that you may have to reduce some of your figures for Basic, Option A and Option B insurance:

- Basic Insurance — If you chose the 50 percent reduction at retirement, your insurance will be reduced by 1 percent per month beginning at age 65 until half the amount of your Basic Insurance remains. If you chose the 75 percent reduction, your insurance will be reduced by 2 percent per month beginning at age 65 until one-quarter of your Basic Insurance remains.
- Option A-Standard — Beginning at age 65, your coverage will be reduced by 2 percent each month until it reaches 25 percent of its initial value, which is $2,500.
- Option B-Additional — Beginning at age 65, your coverage will be reduced by 2 percent each month for 50 months, when coverage will end.

Designation of Beneficiary

If you want to have your survivors receive benefits in the standard Order of Precedence, you do not have to name a beneficiary. Otherwise, you will have to specify a beneficiary or beneficiaries by completing a Designation of Beneficiary form (SF-2823).

You may want to consider changing your designation if you have not already included a survivorship condition. This type of restriction specifies that in order to receive payment of insurance proceeds, your beneficiary must survive you for a certain length of time, which is designated by you but may not exceed 30 days. This may provide significant tax advantages for your survivors. Contact your employing office's human resources or personnel office for a copy of this form and guidance on how to include this special provision.

Note: Under Option C—Family insurance, the only beneficiary is the employee. There can be no other designation.

Standard Order of Precedence

In the absence of a designation of beneficiary, the awarding of survivor benefits will follow the standard Order of Precedence mandated by law. Under this system, your widow or widower would receive your benefits. If you have no spouse or your spouse dies before you, the payment would automatically pass to your child or children, and so forth.

You may change your beneficiary/beneficiaries at any time by completing a SF-2823. In order to be officially recognized as valid, this revised Designation of Beneficiary form must be:

LIFE INSURANCE WORKSHEET

1. Your current actual rate of annual basic pay $_____

2. If not an exact thousand, round to the next higher thousand $_____

3. Add $2,000 $_____2,000

4. Your Basic Insurance Amount
   (The total of lines 2 and 3, or $10,000, if greater) $_____

EXTRA BENEFIT (IF ANY)

See table below

5. Your Basic Insurance Amount (from line 4) $_____

6. Age Multiplication Factor (from table below, times amount on line 5)   X

7. Total amount of Basic Life Insurance at your present age, including
   the EXTRA BENEFIT (if any) $_____

OPTION A—STANDARD

8. Amount of Insurance ($10,000) $_____10,000

OPTION B—ADDITIONAL

9. Your current actual rate of annual basic pay $_____

10. If not an exact $1,000, round to the next higher $1,000 $_____

11. Number of Multiples you elect   X

12. Amount of Option B—Additional insurance (line 10 times line 11) $_____

Extra Benefit Calculation Table

Your Current Age	Age Multiplication Factor
35 or under	2.0
36	1.9
37	1.8
38	1.7
39	1.6
40	1.5
41	1.4
42	1.3
43	1.2
44	1.1
45 and Over	1.0

Figure 10-4

- Signed by you,
- Signed by two witnesses (neither one can be a beneficiary), and
- Received by your employing office's personnel office or by OPM's Employee Service and Records Center if you are an annuitant.

Pointers for Naming Beneficiaries

Some general guidelines for naming beneficiaries:

- If you name more than one beneficiary, designate their respective shares (one-half, three-quarters, etc.) unless you want them to receive equal shares. There are no limitations on the number of eligible beneficiaries you may name or the amount of each share, as long as it totals to 100 percent.
- Should one of these designated beneficiaries die before you or become disqualified to receive a share for any reason, that share will be distributed equally among the remaining beneficiaries.
- If a designated beneficiary dies before you do, his/her rights and interests in your insurance benefits end automatically. This means that there would be no distribution to his or her estate.
- If the last SF-2823 that you execute before your death is determined to be invalid for any reason, the prior form that you filed will be used to distribute your insurance benefits. If there is no prior form, proceeds will be distributed in accordance with the standard Order of Precedence.
- If you have a trust arrangement established as part of your Last Will and Testament or under the provisions of a formal Trust Agreement, arrangements may be made to designate the Trustee, in his/her capacity as trustee, as your beneficiary. (Contact your employing office's personnel office or, if you are an annuitant, OPM's Retirement Operation Center, Boyers, PA 16017, to make special arrangements.)
- In the absence of a properly executed SF-2823 (or an SF-54, the older version of the SF-2823), your beneficiary may be required to furnish documentation of his/her rights to payment.

Assignment of Benefits

Private-sector employees have long been able to assign their life insurance coverage to another person or persons, including an individual, a corporation or an irrevocable trust. As a result, they could:

- Reduce estate taxes or eliminate probate;
- Comply with a court-ordered division of property in a divorce settlement; or
- Obtain cash before their death.

Since October 3, 1994, that option has been available to all federal employees, retirees and other individuals covered by FEGLI.

Assignment means that you transfer ownership and control of your Basic, Option A, and Option B insurance (if you have these coverages) to the assignee(s). Thereafter, life insurance premiums will continue to be withheld from your annuity.

Once assigned, you may not cancel your insurance or designate beneficiaries. The assignee becomes the beneficiary unless the assignee designates someone else.

Note: If you have assigned your insurance, neither you nor the assignee(s) may elect a living benefit. (See below.)

If you are a current employee you may get more information by going to your personnel office and asking for a copy of OPM Form RI 76-10. Retirees should write to the following address:

Office of Personnel Management
Retirement Operations Center
Attn: RI 76-10
P.O. Box 45
Boyers, PA 16017-0045

Living Benefits

Living benefits are life insurance benefits paid to you while you are still alive, rather than paid to your beneficiary or survivor after your death. The early receipt of this money could be a blessing to you and your loved ones, allowing medical bills to be paid in a timely fashion and reducing the threat of bankruptcy.

Effective July 25, 1995, any federal employee, annuitant or compensationer covered by the FEGLI program who has been diagnosed as terminally ill with a life expectancy of nine months or less may elect a living benefit.

Only Basic Insurance is available for living benefits. An employee may elect either a full living benefit — i.e., all of his/her Basic benefit — or a partial living benefit (in multiples of $1,000). A retiree or compensationer may only elect a full living benefit. With a full benefit, withholding for premiums stops; with a partial benefit, it's recalculated.

Living benefits may be elected only once and an election cannot be retracted. If a full living benefit is elected, no basic insurance will remain. If a partial living benefit is taken (an option only available to employees), the amount of the remaining basic insurance will be frozen. It will not change, even if the employee's salary increases.

Note: If you elect a living benefit, whether full or partial, you can't later assign any remaining insurance, either Basic or Optional.

If you are terminally ill and believe you qualify for and wish to elect living benefits, write or call:

Office of Federal Employees' Group Life Insurance
200 Park Avenue
New York, NY 10166-0188
1-800-633-4542

That office will send you an application form (FE-8, Claim for Living Benefits) and a calculation sheet, so you can determine the amount of basic insurance available to you.

Note: By the way, if your medical prognosis is wrong and you live longer than nine months, you will not have to repay the amount you withdrew as a living benefit.

Filing an Insurance Claim

If You Die While an Employee — Your beneficiary or other survivor must complete a claim form, Claim for Death Benefits and furnish a certified copy of your death certificate. The instructions provided on this claim form must be carefully followed. Your employing office's personnel office will provide this form and review it for proper completion, prior to forwarding it for processing to the:

Office of Federal Employees' Group Life Insurance
200 Park Avenue
New York, NY 10166-0188

If You Die While Retired — Your survivor, another family member, or a friend may call OPM at (202) 606-0500 to report your death and begin the process of securing your life insurance benefits. This telephone service is available Monday through Friday (except federal holidays) from 7:30 a.m. to 5 p.m. Eastern time. The caller will be asked to provide the following information:

- Your full name,
- Your annuity claim number (CSA number),
- Your date of birth,
- The date of your death, and
- The name and address of the person(s) who may be entitled to death benefits.

Or write OPM at the following address:

Office of Personnel Management
P.O. Box 45
Boyers, PA 16017-0045

When it receives notification, OPM will send an application form for FEGLI benefits. Your certified death certificate must be included with the completed FE-6 and sent to this address:

Office of Federal Employees' Group Life Insurance
200 Park Avenue
New York, NY 10166-0188

The funeral director or a third party helping to settle your estate will assist your survivor to obtain certified copies of the death certificate for this and other required notification purposes, such as an application for a survivor annuity.

When Benefits Are Paid

The amount of your life insurance is payable in full in the event of your death.

Accidental death and dismemberment benefits are payable if you receive bodily injuries solely through violent, external and accidental means (except as noted below) and lose your life, limb, or eyesight as a direct result of them within 90 days afterwards. Your loss must be independent of all other causes.

The full amount of Accidental Death and Dismemberment insurance is payable if you lose your life under such circumstances. Half the amount is payable to you for the loss of one limb or sight of one eye, or the full amount for two or more such losses. If the accident does not result in your death, the full amount of your insurance remains in effect and is payable when you die at a later date.

For all such losses resulting from any one accident, no more than the full amount of accidental death and dismemberment insurance is payable.

Exceptions — Not surprisingly, there are circumstances under which payment for accidental death or dismemberment will not be made. Most of them would rarely apply. Still others are so odd that the reasons for their inclusion are probably lost in the mists of time. However, there are three exceptions covering situations that occur more often than any of us would like. Simply stated, payment will not be made when the death or loss is caused:

- "Wholly or partly, directly or indirectly, by disease or bodily or mental infirmity, or by medical or surgical treatment or diagnosis thereof;" or
- "By or as a result of intentional self-destruction or intentionally self-inflicted injury, while sane or insane;" or
- "By or a result of the self administration of illegal or illegally obtained drugs."

Discontinuing FEGLI Coverage

You may discontinue your coverage for Basic or Optional insurance coverage at any time by providing a written waiver of insurance coverage to your employing office (or OPM in the case of a retiree). However, with the exception of Option B—Additional coverage, which eventually reduces to zero, there are only five situations in which your insurance can be discontinued without your consent. All but one of them involve a change in employment status:

1. Separation from the service other than for retirement.
2. After 12 months of continuous non-pay status.
3. Any other employment change that results in your ceasing to be a FEGLI-eligible employee.
4. Termination of your annuity.
5. Reemployment in a position that makes you eligible for FEGLI coverage. This gives you a new election opportunity.

Converting to an Individual Policy

If your coverage stops under (1), (2), (3) or (4) above, you have the right to convert your FEGLI coverage under Basic and Options A and B to an individual life insurance policy. If you do, you will be responsible for the full amount of the premiums. There will be no government contribution. You will make your payments directly to the insurance company. Premiums will be retroactive to the date your coverage was terminated. The amount of those premiums will depend on four factors:

- The amount of insurance you apply for;
- The type of policy you apply for;
- Your age; and
- The class of risk you fall into on the day following the termination of group coverage.

You also have the right to purchase conversion policies for family members insured under Option C—Family. If you lose or terminate your group coverage, you have 31 days in which to convert this coverage to individual policies. In the event of your death, your family members will also have a 31-day period in which they may apply for their own conversion policies.

At the time your insurance stops, you may obtain detailed information concerning your right to apply for an individual policy by writing to the Office of Federal Employees' Group Life Insurance, 200 Park Avenue, New York, N.Y. 10166-0166.

If you should die during the 31 days after the date your insurance coverage stops, a death benefit will be payable for the maximum amount for which an individual policy could have been issued, whether or not you had applied for such individual policy or paid the first premium for it.

However, if you become reemployed and covered under FEGLI during the 31-day period, this death benefit will be reduced by whatever life insurance benefit is then in force. Furthermore, if an individual policy is issued before your death during that 31-day period, this death benefit will be reduced by the amount of insurance for which the individual policy is issued, unless the individual policy is surrendered without claim to the insurance company which issued it.

Note: If you drop your FEGLI coverage as a retiree, you may never again be covered unless you are reemployed in a position that provides it. However, if you drop your FEGLI coverage while an employee, you may pick it up at a later date, provided you are found to be medically insurable. Medical insurability must be determined by a physical examination for which you pay. Exam results are attached to an SF-2822, Request for Insurance, which your personnel office can supply and forward to OPM once you've filled it out.

Where to Go for More Information

As an employee, your best point of contact is your local benefits officer. In addition to answering your questions, that person should have copies of OPM's official publication, Certification of Enrollment in the FEGLI Program (RI 76-21).

Retirees who have questions or want copies of forms may call (202) 606-0500 or write:

OPM
P.O. Box 45
Boyers, PA 16017-0045

Private Insurance Considerations

In addition to your government-sponsored life insurance you may, of course, wish to purchase privately offered insurance. Possibly you already have one or more such policies. The period of assessing your finances is a good time to assess what you already own, what you need and what you should do to set up your insurance assets in the most favorable way for you and your family.

In the short run, life insurance can be used as a tool to provide needed cash shortly after your death. As discussed earlier, your survivors will need ready assets to cover the costs associated with your death and the closing of your estate. Without the proper cash reserves, they could be forced to sell off assets that they would prefer to keep—sometimes, even their house. Life insurance can provide the funds to prevent this.

Assuming that your government-sponsored insurance will cover this short-term need with some to spare, the question becomes: how much, if any, additional life insurance should you provide for longer term purposes? There are many estimating methods used by the insurance industry, but the only way to correctly answer that question is to review your own situation.

Refer back to your calculations of family income and living expense requirements that will be needed upon your death. If there is a gap on the negative side, life insurance is one possible way to fill it. The benefit money could be invested by your survivors to provide them with an income that would help make up part of the loss of your income.

Or possibly your survivors will need money for a specific, limited purpose, such as college education for the kids. Or they may wish to pay off a mortgage up front so that they don't have to continue making monthly payments from a reduced income.

Another concern is estate taxes. If your estate will be above the $600,000 federal tax threshold, it may be possible to bring the value of your estate below that figure by converting some of your assets into life insurance exempt from such taxation.

Tax law is highly complicated, so it is recommended that you discuss these issues with your family and your personal financial adviser. Financial planners typically have computer programs and other models that can help you decide the proper role of life insurance among your assets. The adviser ideally should be a disinterested party, with no stake in the amount of life insurance you hold, or in any decision to purchase more.

Life insurance can have value as an investment, but so do a number of other potential places for your money. You must assess each according to its own merits and according to how it fits into your entire portfolio. Remember, the primary purpose of life insurance is to protect your dependents. Other considerations, such as the accumulation of cash value in a policy, the ability to borrow against it and so on, should be secondary in your mind.

If you should decide to purchase private insurance, you should sort through the often bewildering array of insurance products offered in the private market. These include, but are not limited to:

- Term policies, which typically have low premiums but accumulate no cash value and require the holder to continue paying (ever-increasing) premiums indefinitely in order to keep the policy in effect.
- Whole life insurance, whose premiums don't rise and which does accumulate cash value and is paid in full after a set number of years. The premiums for a whole life policy usually are higher than those for a term policy with the same face value.
- Universal life insurance, which combines term insurance with a tax-deferred savings account that pays a variable interest rate, typically with premiums lower than whole life insurance. These policies also usually allow you to vary the amount of your premium going toward insurance coverage and the amount toward investments.
- Variable life insurance, a form of whole life coverage whose earnings on the accumulating cash are tied to an investment market that you choose, such as stock or bond funds—and rise and fall with them. The value of the benefit payable to your survivors also will vary according to the performance of the investments, although it could not fall below the amount of coverage you initially buy.
- Variable universal life insurance, a combination that offers the flexible premium feature of universal life insurance and the fund-switching options of variable life insurance.

All of these types of insurance—as well as the others on the market—have pros and cons that you will have to assess. During this period you may find it advantageous to convert a policy you already own from one type to another. This usually can be done for a fee.

Also remember that as time passes the needs of your survivors will change. As you update your financial plan from time to time, reassess life insurance's role in it; it may be that you should have more, less or a different type several years from now.

A final consideration in purchasing private life insurance is to make sure that the company you are dealing with is financially sound. Several companies have failed in past years, mainly because of poor investments by the company. Such a failure can render much of your planning worthless.

Insurance companies are not federally insured. The industry self-insures through guarantee funds, which exist in all states except New Jersey, Louisiana, and the District of Columbia.

If you find that you own policies that are issued by a financially unsound company, leaving that company can prove to be expensive. Most permanent policies and annuities carry surrender charges in the early years of the contract.

When making the decision to switch, you should consult with your financial adviser to determine what costs and tax consequences are involved in making such a move.

Federal Employees Health Benefits Insurance (FEHB)

Overview

The FEHB is a voluntary program that is jointly paid for by the participants and the government. If you are enrolled in a "Self and Family Option," it can provide your family with group health insurance protection even after you die. This is an extremely important benefit. Think long and hard before giving it up.

While it may be tempting to be covered by your spouse's non-federal health insurance and save the money you would be shelling out for FEHB coverage, beware. That coverage could be significantly altered or even discontinued, something that will not happen under the FEHB program. In addition, many private-sector employers do not provide insurance coverage for retirees.

As for buying health benefits coverage on your own, many of these policies are too expensive or hemmed in by too many restrictions, such as waiting periods or prohibitions against payment for pre-existing conditions.

Employee Coverage

The vast majority of federal employees have elected to be covered by the FEHB, which gives them an annual opportunity to evaluate their family medical needs and change from one option or plan to another. Also during an open season, any employee who is not currently enrolled may join the FEHB program.

Retiree Coverage

With few exceptions, retirees have elected to continue their FEHB coverage. Just as with employees, the annual open season gives them an opportunity to evaluate their family medical needs and change from one option or plan to another.

Note: If you don't elect a survivor annuity, your spouse could lose your federal health insurance after you die. For that reason, some couples who don't feel that a survivor annuity is financially necessary still elect a minimum survivor annuity to qualify the spouse for FEHB coverage in the future. Similarly, federal workers and retirees who are covered by their spouse's private-sector health plan often select the cheapest FEHB plan just to keep their options open.

Eligibility Requirements to Continue Coverage in Retirement

If you retire on an immediate annuity and have been continuously covered by the FEHB for the five-year period before your retirement date (or if less than five years, since you first became eligible for enrollment), you can continue coverage. You need not have been enrolled in the same plan or option to be eligible to continue coverage. Any combination of plans or options for the five years preceding retirement will do.

Note: Past coverage under the military-sponsored health benefits program (CHAMPUS) may be creditable toward meeting the five-year or first opportunity requirement. See your personnel office for details.

If you retire on a deferred annuity under CSRS, your FEHB coverage will end. You may not later enroll in the FEHB when you become eligible for such an annuity. Similarly, if you drop your FEHB coverage while retired, you may never enroll again, unless you are reemployed in a position that offers you an opportunity to rejoin the FEHB program.

If you are a FERS employee who takes a deferred retirement (Minimum Retirement Age plus 10), your FEHB coverage stops when you leave government. However, you can resume coverage when you reach the age and service requirements specified for Standard Retirement.

Conversion Rights

If you are unable to meet the eligibility requirements to continue FEHB coverage in retirement, you will be given a 31-day extension of coverage, without cost. During this time you may convert to non-group coverage with the same insurer without giving evidence of your good health. Similarly, any member of your family who was covered by your enrollment may also convert to non-group coverage.

Even if you meet the eligibility requirements for continued coverage in the FEHB program, this conversion privilege may still be useful to you. Children who reach age 22 are no longer eligible for coverage under a family enrollment. If you have any children who reach that age and haven't yet gotten a job which provides them with health benefits, purchasing a conversion contract may be just the ticket. Doing this won't affect your own coverage under FEHB.

Non-group coverage under a conversion contract is available only from the FEHB plan you were enrolled in before you separated from the service. You must pay the full amount of the premium directly to the plan. There is no government contribution.

Temporary Continuation of Coverage (TCC)

If any member of your family loses FEHB coverage, there is an alternative to purchasing a conversion contract for them. They will be eligible to temporarily continue health benefits coverage under the FEHB program. (The same holds true for you if you have separated from the government for any other reason, except gross misconduct.)

TCC continues for up to 18 months after you separate from service (up to 36 months for eligible children), and you must pay the full cost (both the government and employee share), plus 2 percent for administrative expenses. When your temporary coverage ends (except for nonpayment of premiums), you will still be entitled to a 31-day extension of coverage for conversion to non-group coverage without giving evidence of good health. This conversion contract coverage is only available from the plan in which you are enrolled when the TCC coverage expires.

Note: Under TCC your health benefits coverage will be the same as it was when you were an employee. A non-

group conversion contract will rarely have the same level of benefits for an equivalent price.

Opportunities to Change Enrollment

There are a variety of situations in which you can change your enrollment in FEHB other than through an open season. For example, if you become eligible for Medicare coverage at age 65, you may convert your FEHB coverage from a higher cost plan option to a lower cost one. Because the combination of Medicare and FEHB coverage generally eliminates the difference between low option and high option coverage, it may no longer make financial sense for you to pay the cost of the higher premium.

You may file a form with OPM asking them to make that coverage change at any time beginning 30 days before becoming eligible for Medicare.

Active Employee and Employee Survivor Coverage

Survivors who may be enrolled in the FEHB include your spouse and unmarried dependent children under the age of 22, such as legally adopted children, recognized illegitimate children, stepchildren, and foster children who lived with you in a regular parent-child relationship. A child who is incapable of self support due to a physical or mental disability is covered at any age, provided that the disability occurred before age 18. If these family members are entitled to CSRS or Federal Employees' Compensation Act (FECA) survivor benefits, they are eligible to participate in the FEHB program. However, monthly premium payment requirements must be met through deductions from their survivor payments.

Note: In those rare cases where survivor benefit payments are not sufficient to cover the cost of the premium, the enrollee may pay OPM directly for coverage each month.

Just as it is possible for you to convert your FEHB insurance coverage from a higher cost plan option to a lower one when you become eligible for Medicare at age 65, so too may your surviving spouse. Accordingly, your spouse may file a change of coverage form with OPM, asking to make that change at any time beginning 30 days before becoming eligible for Medicare.

When You or Your Spouse Die

When you or your spouse dies, the following FEHB changes are permitted during the 60 day period following the death:

- A change from Self and Family to Self Only coverage.
- A change from Self Only to Self and Family.
- A change from one health benefits plan or option to another.

In addition, employees who are not enrolled in FEHB may do so at that time.

Note: Retirees who are not enrolled in the FEHB may never enroll or reenroll unless they are rehired in a position that provides coverage.

Where to Go for More Information

For more details about FEHB, request a copy of "FEHB Program Information for Federal Civilian Employees and U.S. Postal Service Employees" (SF-2809-A) from your personnel office. Retirees can get a copy of this form by calling (202) 606-0500 or by writing to the following address:

Office of Personnel Management
P.O. Box 45
Boyers, PA 16017-0045

Medicare

Overview

In addition to the FEHB benefits provided for annuitants, a 1982 law provides federal and postal employees who retired after January 1, 1983, with Medicare coverage beginning at age 65. This coverage also is provided to their spouses when they reach age 65. A mandatory contribution of 1.45 percent of salary pays for this coverage.

There are two parts to Medicare: hospital insurance and medical insurance. The hospital insurance part of Medicare—called Part A—helps pay the cost of four kinds of care:

- Inpatient hospital;
- Skilled nursing facility;
- Home health; and
- Hospice.

The medical insurance part—called Part B—helps pay the cost of:

- Doctors' services;
- Outpatient hospital services;
- Home health visits;
- Diagnostic, X-ray, laboratory, and other tests;
- Necessary ambulance service; and
- Other medical services and supplies.

About three-fourths of the cost of the medical insurance is paid from the general revenues of the federal government. Because Part B coverage is optional, if you choose to enroll you will pay a monthly premium of $43.80 a month (through 1997). This premium rises each year.

102 Your Financial Guide

Note: Congress has been discussing changes in Medicare which could result in reduced benefits and higher premiums for Part B coverage.

Relationship to the FEHB Program

Since Medicare typically provides protection against the same kinds of expenses as FEHB, if you are an employee age 65 or older who is eligible for Medicare, your FEHB plan will be the primary payer and Medicare the secondary payer. Naturally, this primary/secondary relationship only exists where there is an overlap in benefits between the two forms of coverage. Medicare also will be the secondary payer of mutually provided benefits for your covered spouse, regardless of your age, if he or she is age 65 or over and has Part A.

If you are retired when you reach age 65, Medicare will become the primary payer and your FEHB plan will be the secondary payer for you and your covered spouse, if he or she is age 65 or older. This means that all claims will be processed first by Medicare and then referred to your supplemental carrier if Medicare does not cover the full amount.

Where to Go For More Information

Medicare is handled by the Health Care Financing Administration, not by Social Security. But the people at Social Security offices will help you apply for Medicare and answer your questions about the program. Social Security maintains a toll-free number (1-800-234-5772) and answers calls between 9 a.m. and 4:30 p.m. (EST) Monday through Friday.

The Social Security Administration recommends you apply for Medicare three months before you become eligible for benefits, even if you do not plan to retire.

CHAPTER ELEVEN

THRIFT SAVINGS PLAN

The Thrift Savings Plan is a tax-advantaged retirement savings program, which could have considerable value to you and your survivors. As a federal employee, you are allowed to invest in a variety of money-making opportunities which, on your retirement, can be withdrawn, rolled over into an IRA, or used to purchase an annuity.

You can mix and match among the TSP's investment options, and build retirement savings on a tax-advantaged basis, with no taxes due on your TSP account contributions or earnings until you begin withdrawing the funds.

The TSP offers a golden opportunity to create or supplement your retirement and survivor nest egg. For most employees under the FERS retirement system, TSP investing is necessary to accumulate retirement benefits comparable to a similarly situated CSRS employee. For CSRS employees, the TSP also offers an opportunity to save for retirement. Although CSRS employees don't get any automatic government contribution or matching funds the way FERS employees do, they can invest up to 5 percent of their salaries with the same fund choices and tax deferral advantage.

The number of TSP accounts has more than doubled since 1987 and now exceeds two million. There are more than 600,000 CSRS employees regularly contributing to their TSP accounts every pay period, and many former employees have decided to leave their TSP accounts in place as a continuing source of retirement income and investment earnings.

The Need for TSP Investments

If you are not currently investing in the TSP, you could be making a serious mistake. This tax-advantaged retirement savings program similar to private sector 401(k) plans, could have considerable value to you. It allows you to choose among three investments:

- The G fund, which is based solely on U.S. government securities;
- The F fund, essentially a bond account consisting of a mix of government and high-quality corporate bonds and mortgage-backed securities; and
- The C fund, which is a stock-based account that reflects U.S. stock market performance as measured by Standard & Poor's 500 Index.

You can mix and match among these three investment options and build retirement savings without paying taxes on the contributions or earnings until you begin withdrawing the funds. You also should be on the lookout for two additional investment options the TSP will soon be introducing: an international stock fund and a small company stock fund.

Eligible FERS employees receive an automatic 1 percent government contribution without having to contribute anything. They may invest up to 10 percent of their own salaries with the government matching their contributions dollar-for-dollar up to 3 percent of basic pay per pay period, and 50 cents on the dollar on the fourth and fifth percent of basic pay. This is like receiving a 5 percent salary boost without having to pay taxes on it until after retirement.

CSRS employees don't get any automatic contribution or matching funds, but they can invest up to 5 percent of their salaries with the same choices and tax deferral.

TSP money transfers from you to your beneficiaries upon your death. For more details on how the accounts are distributed, see below.

The TSP Tax Advantage

Your contributions to the TSP reduce your taxable current income. In effect, your contributions reduce your gross salary for federal income tax purposes. For example, if you earn $30,000 and invest 5 percent of salary in the TSP ($1,500), your gross income is reduced to $28,500 for federal income tax purposes. Most state and local governments apply the same rule. To be sure about your state and local taxes, you should check with state and local government taxing authorities.

Social Security taxes, however, continue to apply. Thus, in the example above, the Social Security tax would be applied to the $30,000 base salary.

All agency contributions and earnings in your accounts are sheltered from taxes until withdrawn.

Your Financial Guide

Upon withdrawal employee accounts are subject to different tax rules depending upon how the account is withdrawn.

The taxation of TSP withdrawals is fairly simple. TSP payments are taxed as ordinary income as you receive the payments. Amounts paid to you directly from your TSP account are taxable income to you for federal income tax purposes in the year or years in which payments are made. Direct transfers by the TSP to an IRA or other eligible plan are not payments made directly to you and therefore aren't taxable until you receive payments from that IRA or plan. There are no capital gains considerations.

The rules governing tax withholding on payments from plans such as the TSP are more complex. So, it's a good idea to make your tax consultant aware of the TSP program.

Note: *If your distributions from all tax-qualified plans (including the TSP, an IRA, a private-sector plan, or the CSRS or FERS basic annuity) exceed a certain limit in one calendar year, you may be subject to a federal excise tax of 15 percent. The limit is the greater of $150,000 or a base amount of $112,500 adjusted annually for inflation. You should reference IRS Form 5329, Return for Additional Taxes Attributable to Qualified Retirement Plans (Including IRAs), Annuities, and Modified Endowment Contracts, as well as TSP-536, Important Tax Information About Payments From Your Thrift Savings Plan Account.*

TSP Account Withdrawals

Current Employees
Although employees may not withdraw money from a TSP account, they may obtain loans at any time. Depending on your account balance, you may borrow from $1,000 to a maximum of $50,000. You can have two loans outstanding at the same time. The interest rate you will pay is the most recent G Fund rate at the time your application is received. Loans are repaid through regular payroll deductions.

In effect, when you obtain a TSP loan, you are borrowing your own money from your account, and promising to restore the account, with interest, over the repayment period. The application paperwork for loans is minimal.

Note: *If you leave the government and have an outstanding loan balance, you can elect either to repay the loan in full or have the unpaid balance considered as taxable income in the year you separate.*

Retirees
When you separate from federal service, you become eligible to withdraw your TSP account. On separation, you should receive a package of withdrawal information from your agency. The package contains a booklet entitled "Withdrawing Your TSP Account Balance" and various forms. After your agency notifies the TSP that you have separated, the TSP Service Office will send you a comprehensive packet of information about your options and the forms needed to make an election.

The TSP program offers considerable flexibility in the ways you may withdraw your account. You can choose to receive a TSP life annuity (with or without a survivor annuity), a single payment, or a series of monthly payments. You can have your payment(s) begin as soon as possible or you can specify a future date. You can have the TSP transfer all or part of it in a single payment (or in some cases a series of monthly payments) to an IRA or other eligible retirement plan. You may also leave your account in the TSP when you separate, and make a withdrawal decision later on.

You are entitled to select any of the options above that you feel best meets your needs. Keep in mind, however, that the TSP will comply with any valid court order that awards a portion of your retirement benefits to a former or separated spouse, or that enforces payment of child support or alimony.

Early Withdrawal Penalty
In addition to the ordinary income tax that you must pay on TSP distributions, in certain situations you must also pay an early withdrawal penalty tax of 10 percent of the total amount you receive directly from the TSP.

If you separate or retire before the year in which you reach age 55, the penalty tax will apply to all amounts that you receive from the TSP before you become age 59 1/2. However, the penalty tax does not apply in the following situations:

- If you have the TSP purchase an annuity for you even if you are under age 55, which could happen if you took an early retirement;
- Where the payments are made because of your death, made pursuant to a court order, or if you retired on disability; or
- If you choose to receive equal payments by having the TSP compute your payments based on the IRS life expectancy tables.

Types of Annuities
You can direct the Federal Retirement Thrift Investment Board to purchase a life annuity for you with your account balance. The Board purchases annuities through the Metropolitan Life Insurance Company (MetLife), a national insurance company chosen by the Board.

A TSP annuity is a life annuity. It provides you with monthly payments for life, with or without survivor benefits. There is only one restriction. You must have at least $3,500 in your TSP account to purchase an annuity.

The amount of your annuity will depend on a number of factors, including: your TSP account balance, the type of annuity you choose, your age, the age of any survivors for whom you elect continued benefits, and applicable interest rates.

Single Life Annuity

A single life annuity either pays a fixed monthly amount for the duration of your life or a monthly benefit that may change each year of your life based on the Consumer Price Index with a 3 percent cap. The change is made each year on the anniversary date of the first annuity payment. If you choose the increasing benefit, your starting annuity will be reduced to compensate for the subsequent increases.

You also may select two other features, both of which also reduce monthly annuity payments:

The Cash Refund Feature — Guarantees payment to a beneficiary in the amount of the account balance used to purchase the annuity minus actual annuity payments made if you die before the value of the original account balance is exhausted. No further annuity payments are made even if death occurs shortly after annuity payments begin.

The 10-Year Certain Feature — You and your beneficiaries can be guaranteed that the benefit will be paid for at least 10 years regardless of the date of your death.

Comparison of TSP Annuity with Level and Increasing Payments
Assumes Inflation of 3% Per Year
Monthly Annuity Payments Beginning at Age 62

Actual Payment Amounts			Real Purchasing Power	
Level	Increasing		Level	Increasing
$500	$394	At Age 62	$500	$394
$500	$431	At Age 65	$456	$394
$500	$500	At Age 70	$394	$394
$500	$579	At Age 75	$337	$394
$500	$671	At Age 80	$289	$394

Figure 11-1

Joint Life Annuity

A joint life annuity involves the payment of an annuity while you and your spouse are alive. When either of you dies, an annuity will be paid to the survivor for his or her lifetime. A joint life annuity may provide (1) a 100 percent survivor annuity, (2) a 50 percent survivor annuity, (3) a 100 percent survivor annuity with a cash refund feature, or (4) a 50 percent survivor annuity with a cash refund feature.

An increasing payment feature is also available. This involves having the amount of the monthly payment changed each year on the anniversary date of the first annuity payment based on the Consumer Price Index. Such increases are capped at 3 percent per year. In both cases, your starting annuity will be reduced to compensate for the increased costs of these features. (See Figure 11-1 for a comparison of steady versus increasing payment levels.)

Annuity for an Insurable Interest

You also can choose an annuity that provides for a joint annuitant for someone, other than your spouse, who has an "insurable interest" in you. The terms and conditions of payment for an insurable-interest annuity are the same as those for a Joint Life Annuity.

The following persons are presumed to be eligible because they have an "insurable interest" in you:

- A blood or adoptive relative closer than first cousins
- A former spouse
- A person with whom you are living in a relationship that would constitute a common-law marriage in those jurisdictions that recognize common law marriages.

If you want to provide for someone other than your spouse or a person listed above, you must submit with your annuity request an affidavit from at least one person (other than the joint annuitant) who has personal knowledge that the person you have chosen has an insurable interest in you. The certifier must know the relationship between you and that person and must state why he or she believes that the named individual might reasonably expect to benefit financially from your continued life.

If you name a joint annuitant other than your spouse who is more than 10 years younger than you, you must choose a joint annuity with the 50 percent survivor benefit.

Note: TSP annuity payments are taxable as ordinary income in the year they are received. However, the law exempts the purchase of a TSP annuity from state and local premium taxes that sometimes apply to other annuity arrangements.

Calculating Your TSP Annuity

Your age, the amount in your TSP account, the annuity option chosen and any additional features added to the annuity are the main determinants of how much your monthly annuity will be.

Another variable is market interest rates, to which annuity payouts are tied. The TSP from time to time releases revised tables reflecting interest rate changes that affect annuities newly purchased. Those periodic

Monthly Annuity Factors Per $1,000 Account Balance

Annuity Interest Rate = 7%

Age When Annuity Begins	Single Life Annuity No Added Features
50	$6.90
51	6.97
52	7.03
53	7.11
54	7.18
55	7.27
56	7.35
57	7.45
58	7.55
59	7.66
60	7.77
61	7.90
62	8.04
63	8.18
64	8.34
65	8.51
66	8.69
67	8.88
68	9.09
69	9.32
70	9.57
71	9.83

Figure 11-2

changes don't affect previously purchased annuities, however, only those bought from that point on.

Figure 11-2 shows how much monthly annuity each $1,000 in your TSP account will buy at the current rates and at different ages when you might begin to receive the annuity (if you choose a single-life annuity with no optional features).

If you're still some time away from potentially receiving a TSP annuity, these payout factors likely will change before you retire, but they will give you a rough idea of your potential base annuity. Also remember to watch changes in interest rates (future annuity rates will go up or down with them) and to factor in the expected growth of your TSP account before your payout begins.

Consider the single life-only option your base amount. Choosing options will reduce that base. Once you have an estimate of your potential base annuity, see Figure 11-3 to estimate the reductions from various options. For example, if your base annual annuity would be $10,000, choosing the 10-year certain feature with single life would reduce the annual payout to $9,700, choosing a joint life annuity with a 100 percent benefit to your survivor would reduce it to $8900, and so on.

Detailed dollar tables are found in the TSP publication "Annuities," which is available at personnel offices.

Purchasing an Annuity

You choose your annuity option by completing form TSP-70, Withdrawal Request (see Appendix). The form must be sent to the TSP Service Office at the following address:

Amount of Initial Payments For Various Annuity Options
(As % of Single Life Annuity)
7% Interest

If You Purchase Your Annuity at Age:

	55	60	62	65	70
Single Life Annuity					
No Options	100%	100%	100%	100%	100%
with Cash Refund	96%	94%	94%	91%	87%
with 10-Year Certain	98%	98%	97%	96%	93%
with Increasing Payments	73%	75%	76%	78%	80%
with Cash Refund and Increasing Payments	68%	69%	70%	69%	68%
with 10-Year Certain and Increasing Payments	72%	74%	74%	75%	75%
Joint Life Annuity, 100% to Survivor					
with Level Payments	91%	89%	88%	87%	84%
with Level Payments and Cash Refund	90%	88%	87%	86%	83%
with Increasing Payments	64%	65%	65%	65%	66%
with Increasing Payments and Cash Refund	63%	64%	64%	64%	64%
Joint Life Annuity, 50% to Survivor					
with Level Payments	100%	100%	100%	100%	100%
with Level Payments and Cash Refund	98%	97%	97%	96%	94%
with Increasing Payments	73%	75%	76%	78%	80%
with Increasing Payments and Cash Refund	71%	72%	73%	73%	74%

Figure 11-3

Your Financial Guide

TSP Service Office
National Finance Center
P.O. Box 61500
New Orleans, LA 70161-1500

After you submit the TSP-70 to the TSP Service Office, it will send you an Annuity Request Package, which contains the following forms:

- TSP 11-A, Annuity Request;
- TSP-11B, Beneficiary Designation for a TSP Annuity;
- TSP-11C, Spouse Information and Waiver.

If you decide to defer your request for an annuity, the package will be sent a few months before the date you have selected for your annuity to begin. Make sure that you keep your address up to date so that you will receive the Annuity Request Package.

Note: You cannot change the annuity option or the joint annuitant after the annuity has been purchased.

Designation of Beneficiary

Whether you are currently employed or retired, Form TSP-3 (see Appendix) permits you to name those persons you want to receive your account balance when you die. It is extremely important for you to keep your beneficiary designation current in order to ensure that TSP officials will be able to locate them. If there are any changes in your family status, such as marriage, divorce, or the birth of a child, you may want to make changes in your beneficiary designation.

To file or change a designation of beneficiary, fill out form TSP-3 and mail it directly to the TSP Service Office. If you are planning to leave your money in your TSP account when you retire, it is a good idea to complete a TSP-3 at that time to ensure that the TSP service office has current information on your beneficiaries.

Note: A completed TSP-3 is valid only for your TSP account. It does not establish beneficiaries for other benefits, such as life insurance or annuity entitlement. It also has no effect on an annuity that was purchased with funds from your TSP account. If you request an annuity purchase, you will be sent a new designation of beneficiary form (TSP-11B). You must complete this form if you elect an annuity type (e.g., cash refund or 10-year certain) that requires it.

What Happens if You Don't Designate a Beneficiary

In the event you did not complete a form TSP-3, your account will be distributed in accordance with the standard Order of Precedence required by law. Under this system, your widow(er) would receive your benefits. If you have no spouse, or your spouse dies before you, the payment would automatically pass to your child or children, and so forth.

What Happens to Your TSP Account When You Die

If you die before having made an election to withdraw your TSP account, your designated beneficiary (or if none, your survivor(s) under the statutory Order of Precedence) will be paid the balance in your TSP account. If the recipient of this payment is your widow(er), he or she may be able to "roll over" the payment into his or her own IRA. This will defer payment of taxes until a time when he or she may be in a lower income tax bracket. Federal income taxes must then be paid on the funds as they are withdrawn, according to IRS rules.

Procedures Your Beneficiaries Must Follow in Order to Receive Your TSP Account

Eligible persons applying for your account balance, including a third party acting on behalf of a beneficiary, must complete form TSP-17, Application for Account Balance of Deceased Participant (see Appendix). This form and a certified copy of your death certificate must be submitted to the TSP service office. If the TSP service office has a valid TSP-3 on file for you, your account balance will be paid to the beneficiaries you designated on that form. If you did not file a valid TSP-3, benefits will be paid in accordance with the Order of Precedence.

What Happens to Your TSP Annuity After You Die

If you die after purchasing a TSP annuity, benefits will be paid out in accordance with your annuity selection. Your survivor(s) should get in touch with the Metropolitan Life Insurance Company at the following address:

Metropolitan Life Insurance Company
200 Park Avenue
New York, NY 10166-0188

MetLife will provide procedural instructions for reporting your death. The Thrift Savings Plan does not have to be notified.

Where to Go for More Information

TSP booklets, fact sheets, and forms generally are available to employees from their employing agency personnel offices. Separated participants may obtain TSP materials from the TSP Service Office.

Your Financial Guide

The Federal Employees News Digest Inc. has published the only comprehensive guide to understanding investment options, strategies, and withdrawal rules called *Your Thrift Savings Plan*. Instructions for ordering a copy are in the back of this book.

The TSP Service Office is the primary contact for participants who have left federal service and who have questions concerning the maintenance or withdrawal of their accounts. If you have questions concerning your account or benefits or need to report a change of address after you have separated from service, your letter must include your signature and the following information:

- Full name
- Social Security number
- Date of birth
- Daytime telephone number
- Return address

The address is:

TSP Service Office
National Finance Center
P.O. Box 61500
New Orleans, LA 70161-1500

The address for interfund transfers is:

TSP Service Office
National Finance Center
P.O. Box 60012
New Orleans LA 70161-0012

Handy TSP Telephone Numbers:

TSP Service Office (504) 255-6000
TSP Inquiry Line (504) 255-8777

Telecommunications Device for the Deaf (TDD) (504) 255-5113, Monday-Friday, 7:45 a.m.-4:15 p.m. (Central time).

Large print versions of the summary of the Thrift Savings Plan for Federal Employees are available. If you are visually impaired, ask your agency employing office to request a copy for you from your agency's TSP coordinator.

CHAPTER TWELVE

FUNERAL CONSIDERATIONS

Your loved ones will be grief-stricken and in a state of shock after your death—and it's during this time that they will have to decide how much to spend on your funeral. They will have to choose a package when they might not exercise their usual cost judgment, and may get carried away buying extras. Therefore, it's wise to arrange in advance for a funeral, cremation and/or burial, at a time when emotion is not as large a factor.

Some families would have nothing less than the top-of-the-line funeral, complete with brass-trimmed mahogany casket, dozens of mourners, the best burial plot in the most prestigious cemetery around, and so on. Others would prefer to save that expense in order to better provide for the survivors.

Either way, you will be well advised to discuss your preferences now with your loved ones and then shop around for the best deal.

Chances are pretty good that one day you'll receive a solicitation from a local funeral parlor strongly suggesting that you should purchase a "Pre-Need Plan." For about $6,000, or so, including cemetery fees, you can arrange to pay for your funeral in advance. An obvious advantage of this approach is that you freeze your funeral costs at today's prices, although some plans won't allow this.

But such plans can be surprisingly expensive, and you may find that investing your money instead may pay for your future funeral and leave some money for your survivors, as well. Make sure you can cancel your advance funeral arrangements if you change your mind, or move away.

After discussing the provisions for your funeral plan with your spouse and other mature members of the family, document your decision in the "Funeral Instructions" form you'll find in the Appendix. This will provide ready information on the funeral arrangements you have made.

Coffin and Burial Costs
The following figures are national averages. Prices and fees vary from state to state and from location to location.

The average cost of a single plot reportedly is about $500 with a range of approximately $400 to $700. These plots customarily are lined or contain a vault made out of concrete or steel. The average cost for liners is about $350 and $550 for a fully enclosed vault. A stone or other grave marker costs an average $700. For opening and closing the gravesite, the cost is roughly $400. That can double if burial is on a holiday or weekend. "Perpetual care" of the burial site usually adds about 15 percent of the cost of the grave site.

So, a "typical" expectation for total burial site-related costs would be about $2,000.

How Much Funerals Cost
A simple wooden casket and a traditional funeral can be arranged for about $1,500 in many locations; others a little more, others somewhat less. But you could easily pay $5,000 for the same package.

The Federal Trade Commission's "funeral rule" requires funeral directors to provide their clients, *if requested*, detailed pricing information. Demand it if it is not offered to you. However, you must avoid being manipulated into signing up for more than you have planned and can afford. It's unbelievably easy to jump from $2,000 to $10,000 for a funeral package. And some can go even higher.

Costs for transporting the deceased to and from the funeral home (hearse, etc.) amount to about $250. Charges for embalming, which may be required only if there is an open casket viewing, run about $300. Viewing and ceremonies run another $400. The funeral director also charges around $600 for his or her personal services. The total runs close to $3,000 if costs are kept at a moderate level.

When extras such as special coffins; funeral director-provided lead cars, limos, and special vehicles such as flower cars and motorcycle escorts; music, special flowers and ceremonies at the funeral parlor; unusual burial arrangements and special graveside decorations; exclusive cemeteries; marble headstones with statuary; or elaborately decorated mausoleums are factored into the equation, the costs can easily escalate to five figures.

Your Financial Guide

Cremation with ceremony is becoming an ever increasingly popular alternative to traditional funeral arrangements. Many people prefer cremation for its simplicity, and others find that the cost of cemetery lots has made traditional burials economically prohibitive. The average cost of this approach with a basic ceremony is approximately $2,000.

Body or Organ Donation Arrangements

As an alternative to burial or cremation, you may wish to donate your organs for transplant purposes or your entire body for medical research.

For the purpose of organ donations, which require quick action following your death, some states include a uniform donor card as part of a driver's license. The donation of your organs or tissues should be stipulated in your will.

This obviously can be a touchy subject among family members. Make sure you have a solid understanding with them before you opt for this program.

Veterans Burial Benefits

Certain burial benefits are available to deceased veterans of wartime or peacetime service (other than for training) who were honorably discharged and their survivors. Members of the Reserve and the Army and Air National Guard who die while performing or as result of performing active duty for training may also be eligible. You may apply at any VA office.

Benefits, described below, are available to assist with the burial expenses of veterans and certain dependents or survivors. Assistance for burial of dependents and survivors is limited to interment in a national cemetery.

Service-Connected Death Burial Allowance

Eligibility is established if the veteran died as a result of service-connected disability.

Nonservice-Connected Death Burial Allowance

Eligibility is established if the veteran was entitled at the time of death to pension or compensation (or but for the receipt of military pay would have been entitled to compensation). Eligibility is also established if the veteran died while hospitalized or domiciled in a VA facility or other facility at VA expense.

Plot or Interment Allowance

Eligibility for the plot or interment allowance is established if the requirements for the burial allowance are met. Eligibility is also established when the deceased veteran was discharged or retired from the service because of a disability that was incurred or aggravated in the line of duty. The amount of the payment varies.

Burial in National Cemeteries

Burial in a VA national cemetery is available to any eligible veteran, spouse, unremarried widow(er), minor children, and, under certain conditions, unmarried adult children.

Detailed information regarding eligibility and interments is contained in VA pamphlet, "Interments in National Cemeteries." You can get a copy from any VA regional office. It also will provide information and other assistance in filing burial benefit claims.

Arlington National Cemetery is under the jurisdiction of the Department of the Army, and burial is limited to specific categories of military personnel and veterans (except in the case of cremated remains to be placed in the columbarium). For information you should write to the Superintendent, Arlington National Cemetery, Arlington, VA 22211 or telephone (703) 695-3253 or 3250.

Headstone or Grave Markers

Headstones and markers are provided for the gravesites of eligible veterans buried in private or national cemeteries. An application is not required for national cemeteries. Applications—VA Form 40-1330, available at VA regional offices—should be sent to the Director, Office of Memorial Programs (403), National Cemetery System, Department of Veterans Affairs, Washington, DC 20420. VA regional offices will provide information and other assistance.

Information regarding the status of a headstone/marker application for placement in a private cemetery can be obtained by writing to the Director, Office of Memorial Programs (403) at the address above, or by calling 1-800-697-6947.

CHAPTER THIRTEEN

TAXES

Federal Estate Taxes

If you have extensive assets, you should take full advantage of your opportunities under the law to minimize future estate tax obligations. For example, you can give away $10,000 a year to anyone without tax consequences. This is an excellent way to pass on inheritances before your death and to reduce the amount of your estate to the point where it either is no longer taxable, or only minimally taxable.

You are entitled to an automatic credit of $192,800 against any federal estate taxes that may be due at the time of your death. This is sufficient to offset the tax on any estate worth $600,000 or less.

But you should take a close look at your situation if you own an expensive home or other real estate that has gained significantly in value. Other factors to be considered are the increased value of other investments such as securities, your Thrift Savings Plan Account, and the face value of life insurance policies. You may be pushing or exceeding your non-taxable limit. You might be facing federal taxes that could reduce the value of your estate by as much as half or more.

Here are some of the many financial planning considerations to keep in mind:

- What is the face amount of life insurance policies on your life and owned by you?
- Are you planning to retire at age 55 and take a well paying position, one that when combined with your pension will rapidly increase your assets during the 10 years or more that you may continue to work?
- Are your children either in college or on their own? Do you now find yourself with extensive funds to invest?
- Does your spouse also work?
- Is there a possibility that you will be inheriting a substantial amount from parents or other relatives?
- How much will your Thrift Savings Plan be worth when you retire?
- Do you have other substantial assets that you have accumulated over the years, through sound investments, a consistent and extensive savings program, etc.?

Periodically take a close look at your situation by using the following table to calculate your current liability:

How to Calculate Your Federal Estate Taxes

1. Calculate Your Gross Estate $_____

Include the total value of everything you own yourself plus 50 percent of what you and your spouse own together. Use your best estimate of fair market value in these calculations. You should include the value of any assets held in a revocable living trust. Also add the value of any life insurance (death benefits only) you own. Factor in amounts for bonds, stocks and cash accounts, automobiles, household furnishings, jewelry, antiques and other collectibles and the value of retirement-related savings plans at work.

2. Estimated Debts and Expenses $(_____)

Deduct expenses that your estate will incur, such as funeral and burial costs; debts for consumer credit, loans, mortgages, and unpaid taxes; and expenses for settling your estate, such as executor and legal fees and court costs (anywhere from 2 to 10 percent, depending on the state in which you reside). You'll find information, tables, and worksheets throughout this book that will help you determine these amounts. In estimating estate settlement costs, factor in approximately 10% of item 1.

3. Estimated Deductions $(_____)

Anything you leave your spouse is 100 percent deductible (referred to as the "marital deduction"). This also may include certain assets left to your spouse in a trust. Charitable contributions also are deductible.

4. Taxable Portions of Gifts $_____

Figure 13-1

Your Financial Guide

How to Calculate Your Federal Estate Taxes, cont'd.

Add up all the taxable portions of gifts you have made since 1976. This means that if you gave one individual more than $10,000 in a single year ($3,000 before 1981), the excess over this amount is included in this section.

5. Taxable Estate $ _____
(Item 1, minus items 2 and 3, plus item 4)
6. Calculate Potential Federal Estate Tax Due
   (See Figure 13.2 Federal Gift & Estate Tax Table) $ _____
   Your Federal Estate Tax Due (if any) $ _____

Example: Taxable estate - $975,000.
Estate tax	$336,050
Less Unified Credit	($192,800)
Estate Tax	$143,250
Less: State Tax Credit*	($31,800)
Net Estate Tax	$111,400

*Computed by subtracting $60,000 from the taxable estate ($975,000 - $60,000 = $915,000) = credit (see Figure 13.3, State Death Tax Credit Table).

Figure 13-1

Federal Gift and Estate Tax Table Estate Tax Bracket

Tentative rate on:

From	To	Tax	Excess
$0	$10,000	$0	18%
10,001	20,000	1,800	20%
20,001	40,000	3,800	22%
40,001	60,000	8,200	24%
60,001	80,000	13,000	26%
80,001	100,000	18,200	28%
100,001	150,000	23,800	30%
150,001	250,000	38,800	32%
250,001	500,000	70,800	34%
500,001	750,000	155,800	37%
750,001	1,000,000	248,300	39%
1,000,001	1,250,000	345,000	41%
1,250,001	1,500,000	448,300	43%
1,500,001	2,000,000	555,800	45%
2,000,001	2,500,000	780,800	49%
2,500,001	3,000,000	1,025,800	53%*
3,000,001	and up	1,290,800	55%*

* Under current law, the top rate is reduced to 50 percent for decedents dying in 1993 and thereafter. Also, the benefits of the graduated rates and the unified credit are phased out, beginning with transfers above $10,000,000.

Figure 13-2

114 Your Financial Guide

State Death Tax Credit Table

Adjusted Taxable Estate*

At Least	But Less Than	Credit	+ %	Of Excess Over
$0	$40,000	$0	0.0	$0
40,000	90,000	0	0.8	40,000
90,000	140,000	400	1.6	90,000
140,000	240,000	1,200	2.4	140,000
240,000	440,000	3,600	3.2	240,000
440,000	640,000	10,000	4.0	440,000
640,000	840,000	18,000	4.8	640,000
840,000	1,040,000	27,600	5.6	840,000
1,040,000	1,540,000	38,800	6.4	1,040,000
1,540,000	2,040,000	70,800	7.2	1,540,000
2,040,000	2,540,000	106,800	8.0	2,040,000
2,540,000	3,040,000	146,800	8.8	2,540,000
3,040,000	3,540,000	190,800	9.6	3,040,000
3,540,000	4,040,000	238,800	10.4	3,540,000
4,040,000	5,040,000	290,800	11.2	4,040,000
5,040,000	6,040,000	402,800	12.0	5,040,000
6,040,000	7,040,000	522,800	12.8	6,040,000
7,040,000	8,040,000	650,800	13.6	7,040,000
8,040,000	9,040,000	786,800	14.4	8,040,000
9,040,000	10,040,000	930,800	15.2	9,040,000
10,040,000	---------	1,082,800	16.0	10,040,000

*The adjusted taxable estate is computed by subtracting $60,000 from the taxable estate.

Figure 13-3

Gift (Transfer) Tax Exemption

You are permitted by law to give $10,000 gifts to any number of people each year without having to pay a gift (actually, called a *transfer*) tax. If your spouse joins you in each such gift, the amount per recipient can be increased to $20,000. For a gift to qualify for the annual exclusion, the individual receiving the gift must have the immediate right to use it without any restrictions. If your estate is large enough to approach the taxable level, some well-planned gifts may help solve your potential tax problem.

State Death Taxes

Pickup Taxes

Consider yourself fortunate from an estate death tax standpoint if you live in Alabama, Alaska, Arizona, Arkansas, California, Colorado, the District of Columbia, Florida, Georgia, Hawaii, Idaho, Illinois, Maine, Missouri, Nevada, New Mexico, North Dakota, Oregon, Rhode Island, Texas, Utah, Vermont, Virginia, Washington, West Virginia, or Wyoming. With the exception of Nevada, these states only levy death taxes against estates that are subject to federal tax. These states collect a part of what the federal government would normally receive; therefore, your overall estate tax obligation, if any, is not increased. This type of tax is referred to as the "pickup tax" because it equals the maximum credit for state death taxes allowed for federal estate tax purposes. Accordingly, estates under $600,000 will escape both state and federal taxes in these states.

Death Taxes Imposed by Other States

The other states also have death taxes such as inheritance taxes and estate taxes that are levied against beneficiaries. As these state laws vary significantly in terms of their exemptions, you should check with your attorney or accountant concerning the specifics that will apply in your situation. For general information concerning the inheritance and estate taxes that apply in these states, see **Special State Inheritance and Estate Tax Laws.**

Inheritance Tax
Your heirs will be liable for the payment of their inheritance taxes based on the taxable value of their respective shares of the estate. For example, if someone inherits property worth $100,000, this is the value that will be used for computing the inheritance tax.

Annuity proceeds are generally not considered to be insurance proceeds; therefore, they do not enjoy the same special exemption. Payments made to designated beneficiaries in lump-sum or on a long-term basis will be taxed.

Taxable properties are taxed on their established "Fair Market Value." In taxing your beneficiary's gross share of an estate, a state recognizes that part of this share must be used to pay debts and other estate expenses. Accordingly, certain deductions are allowed and taxes apply to the resultant net amount that you actually receive. Typical allowable deductions include: property and income taxes, medical expenses, funeral expenses, your personal debts, and the expenses required to settle the estate (attorney costs, probate court costs, etc.) States also typically allow exemptions which permit deducting amounts from the value of the property being transferred before inheritance tax rates are applied. These amounts vary depending on the relationship of the beneficiary to the deceased; for example, a wife or husband may receive a $50,000 exemption and a child would only be entitled to a $5,000 exemption. Each state's laws are different, however, and you should check with an attorney to determine a particular state's exemptions.

Estate Tax
An estate tax applies to the net value of an estate rather than the value of the shares passing to each beneficiary. The net value is the amount remaining in an estate after deductions and exemptions have been subtracted. This concept is very similar to the one used for federal estate tax purposes.

Credit Estate Tax
In addition to imposing either an inheritance or an estate tax, most states also require the payment of an additional death tax. This is the *credit estate tax*. This type of tax is designed to take advantage of the credit provided by the federal government on a estate tax return for paying state inheritance or estate taxes. The way it works is that the Internal Revenue Service allows a credit on the federal estate tax return for death taxes actually paid up to specified limits. This credit is only available for an "Adjusted Taxable Estate" which equals or exceeds $40,000. The "Adjusted Taxable Estate" is the taxable estate for federal tax purposes reduced by $60,000. (See Figure 13.3 State Death Tax Credit Table for the technique to be used in calculating the amount of credit available for state death taxes paid for property involved in settlement of an estate.)

Special State Inheritance and Estate Tax Laws
Note: Every effort was made to include the most current information on state tax laws. You should check with your state tax authority to make sure details haven't changed.

Connecticut
Connecticut taxes each class of beneficiary, not the specific share that each person receives. This tax consists of a basic tax plus a surtax of more than 30 percent.

- Spouse is not taxed.
- Parents, grandparents, grandchildren, children and other natural or adopted descendants receive a $50,000 exemption as a class before a progressive tax is levied.
- Brothers, sisters, sons-in-law, daughters-in-law, aunts, uncles, nieces, nephews and other bloodline relatives receive a $6,000 exemption as a class.
- All others receive a $1,000 exemption as a class.
- Life insurance and bequests to charity are not taxed. However, death benefits are taxed (subject to limitations).
- The state also levies an estate tax, which is the difference between the total inheritance taxes and the maximum credit allowed for state death tax by the federal estate tax laws.
- Returns are due within six months after death.

Delaware
Delaware taxes the specific share received by each beneficiary. A progressive tax is levied and varies according to the class in which the beneficiary is in.

- Spouse receives a $70,000 exemption after taking into effect the full marital deduction.
- Parents, grandparents, grandchildren, children and other natural or adopted descendants receive a $25,000 exemption per share before a progressive tax is levied.
- Brothers, sisters, nieces, nephews and first cousins once removed receive a $5,000 exemption per share before a progressive tax is levied.
- Others (including brothers-in-law and sisters-in-law) receive a $1,000 exemption per share before a progressive tax is levied.
- Life insurance and bequests to charity are not taxed (subject to limitations). The state also levies an estate tax equal to the difference between the total inherit-

ance taxes and the maximum credit allowed under the federal estate tax law.
- Returns are due within nine months after death.

Indiana
Indiana has an inheritance tax on the specific share received by each beneficiary as follows:

- Spouse is not taxed.
- Parents, children, grandchildren and all other lineal ancestors or lineal descendants are all in the same class, but receive different exemptions per share before a progressive tax is levied.
- Brothers, sisters, sons-in-law and daughters-in-law are in a separate class; they receive a $500 exemption per share before a progressive tax is levied.
- Aunts, uncles and others are in the same class: they receive a $100 exemption per share before a progressive tax is levied.
- Bequests to charity and life insurance are not taxed (subject to limitations). The state also levies an estate tax equal to the difference between the total inheritance taxes and the maximum credit allowed for state tax by the federal estate tax laws.
- Returns are due within 12 months after death.

Iowa
Iowa taxes the specific share received by each beneficiary as follows:

- Spouse is not taxed.
- Parents, children, grandchildren, and other lineal descendants receive different exemptions per share before a progressive tax is levied.
- Brothers, sisters, sons-in-law, daughters-in-law, and stepchildren are in a separate class: they do not receive an exemption and a progressive tax is levied.
- All other persons are in a separate class: they do not receive an exemption and a progressive tax is levied.
- Institutions organized in other states for charitable, educational, or religious purposes are in a separate class. They do not receive an exemption. A tax of 10% is levied.
- Firms, corporations, and societies organized for profit are in a separate class. They do not receive an exemption. A tax of 15% is levied.
- Life insurance and bequests to charity are not taxed (subject to limitations). This state also levies an estate tax equal to the difference between the total inheritance taxes and the maximum credit allowed under the federal estate tax law.

Kansas
Kansas has an inheritance tax on the specific share received by each beneficiary. The following rules apply:

- Spouse is not taxed.
- Parents, children, grandchildren, and other lineal ancestors and descendants, sons-in-law and daughters-in-law are in the same class and receive a $30,000 exemption per share before a progressive tax is levied.
- Brothers and sisters are in a separate class: they receive a $5,000 exemption before a progressive tax is applied.
- Others do not receive an exemption and a progressive tax is levied.
- No tax is due on shares of $200 or less.
- Bequests to charity and life insurance are not taxed (subject to limitations). The state also levies an estate tax equal to the difference between the total inheritance taxes and the maximum credit allowed for state tax by the federal estate tax laws.
- Returns are due within nine months after death.

Kentucky
Kentucky taxes the specific share received by each beneficiary.

- Spouse is not taxed.
- Parents, children, and grandchildren are all in the same class, but receive different exemptions per share before a progressive tax is levied. For children, the first $20,000 of each share is exempt. For parents and grandchildren, the first $5,000 is exempt.
- Brothers, sisters, sons-in-law, daughters-in-law, aunts, uncles, nieces, nephews, and great grandchildren are in the same class: they receive a $1,000 exemption per share before a progressive tax is levied.
- Others are in a separate class and receive a $500 exemption per share before a progressive tax is levied.
- Life insurance and bequests to charity are not taxed (subject to limitations). The state also levies an estate tax equal to the difference between the total inheritance taxes and the maximum credit allowed for state tax by the federal estate tax laws.
- Reports are due within 18 months after death.

Louisiana
Louisiana taxes the specific share received by each beneficiary. A progressive tax is levied and varies according to the class in which the beneficiary is in.

- Spouses, parents, children, grandchildren, and other direct ascendants and descendants are in the same class and receive a $25,000 per share exemption before a progressive tax is levied.
- Spouse is not taxed.
- Brothers, sisters, and other collateral relations are in the same class and receive a $1,000 exemption per share.

- All others are in a separate class and receive a $500 exemption per share before a progressive tax is levied.
- Bequests to charity are not taxed (subject to limitations). The state also levies an estate tax equal to the difference between the total inheritance taxes and the maximum credit allowed for state tax by the federal estate tax laws.
- If there is no administration, a report is due within nine months after death or discovery of the will. When there is an administration, the return is due within nine months after death when filing a federal estate return.

Maryland

The inheritance tax for Maryland involves:

- All jointly held property with the spouse, all real property passed to the spouse and $100,000 of other property passed to the spouse are exempt. The remainder is taxed at a flat 1%.
- Parents, grandparents, children, grandchildren, and other lineal descendants are in the same class. No exemption is allowed unless the transfer is $150 or less, in which case the entire transfer is tax-free. The tax levied is a flat 1%.
- Others are in the same class. No exemption is allowed unless the transfer is $150 or less in which case the entire transfer is tax-free. The tax levied is a flat 10%.
- Life insurance and bequests to charity are not taxed (subject to limitations). The state also levies an estate tax equal to the difference between the total inheritance taxes and the maximum credit allowed for state tax under the federal estate tax laws.

Massachusetts

Massachusetts does not have an inheritance tax but taxes estates under the following rules:

- An exemption equal to the Massachusetts net estate is allowed if the Massachusetts net estate is $200,000 or less.
- No exemption is allowed if the Massachusetts net estate exceeds $200,000. However, a credit equal to the lesser of the Massachusetts estate tax liability or $1,500 is allowed.
- A deduction is allowed for bequests to charity (subject to limitations).
- An additional estate tax for federal credit absorbs the credit allowed under the federal estate tax.
- Tax return is due within nine months after the decedent's death.

Michigan

Michigan has an inheritance tax that taxes the specific share that each beneficiary receives.

- A transfer made to a spouse who qualifies for a marital deduction under the federal estate tax is exempt. The spouse receives a $65,000 exemption taken from the top applicable bracket and a $10,000 exemption taken from the lowest bracket for other transfers. A widow(er) receives an additional $5,000 for every minor child to whom no property is transferred.
- Grandparents, parents, children, brothers, sisters, sons-in-law, daughters-in-law, and lineal descendants are all in the same class and receive a $10,000 exemption per share before a progressive tax is levied.
- All others are in a separate class and no exemption is allowed.
- There is no tax on shares with a value of $100 or less.
- Bequests to charity and life insurance are not taxed (subject to limitations). The state also levies an estate tax equal to the difference between the total inheritance taxes and the maximum credit allowed under the federal estate tax law.

Minnesota

Minnesota levies an estate tax equal to the proportion of the maximum credit allowed under the federal estate tax law for state death taxes as the Minnesota gross estate bears to the value of the federal gross estate.

- For a resident decedent, the tax is the maximum credit allowed under the federal estate tax law for state death taxes reduced by state death taxes paid to other states if this results in a larger amount of tax.
- The estate tax cannot exceed the maximum credit allowed under the federal estate tax law.

Mississippi

Mississippi does not have an inheritance tax, but taxes estates generally following the federal law.

- Property valued at $600,000 or less is exempt.
- Bequests to charity are exempt (subject to limitations).
- The estate tax is levied at a progressive rate, but shall not be less than the federal estate tax credit.
- An advanced return is due within 60 days after death or qualification of executor and a detailed return is due within nine months after death.

Montana

Montana has an inheritance tax as follows:

- Spouse, children, grandchildren, and other lineal descendants are not taxed.

- Parents and other lineal ancestors are in a separate class and receive a $7,000 exemption per share before a progressive tax is levied.
- Brothers, sisters, their descendants, sons-in-law, and daughters-in-law are in a separate class and receive a $1,000 exemption per share before a progressive tax is levied.
- Uncles, aunts, and first cousins are in a separate class and receive no exemption before a progressive tax is levied.
- All others are in a separate class and receive no exemption before a progressive tax is levied.
- Bequests to charity are not taxed (subject to limitations).
- Transfers of property are exempt if the property was owned by a resident of the United States killed while serving in a combat zone in the line of duty or dying as a result of injuries suffered while serving in a combat zone in the line of duty.

The state also levies an estate tax equal to the difference between the total inheritance taxes and the maximum credit allowed under the federal estate tax laws.

Nebraska

Nebraska taxes the specific share received by each beneficiary as follows:

- Spouse is exempt.
- Parents, grandparents, brothers, sisters, sons, daughters, children, lineal descendants, and the surviving spouse of any such person are all in the same class and receive a $10,000 exemption per share before a progressive tax is levied.
- Uncles, aunts, nieces, nephews, other lineal descendants of the same, or the spouse or surviving spouse of any such person are in a separate class and receive a $2,000 exemption per share before a progressive tax is levied.
- All others are in a separate class and receive a $500 exemption per share before a progressive tax is levied.
- Bequests to charity and life insurance are not taxed (subject to limitations). The state also levies an estate tax equal to the difference between the total inheritance taxes and the maximum credit allowed under the federal estate tax law.
- Return is due within 12 months of death.

Nevada

Nevada does not have an inheritance tax but taxes the estates of resident descendants in an amount equal to the credit allowable under the federal estate tax laws.

- Estates of nonresident decedents are taxed in an amount equal to the credit allowable against the federal estate tax on real and tangible property located in Nevada.
- Returns are due on or before the date the federal estate tax return is required to be filed.

New Hampshire

New Hampshire levies a very limited inheritance tax and uses an estate tax to absorb the difference between the state inheritance tax and the credit allowable against the federal estate tax.

- Spouses, lineal ascendants, lineal descendants, and their spouses are exempt from tax.
- All other beneficiaries receive no exemption and are taxed at a flat 15%.
- Bequests to charities are exempt (subject to limitations).
- Reports are due within six months after death.

New Jersey

New Jersey has an inheritance tax with the following rules:

- Spouse, parents, grandparents, children, grandchildren, and other lineal descendants are not taxed.
- Brothers, sisters, sons-in-law, and daughters-in law are in the same class and receive a $25,000 exemption per share before progressive tax is applied.
- All others are in the same class and receive no exemption.
- No tax is due on shares of less than $500.
- Bequests to charity and life insurance are not taxed (subject to limitations). The state also levies an estate tax equal to the difference between the total inheritance taxes and the maximum credit allowed under the federal estate tax law.
- Returns are due within eight months after death.

New York

New York does not have an inheritance tax, but taxes estates generally following the federal law.

- Bequests to charity are exempt (subject to limitations).
- An additional estate tax is assessed on estates of resident decedents to absorb the difference between the state estate tax and the maximum credit allowed by the federal estate tax law.
- Returns are due within nine months after death. Interest accrues if the tax is not paid within six months of death.

North Carolina

North Carolina taxes are the specific share that each beneficiary receives.

Your Financial Guide

- Spouse is not taxed.
- Parents, children, lineal ancestors, lineal descendants, sons-in-law, and daughters-in-law are in the same class. This class receives a $26,150 credit, which is prorated first for children, then, if any credit remains, among the remaining beneficiaries.
- Brothers, sisters, their descendants, aunts, and uncles are in the same class. No credit is allowed.
- All others are in a separate class. No credit is allowed.
- Bequests to charity are not taxed (subject to limitations).
- Life insurance is normally taxed. The state also levies an estate tax equal to the difference between the total inheritance taxes and the maximum credit allowed under the federal estate tax law.
- Returns are due within nine months of the qualification of the executor or administrator.

Ohio

Ohio applies a progressive estate tax on the adjusted Ohio taxable estate. To determine the adjusted taxable estate, subtract the following items from the federal adjusted gross estate:

- Marital deduction equal to the greater of 50% of the federal adjusted gross estate or $500,000, but not to exceed the modified Federal Marital Deduction.
- All life insurance except that which is payable to the estate.
- Charitable deduction.
- A credit equal to the lesser of $500 or the amount of tax that is applied to the resultant tax.
- An additional estate tax equal to the credit available under federal estate tax law, less death taxes paid in Ohio and other states.

Oklahoma

Although referred to as an estate tax, the state tax is treated like an inheritance tax. The exception is that the tax is levied on classes of beneficiaries rather than the share received by each beneficiary. These general provisions apply:

- Spouse is exempt.
- Parents, children, grandchildren, and other lineal descendants are in the same class and receive a $175,000 exemption.
- All others are in a separate class. No exemption is allowed.
- Bequests to charity are not taxed (subject to limitations).
- Life insurance is taxed. The state levies an additional estate tax equal to the difference between the total inheritance taxes and the maximum credit allowed under the federal estate tax law.
- Returns are due within 15 months after death.

Pennsylvania

Pennsylvania has an inheritance tax as follows:

- Spouse, parents, grandparents, children and other lineal descendants, sons-in-law, and daughters-in-law are in the same class. This class receives what is called a family exemption of $2,000. The remainder of the proceeds is taxed at a flat 6%.
- All others are in a separate class. There is no exemption. The tax is a flat 15%.
- Life insurance and bequests to charity are not taxed (subject to limitations). The state also levies an estate tax equal to the difference between the total inheritance taxes and the maximum credit allowed for state tax by the federal estate tax laws.
- Returns are due within nine months after death.

South Carolina

An estate tax is assessed on resident estates in an amount equal to the credit allowable under the federal estate tax laws in effect on December 31, 1989.

- The estate tax is reduced by the lesser of: 1) Death taxes collected on the state by another state; or 2) an amount equal to the federal credit multiplied by the percentage of the gross estate over which another state has jurisdiction.
- Nonresidents are taxed on an amount equal to the federal credit multiplied by the percentage of the gross estate over which South Carolina has jurisdiction.

South Dakota

South Dakota taxes the specific share received by each beneficiary. A progressive tax is levied and varies according to the class in which the beneficiary is in.

- Spouse is not taxed.
- Children and other lineal descendants are in a separate class and receive a $30,000 exemption.
- Lineal ancestors are in a separate class and receive a $3,000 exemption.
- Brothers, sisters and their descendants, sons-in-law, and daughters-in-law are in a separate class and receive a $500 exemption.
- Aunts, uncles, and their descendants are in a separate class and receive a $200 exemption.
- All others are in a separate class and receive a $100 exemption.
- Bequests to charity are not taxed (subject to limitations).

- Returns are due within nine months after the appointment of a legal representative.

Tennessee

Tennessee has an inheritance tax that is levied on all beneficiaries as a class, rather than on the share received by each beneficiary.

- Spouse receives a marital deduction for one-half the value of the taxable transfer.
- Beneficiaries receive a $600 exemption as a class.
- Bequests to charity are not taxed (subject to limitations).
- Life insurance is taxed.
- Tennessee also imposes an estate tax equal to the difference between the total inheritance taxes and the maximum credit allowed under the federal estate tax law.

Texas

An inheritance tax equal to the maximum credit allowed by the federal estate tax law is imposed on the transfer at death of property of every resident.

- Tax on nonresident estates is assessed on the proportionate share of the net estate that the value of the Texas property bears to the nonresident decedents gross estate value.
- Return is due within nine months after death.

Your Financial Guide

CHAPTER FOURTEEN

RESOURCES & OTHER INFORMATION

Retiree organizations are one of the true bargains available. Their annual membership fees tend to be very low in order to attract the largest number of members possible, and they offer a variety of valuable services in return.

There are many advantages to supporting and participating in the activities of retiree and other associations. Beyond their congressional lobbying efforts to maintain and improve the level of benefits provided to retired workers, they offer social opportunities, discounts on a wide variety of products and services, and personal attention in helping to resolve problems in obtaining benefits.

NARFE

The National Association of Retired Federal Employees has more than 500,000 civilian employees, retirees, spouses, and survivors on its growing membership list. Its primary role is to work with allied organizations in lobbying Congress to preserve or improve retirement benefits—particularly those affecting you. NARFE has increased in power and influence since its inception in 1921.

NARFE helped a coalition of more than 30 organizations to obtain the congressional repeal of the 1988 Medicare catastrophic care surtax. It has successfully beat back attempts to raise the federal employee retirement age and to cancel or reduce retiree cost-of-living adjustments.

Membership is open to civilians eligible for an annuity from the postal service, the federal government, or the District of Columbia. Membership may be extended to retirees, employees with five or more years of vested service, and spouses and survivors of members.

NARFE says its membership benefits include: a subscription to the monthly magazine *Retirement Life*, insurance programs, VISA and MasterCard programs, and travel discounts. Members may obtain assistance in solving benefits-related problems by providing full details in a letter to: Retirement Benefits Department, NARFE, 1533 New Hampshire Avenue, N.W., Washington, DC 20036.

For membership information, write to: NARFE, 1533 New Hampshire Avenue, NW, Washington, DC 20036-1279; or call (202) 234-0832, FAX: (202) 797-9698.

AARP

If you are age 50 or older, you also may want to consider joining the American Association of Retired Persons. Associate membership is available to individuals who are under age 50. Further information may be obtained by contacting AARP Membership Services, 1909 K Street, N.W., Washington, DC 20049.

AARP membership benefits include:

- Publications — *Modern Maturity Magazine*, *AARP Bulletin*, better-living guides and self-help books
- Special local programs — Tax assistance, driver education, etc.
- Insurance programs
- Pharmacy service
- Motoring plan
- Travel services
- Federal credit union and VISA card
- Discounts — Hotels, auto rentals, air travel

Other Special Groups

There are a number of organizations that also provide membership benefits primarily to federal employees and retirees. They generally are fraternal, benevolent, or social nonprofit organizations that offer products and services to government workers. You should write or call them to request printed materials that describe their services, then carefully evaluate the merit of joining their organizations and participating in the programs they offer.

American Association of Government Employees (AAGE) — 15600 Boulder Creek, San Antonio, TX 78247, Mailing: AAGE, P.O. Box 33237, San Antonio, TX 78265. Offers special membership benefits to government workers on various products and services. Phone (512) 496-3375.

American League of Federal Employees — 1331 P Street, NW, Suite 105, Washington, D.C. 20005. Offers

Your Financial Guide

special rates to government employees on various products and services. Phone (202) 319-8075.

Civil Service Employees Advisory Association — 909 Marina Village Parkway, Suite 150, Alameda, CA 94501. Phone (510) 523-2454, (800) 888-8522 (Outside CA) and (800) 640-1714 (inside CA).

Civil Service Employee Association — 3334 S. Sherman St., Suite 101, Englewood CO 80110. Offers special rates to government employees on various products and services. Phone (303) 762-1443.

Federal Employee Associations/Government Employee Association — 1747 Citadel Plaza, San Antonio, TX 78209. Offers special rates to government workers on various products and services. Phone (512) 821-5121.

League of Federal Recreation Associations, Inc. — P.O. Box 70509, Washington, D.C. 20024. A group promoting the welfare and morale of government employees in the Washington Metropolitan area. LFRA says it is often able to secure benefits not readily available to a single association. Phone (202) 479-0089.

National Association of Federal Employees — 3421 M Street, NW, Suite 343, Washington, D.C. 20007. Phone (405) 842-0028.

U.S. Government Employees Association — 19785 West Twelve Mile Rd., Suite 135, Southfield, MI 48076-9938. Offers benefits to federal workers and their families. Phone (313) 358-3530.

Handy Telephone Numbers

Here are some telephone numbers that can help you find out more about your benefits and rights as federal employees and retirees, and help you solve problems relating to them. Virtually all these numbers belong to the Office of Personnel Management in Washington D.C. (The area code for each number is 202.):

Allotments and Assignments of Pay 606-2858
Annuity: (See Retirement)
Appeals:
    Disability Retirement Appeals 606-0288
    Retirement (Other than disability) 606-0777
Central Personnel Data File 606-2868
Court Actions ....
606-1700
Disability Retirement, Appeals 606-0288
Federal Employees Group Life Insurance
    (See Insurance, Life)
Federal Employees Health Benefits Program (See Insurance, Health)
Federal Personnel Manual
    (See Publications and Issuances)

Forms:
    Insurance (Life and Health) 606-0623
    Retirement 606-0623
Garnishment (legal questions) 606-1980
Incentive Awards Program 606-2828
Insurance, Health:
    Disputed Claims (Retirees and Employees) ... 606-0730
    Enrollment Reviews:
        Employees 606-0730
        General Inquiries 606-0500
        Retirees 606-0500
    Policy 606-0191
Insurance, Life:
    Policy 606-0191
    Retired Employees 606-0500
    Survivors 606-0500
Insurance, Program Office 606-0745
Life Insurance (See Insurance, Life)
Litigation (See Court Actions)
Official Personnel Folder Policy 606-1976
Pay:
    Administrative Law Judges 606-0810
    Advances in Pay 606-2858
    Back Pay 606-2858
    Cost-of-Living Allowance 606-2848
    Critical Pay 404-1610
    Federal Wage System 606-2848
    General Schedule Pay Administration 606-2858
    General Schedule Rates and Schedules 606-2838
    Grade and Pay Retention 606-2858
    Hazard Pay 606-2848
    Health Care Occupations 606-2838
    Interim Geographic Adjustments 606-2858
    Law Enforcement Occupation 606-3710
    Locality Pay (FEPCA-GS) 606-2838
    Overtime Pay 606-2858
    Physicians Comparability Allowance 606-1413
    Premium Pay 606-2858
    Recruitment and Relocation Bonuses 606-2858
    Retention Allowances 606-2858
    Salary Offset 606-2858
    Senior Executive Service 606-1610
    Senior-Level Positions 606-1610
    Severance Pay 606-2858
    Special Rates 606-1413
    Supervisory Differentials 606-2858
    Within-grade Increases 606-2858
Personnel Data File:
    Agency Submissions 606-2360
    Personnel records of former federal
        employees 606-1976
    Statistics 606-2546
Personnel Record keeping 606-1976
Public Affairs (General Information) 606-1800
Publications and Issuances:
    Administrative Manual:
        Availability, distribution 606-0536

Retirement:
    Appeals:
        Disability Retirement Appeals 606-0288
        Retirement (Other than disability) 606-0775
        Bankruptcy/Garnishments
        (Civil Service Annuitants Only) 606-0210
    Forms: ....
        Insurance (Life and Health) 606-0623
        Retirement 606-0623
    Insurance, Health
        Accounting 606-0666
        Contracts 606-0770
        Disputed Claims
        (Retirees and Employees) 606-0730
        Enrollment Reviews:
            General Inquiries 606-0500
            Employees 606-0730
            Retirees/Survivors 606-0500
        Policy (Agency Inquiries) 606-0191
        Statistical Data 606-0650
    Insurance, Life:
        Accounting 606-0666
        Contracts 606-0770
        Policy (Agency Inquiries) 606-0191
        Retired Employees 606-0500
        Retirees/Survivors 606-0500
        Statistical Data 606-0650
    Insurance Program Office 606-0770
    Medical Examination:
        In Connection with Disability Retirement
        Cases 606-0290
        Policy 606-0500
    Publications and Issuances:
        Government Claims (Annuitants Only) 606-0214
        IRS levies 606-0214
        Reconsideration of Debt Owed to the Retirement ...
        System 606-0563
        Special Publications and Issuances (Subject-Matter
        Content or Distribution):
        Retirement and Insurance 606-0623
        Tax Withholding Inquiries
        (Annuitants Only) 606-0214
        Waste, Fraud and Abuse Against the Civil Service
        Retirement System 606-0232
    Retirement Information Office:
        Self Service, general information tape recording
        for the following categories: 606-0400
        Change of address
        Death/Survivor Benefits
        Designation of Beneficiary
        Direct Deposit
        Eligibility Surveys
            (Students/Disability Earnings/Martial Status)
        First Retirement Check (When to expect)
        Health Benefits
        Life Insurance
        Non-Receipt of Annuity Check
        Refund of Retirement Contribution

Income Tax Withholding
To Speak Directly to a Retirement Specialist 606-0500
To Report Death of an Annuitant or
Survivor 606-0133
TDD (Hearing-Impaired Retirees) 606-0551

Agency Obligations Concerning Death of Employee on Duty or Official Travel

It's helpful for your loved ones to know what the government should do if you die on duty or during official travel.

The death of an employee under any circumstances requires the immediate attention of agency management. Each personnel office or human resource management (HRM) division maintains standard procedures and essential forms required for notifications and record-keeping in the event of an employee's death. Following is an example of a typical agency policy:

Usual and Customary Actions by Officials at Location Where Death Occurred

- Notify local authorities such as the coroner in accordance with state and local laws concerning the death of an individual.

- Based on directions received from local authorities, assist in the transferring of the body to a morgue or mortuary.

- Make the notifications of death as prescribed in the applicable agency order. Provide the date, time, a brief explanation of the circumstances and cause of death, and details concerning where the body has been taken.

- Upon receiving instructions from the next of kin, provide assistance in making arrangement for the embalming and shipment of the body to the specified location.

- Notify the deceased employee's personnel office concerning the date, time, and location for the arrival of the body. Also provide the name of the next of kin.

- Arrange for a minimum of five certified death certificates; the cost is to be paid by the next of kin, because this is not generally an authorized government expense.

- Arrange to pick up the deceased employee's personal effects, and any government papers, including reports, credentials, and other items such as equipment, and have them transported along with the remains.

- Exercise care in the release of information to the press concerning the circumstances that led to the death of the employee. Normally, no information is to be released until after the next of kin has been notified.

Your Financial Guide

- If the death was due to a job-related injury or disease, the procedures specified in the injury compensation order are to be followed.

Actions by Personnel Office or Employee's Supervisor

- Notify the next of kin concerning the death of the employee and the location of the body (name and location of mortician or morgue).
- Assist in arranging for the release of the body from the coroner's or mortician's establishment.
- Advise next of kin regarding the regulations that apply to the return shipment of the body.
- Notify an official at the temporary duty station of any instructions from the next of kin and actions that have been taken.
- If the employee was charged with a government vehicle or equipment, arrange for the pick-up and return of the vehicle or equipment to the home station.
- Furnish claim forms to the survivors, provide assistance in their completion, and rush their processing upon receipt of these completed claims.
- If death resulted from a job-connected injury or disease, promptly initiate and forward required forms in accordance with the provisions of the Injury Compensation order.

APPENDIX

A-1 Notification Letters Regarding Death of Annuitant p.128
A-2 Personal and Family History 130
A-3 Funeral and Burial Instructions 136
A-4 Financial and Personal Documents 137
A-5 Forms 147

Sample Notification Letter to OPM Regarding Death of Annuitant

Note: This information can also be provided to OPM by phone: (202) 606-0500, (202) 606-0551-TDD; or by FAX (412) 794-1236

Your Name
Address
Telephone number
Date

Office of Personnel Management
Retirement Operations Center
PO Box 45
Boyers, PA 16017

Dear Sir or Madam:

I am very sorry to advise you that my spouse, _____
has died. A certified copy of the death certificate is enclosed for your information.

Please send me the form needed to apply for survivor benefits. To help you research this case, I am providing the following information:

Date of Birth: _____

(His/Her) CSA Number: _____

(His/Her) Social Security Number: _____

I have forwarded the last annuity check he received to the U.S. Treasury Department.

Meanwhile, if you have any questions concerning my claim, please call me at the telephone number shown in the heading. Many thanks for your help.

Sincerely,

Enclosure

Figure A-1

Sample Notification Letter to OPM Regarding Death of Annuitant's Spouse

Note: This information can also be provided to OPM by phone: (202) 606-0500, (202) 606-0551-TDD; or by FAX (412) 794-1236

Your Name
Address
Telephone number
Date

Office of Personnel Management
Retirement Operations Center
PO Box 45
Boyers, PA 16017

Dear Sir or Madam:

I am sorry to advise you that my wife/husband has died. A certified copy of the death certificate is enclosed for your information.

As a federal retiree, here is the information for locating my case file:

(Your) CSA Number: _____

Date of Birth: _____

(His/Her) Social Security Number: _____

Since I elected a reduced annuity at the time of my retirement to provide a survivor's benefit for my wife/husband, a benefit that now no longer will be needed, please restore my annuity to the full unreduced life rate.

As I do not have any other dependents who are covered by my FEHB health insurance, please change my coverage to "SELF ONLY."

Many thanks for your prompt assistance in making these changes and providing the requested forms.

Sincerely,

Enclosure

Figure A-1

Personal and Family History

Personal Data

Full Name: _____

Social Security Number: _____

Also Known As (Name): _____

Former Legal Name: _____

Date Changed: _____

Court Authorizing Change: _____

Date of Birth: _____

Location of Birth: _____

Naturalization Certificate Number: _____

Court Granting Citizenship: _____

Date U.S. Citizenship Granted: _____

Date of Marriage: _____

Location of Marriage: _____

Location(s) of these documents: _____

_____

_____

_____

_____

Veteran Status - Active Military Service

Enlisted Service: _____

Branch of Service: _____

Serial Number: _____

Date of Entry: _____

Highest Grade: _____

Date of Discharge: _____

Figure A-2

Commissioned Service: _____

Branch of Service: _____

Serial Number: _____

Date of Entry: _____

Highest Grade: _____

Date of Discharge: _____

Location of Military Records (DD-214): _____

_____

_____

_____

_____

Family History and Contact Information - Parents

Father's Name: _____

Date of Birth: _____

Location of Birth: _____

_____

Current Address: _____

_____

Telephone Number: (_____)

Mother's Name: _____

Mother's Maiden Name _____

Mother's Remarried Current Last Name: _____

Date of Birth: _____

Location of Birth: _____

_____

Current Address: _____

_____

Telephone Number: (_____)

Figure A-2

Your Financial Guide

Family History and Contact Information - Siblings

Sibling's Name: _____

Date of Birth: _____

Current Address: _____

_____

Telephone Number: (_____)

Sibling's Name: _____

Date of Birth: _____

Current Address: _____

_____

Telephone Number:(_____)

Sibling's Name: _____

Date of Birth: _____

Current Address: _____

_____

Telephone Number: (_____)

Sibling's Name: _____

Date of Birth: _____

Current Address: _____

_____

Telephone Number: (_____)

Family History and Contact Information - Spouse

Current Name: _____

Maiden Name: _____

Social Security Number: _____

Date of Marriage: _____

Location of Marriage: _____

_____

Figure A-2

Special Agreements Concerning Pension Rights: _____

_____

_____

_____

_____

_____

Family History and Contact Information - Children

Child's Name: _____

Date of Birth: _____

Location of Birth: _____

_____

Current Address: _____

Telephone Number:(_____)

Child's Name: _____

Date of Birth: _____

Location of Birth: _____

_____

Current Address: _____

Telephone Number:(_____)

Child's Name: _____

Date of Birth: _____

Location of Birth: _____

_____

Current Address: _____

Telephone Number: (_____)

Figure A-2

Your Financial Guide

Family History and Contact Information - Former Spouse

Current Name: _____

Social Security Number: _____

Date of Marriage: _____

Location of Marriage: _____

_____

Date of Divorce: _____

Court Granting Divorce: _____

_____

Where are divorce papers (decree) located? _____

_____

Special Agreements Concerning Pension Rights: _____

_____

_____

_____

_____

Educational and Other Accomplishments

High School Name, Town, and State: _____

_____

Date of Graduation: _____

College Name, Town, and State: _____

_____

Date of Graduation: _____ Degree: _____

Special Honors/Activities: _____

_____

College Name, Town, and State _____

_____

Figure A-2

Date of Graduation: _____ Degree: _____

Special Honors/Activities: _____

_____

Other Lifetime Achievements/Honors/Awards: _____

_____

_____

_____

_____

_____

Past Addresses and Phone Numbers

From: _____ To: _____ Phone: (_____)

Address: _____

_____

From: _____ To: _____ Phone: (_____)

Address: _____

_____

From: _____ To: _____ Phone: (_____)

Address: _____

_____

From: _____ To: _____ Phone: (_____)

Address: _____

_____

From: _____ To: _____ Phone: (_____)

Address: _____

_____

Figure A-2

Funeral and Burial Instructions

Funeral Home Name & Address: _____

Funeral Director's Name: _____ Phone: (_____)

I have prepaid $_____ for arrangements specified in a receipted document located in:
_____

No arrangements have been planned with the Funeral Director, but my wishes are as follows:

____ Burial   ____ Cremation (Ashes are to be scattered) by _____ at _____

If Burial, I do ___ do not ___ want an open casket.

If Burial, I do ____ do not ___ want a chapel visitation period at the mortuary. If my decision is affirmative, it is based primarily on giving members of my fraternal order an opportunity to conduct their ceremony. Please have

the Funeral Director contact _____ Phone: (_____)
to make these fraternal arrangements. I believe that they have a fund that helps to pay for funeral expenses.

In either case, Burial or Cremation, I do ___ do not ___ want a memorial service conducted at our religious

institution. If my decision is affirmative, please have _____ officiate.
I would like the following readings and musical selections at the memorial ceremony:
_____

If Burial, I want my remains to be interred at the _____ Cemetery.

I have purchased a site at Section _____, Block _____, and Plot _____

The Deed is located in: _____

____ Please purchase a site at this cemetery. Pallbearers should include the following individuals:
_____

___ In view of my status as a veteran, I want to be buried in the _____
National Cemetary with full military honors. My grave should be marked with the traditional military headstone.
In lieu of flowers, I would appreciate donations being made in my memory to my favorite charity:

Name of Charity _____

Address: _____

Special Instructions: _____
_____

Signed _____ Date: _____

Witnessed _____ Date: _____

Figure A-3

Financial and Personal Documents

Wills and Trusts

My most recent will is dated _____

I subsequently added a codicil to this will relating to

_____

It is dated _____

The attorney who assisted me in preparing this will is:

Name _____

Phone (_____)

Address: _____

A copy of the will has been retained by the attorney.

A copy for you is located in: _____

Safety deposit box location: _____

TRUSTS: Trust documents have been prepared for (Names of Recipients)

_____

_____

_____

Copies are located in _____

I have the following policies located in _____
for which you are the beneficiary:

Policy Number: _____

Non-Government Life Insurance Policies

Name & Address of Insurance Company:

_____

_____

Name of Agent: _____ Phone: (_____)

Figure A-4

Your Financial Guide 137

Face Amount of Policy: $ _____

Outstanding Loans: $ (_____)

Estimated Cash Value: $ _____

Policy Number: _____

Name & Address of Insurance Company: _____

_____

Name of Agent: _____ Phone: (_____)

Face Amount of Policy: $ _____

Outstanding Loans: $ (_____)

Estimated Cash Value $ _____

_____

_____

Information on Homeowners or Renters Insurance Policies

Address of Property: _____

City/State/Zip: _____

Insurance Company Name: _____

Address: _____

City/State/Zip: _____

Policy Number: _____

Personal Liability Coverage: $ _____

Dwelling Coverage Amount: $ _____

Personal Property Coverage Amount: $ _____

Other Coverage: $ _____

Other Coverage: $ _____

Agent: _____

Address: _____

City/State/Zip: _____

Figure A-4

Telephone: _____

Policy Premium: $ _____

Month Payable: _____

Claim Notification Telephone Number: _____

Policy Location: _____

Property Inventory & Valuations Location: _____

Other Information: _____

Information on Auto Insurance Policy (Car #1)

Vehicle Year & Make: _____

Body Type: _____ ID# _____

Insurance Company: _____

Address: _____

City/State/Zip: _____

Policy Number: _____

Phone: _____

COVERAGE:

Bodily Injury: _____ Each Person: $ _____

Each Occurrence: $ _____

Property Damage Liability -Each Occurrence: $ _____

Medical Payments - Each Person: $ _____

Comprehensive Actual Cash Value? _____ Personal Effects ___ Yes ___ No

Collision: _____ (Deductible Amount $ _____)

Uninsured Motorists, Each Person = $ _____

Each Accident = $ _____

Property Damage Liability = $ _____ (Deductible Amount $ _____)

___ 6 Months Premium Payment Due in Months of _____

___ 12 Months Premium Payment Due in Month of _____

___ Premium Payments Due Monthly   Amount of Each Premium Payment = $ _____

Figure A-4

Your Financial Guide

Information on Auto Insurance Policy (Car #2)

Vehicle Year & Make: _____

Body Type: _____ ID# _____

Insurance Company: _____

Address: _____

City/State/Zip: _____

Policy Number: _____

Phone: _____

COVERAGE: _____ Bodily Injury: _____

Each Person: $ _____

Each Occurrence: $ _____

Property Damage Liability -Each Occurrence: $ _____

Medical Payments - Each Person: $ _____

Comprehensive Actual Cash Value? _____ Personal Effects ___ Yes ___ No

Collision: _____ (Deductible Amount $ _____)

Uninsured Motorists, Each Person = $ _____

Each Accident = $ _____

Property Damage Liability = $ _____

(Deductible Amount $ _____)

___ 6 Months Premium Payment Due in Months of _____

___ 12 Months Premium Payment Due in Month of _____

___ Premium Payments Due Monthly   Amount of Each Premium Payment = $ _____

Details Concerning Owned Home

Property Location: _____

_____

Purchase Price $ _____

Date Purchased _____

Figure A-4

Your Financial Guide

Mortgage Term: _____

Mortgage Interest _____

MONTHLY PAYMENT: _____ Mortgage Principal Payment = $ _____

Mortgage Interest Payment = $ _____

TOTAL = $ _____

Prorated Taxes = $ _____

TOTAL = $ _____

Prorated Insurance = $ _____

Utility Costs = $ _____

Equity Loan Payment = $ _____

(Second Mortgage)

TOTAL = $ _____

Mortgage Service Company: _____

Address: _____

City/State/Zip: _____

Account Number: _____

Phone: _____

Current Assessed Value for Tax Purposes = $ _____

Estimated Fair Market Value = $ _____

Loans Against Owned Home - Equity Loan(s) or Second Mortgage

Property Location: _____
_____

Lending Institution: _____

Address: _____

City/State/Zip: _____

Account Number: _____ Phone: _____

Representative's Name _____

Figure A-4

Your Financial Guide

EQUITY LOANS:

Amount Borrowed	Date	Interest Rate	Monthly Payment	Purpose
$ _____	_____	____%	$ _____	_____
$ _____	_____	____%	$ _____	_____
$ _____	_____	____%	$ _____	_____
$ _____	_____	____%	$ _____	_____
$ _____	_____	____%	$ _____	_____
$ _____	_____	____%	$ _____	_____

Total Monthly Payment = $ _____

Date Monthly Payment Due = _____

Loans

Lending Institution: _____

Address: _____

City/State/Zip: _____

Account Number: _____

Representative's Name: _____ Phone: _____

Purpose of Loan: _____

Amount Borrowed $ _____ Interest% _____

Date Borrowed: _____ Total Payments Due: _____

Monthly Payment = $ _____ Date Payment Due: _____

Lending Institution: _____

Address: _____

City/State/Zip: _____

Account Number: _____

Representative's Name: _____ Phone: _____

Purpose of Loan: _____

Amount Borrowed $ _____ Interest% _____

Figure A-4

Date Borrowed: _____ Total Payments Due: _____

Monthly Payment = $ _____ Date Payment Due: _____

Lending Institution: _____

Address: _____

City/State/Zip: _____

Account Number: _____

Representative's Name: _____ Phone: _____

Purpose of Loan: _____

Amount Borrowed $ _____ Interest % _____

Date Borrowed: _____ Total Payments Due: _____

Monthly Payment = $ _____ Date Payment Due: _____

Bank Accounts

Bank/S&L/Credit Union: _____

Address: _____

City/State/Zip: _____

Account Number: _____ ____ Savings ____ Checking

Name(s) on Account: _____

Bank/S&L/Credit Union: _____

Address: _____

City/State/Zip: _____

Account Number: _____ ____ Savings ____ Checking

Name(s) on Account: _____

Bank/S&L/Credit Union: _____

Address: _____

City/State/Zip: _____

Account Number: _____ ____ Savings ____ Checking

Name(s) on Account: _____

Figure A-4

Bank/S&L/Credit Union: _____

Address: _____

City/State/Zip: _____

Account Number: _____ ___ Savings ___ Checking

Name(s) on Account: _____

Credit Cards

TYPE OF CARD: ___ VISA ___ MasterCard ___ Diners Club ___ Discover ___ Other: _____

Issued By (Bank/Company) _____

Address: _____

City/State/Zip: _____

Issued To (Name): _____

Account No.: _____ Expiration Date: _____

Telephone Number to Call if Lost: _____

TYPE OF CARD: ___ VISA ___ MasterCard ___ Diners Club ___ Discover ___ Other: _____

Issued By (Bank/Company) _____

Address: _____

City/State/Zip: _____

Issued To (Name): _____

Account No.: _____ Expiration Date: _____

Telephone Number to Call if Lost: _____

TYPE OF CARD: ___ VISA ___ MasterCard ___ Diners Club ___ Discover ___ Other: _____

Issued By (Bank/Company) _____

Address: _____

City/State/Zip: _____

Issued To (Name): _____

Account No.: _____ Expiration Date: _____

Telephone Number to Call if Lost: _____

Figure A-4

Investment Information - Stocks, Bonds, U.S. Savings Bonds, etc.

Type of Purchase	Amount Paid	Purchase Date	Number	Present Value
_____	$_____	_____	_____	$_____
_____	$_____	_____	_____	$_____
_____	$_____	_____	_____	$_____
_____	$_____	_____	_____	$_____
_____	$_____	_____	_____	$_____
_____	$_____	_____	_____	$_____
_____	$_____	_____	_____	$_____
_____	$_____	_____	_____	$_____
_____	$_____	_____	_____	$_____
_____	$_____	_____	_____	$_____
_____	$_____	_____	_____	$_____

Debts Owed to Me/Business Interests

Borrower: _____

Address: _____

City/State/Zip: _____

Phone: _____

Amount Borrowed: $ _____ Date Borrowed: _____

Amount Paid:$ _____ Interest Rate: _____

Balance Due:$ _____ Payments Due: $ _____

_____ Weekly _____ BiWeekly _____ Monthly

Borrower: _____

Address: _____

City/State/Zip: _____

Phone: _____

Amount Borrowed: $ _____ Date Borrowed: _____

Figure A-4

Your Financial Guide

Amount Paid:$ _____ Interest Rate: _____

Balance Due:$ _____ Payments Due:$ _____

____ Weekly ____ BiWeekly ____ Monthly

Borrower: _____

Address: _____

City/State/Zip: _____

Phone: _____

Amount Borrowed: $ _____ Date Borrowed: _____

Amount Paid:$ _____ Interest Rate: _____

Balance Due:$ _____ Payments Due:$ _____

____ Weekly ____ BiWeekly ____ Monthly

Contents of Safe Deposit Box

Bank: _____

Address: _____

Location of Key: _____

ITEM (Document/Jewelry/Coins)	VALUE
_____	$ _____
_____	$ _____
_____	$ _____
_____	$ _____
_____	$ _____
_____	$ _____
_____	$ _____
_____	$ _____
_____	$ _____
_____	$ _____
_____	$ _____

Figure A-4

Standard Form 2800
Revised March 1992
Previous editions are not usable

Form Approved
OMB No. 3206-0156
NSN 7540-00-634-4249
Office of Personnel Management
FPM Supplement 830-1

CSRS
Civil Service Retirement System

Application for Death Benefits

Help in Filling Out Your Application

If you need help to complete this application:

a. Contact the personnel office in the agency where the deceased was working if he or she died while still employed; otherwise

b. Contact the Office of Personnel Management
   Civil Service Retirement System
   1900 E. Street, N.W.
   Washington, D.C. 20415

You may visit the Retirement Information Office at the above address.

General Information

The Office of Personnel Management prepared this package for individuals who want to apply for survivor benefits based on the death of a Civil Service employee, former employee, or annuitant who was covered by the Civil Service Retirement System (CSRS). The package contains information, instructions, and a claim form. Each person who expects to be paid a benefit must fill out an application. (See Instructions, Section C regarding applications in behalf of minor children.)

This application is not for use by former (i.e., divorced) spouses who are applying for survivor annuity benefits (1) for themselves alone or (2) for themselves and children of the deceased. To obtain the former spouse's application form write to:

Office of Personnel Management
Civil Service Retirement System
Retirement Operations Center
Boyers, PA 16017

The survivors of employees and annuitants who were subject to the Federal Employees Retirement System (FERS) must use Standard Form 3104 to apply for death benefits.

Type of Death Benefits

The two kinds of benefits possible are "survivor annuity" and "lump sum payment." Monthly survivor annuities may be payable, upon the death of an employee or annuitant, to a spouse, former spouse, children or a person elected by the annuitant (i.e., insurable interest). Monthly survivor annuity benefits are usually payable commencing the day after the death of the employee or annuitant. Survivor annuity payments to widows, widowers, and former spouses end when the survivor annuitant remarries before reaching age 55 or dies. Survivor annuity payments for a child end when the child marries, dies, reaches age 18 (unless the child is disabled; see instructions for Section C.1.a) and is not a full-time student, or reaches age 22. Insurable interest survivor annuity benefits end when the survivor annuitant dies.

If no one is eligible for a monthly benefit or when monthly annuity payments to all eligible survivors end, a one-time lump sum benefit is payable if all the money the deceased paid into the Civil Service Retirement Fund has not been paid out. Also, a lump sum is payable upon the death of an annuitant who does not receive all the annuity payable through the date of death. Lump sums are paid in the following order:

a. Any beneficiary named by the deceased in a written designation received by the Office of Personnel Management or its predecessor, the U.S. Civil Service Commission, prior to death;

b. Widow or widower of the deceased;

c. Child or children (descendants of a deceased child may qualify);

d. Parents in equal shares or all to the surviving parent (attach a statement telling what happened to the other parent);

e. Executor or administrator of the deceased's estate;

f. If none of the above apply, payment will be made to the next of kin according to the laws of the deceased's State of residence.

Attachments

ALWAYS attach a copy of the deceased's DEATH CERTIFICATE. We may need other documents such as proof of marriage, divorce, birth, guardianship, etc., depending on your situation. These documents are discussed in the instructions for each item on the application. If you don't have the additional documents, send in your application and the death certificate without them. We will notify you if we can't proceed without additional information or evidence. If we have to request additional documentation, this will delay the processing of your claim.

ATTACH the death certificate and the other documents to the application.

Federal Employees' Group Life Insurance

The Civil Service Retirement System does not pay the life insurance claims. To apply for any Federal employees' life insurance which may be payable, use Form FE-6, Claim for Death Benefits, Federal Employees Group Life Insurance. Life insurance isn't always payable. Form FE-6 has complete instructions on how to file and where to mail the Form FE-6. You can get Form FE-6 from the Office of Personnel Management or from Federal agency personnel offices. You must send a **certified** death certificate with Form FE-6.

SF-2800

Uncashed Annuity Checks

Any uncashed checks payable to the deceased must be returned to the following address:

> Director, Regional Financial Center
> U.S. Treasury Department
> Post Office Box 8670
> Chicago, IL 60680-8670

If annuity payments were deposited directly into an account through Electronic Fund Transfers, immediately notify the financial institution of the death of the annuitant. The U.S. Treasury Department will request that the financial institution recover the direct deposits made to the annuitant's account after the date of death. If the annuity payments are still in the account, the financial institution will simply reimburse the Treasury Department in the amount requested. If the payments have been withdrawn, the financial institution and/or OPM will contact the withdrawer for reimbursement.

Information Regarding Federal Income Tax Withholding

Federal law requires that income tax be withheld, under certain circumstances, from survivor annuity and/or lump sum payments unless the payee requests in writing that we not withhold the tax. We withhold Federal income tax from the first survivor annuity payment and send the payee information about the right to change the amount of withholding or have it stopped.

Survivors of Deceased Annuitants or Former Employees

Send your completed, SIGNED application, the deceased's DEATH CERTIFICATE, and any required additional documents to the following address:

> Office of Personnel Management
> Civil Service Retirement System
> Retirement Operations Center
> Boyers, PA 16017

Survivors of Deceased Employees

Send your completed, SIGNED application, the deceased's DEATH CERTIFICATE, and any required additional documents to the personnel office of the deceased's employing agency.

Privacy Act Statement

Solicitation of this information is authorized by the Civil Service Retirement law (Chapter 83, title 5, U.S. Code). The information you furnish will be used to identify records properly associated with your application, to obtain additional information, if necessary, to determine and allow present or future benefits, and to maintain a unique identifiable claim file. The information may be shared and is subject to verification, via paper, electronic media, or through the use of computer matching programs, with national, state, local or other charitable or social security administrative agencies in order to determine benefits under their programs, to obtain information necessary for determination or continuation of benefits under this program, or to report income for tax purposes. It may also be shared and verified, as noted above, with law enforcement agencies when they are investigating a violation or potential violation of the civil or criminal law. Executive Order 9397 (November 22, 1943) authorizes use of the Social Security Number. Furnishing the Social Security Number, as well as other data, is voluntary, but failure to do so may delay or make it impossible for us to determine your eligibility to receive death benefits.

Public Burden Statement

We think this form takes an average 30 minutes per response to complete, including the time for reviewing instructions, getting the needed data, and reviewing the completed form. Send comments regarding our estimate or any other aspect of this form, including suggestions for reducing completion time, to the Office of Management and Budget, Paperwork Reduction Project, (3206-0156), Washington, D.C. 20503.

Instructions for Completing Standard Form 2800

Please Carefully Follow the Instructions Below

TYPE OR PRINT CLEARLY. If you need more space in any section, use a plain piece of paper with your name, date of birth, and Social Security Number and the deceased's name, date of birth, Civil Service Claim (CSA) Number (if applicable), and Social Security Number written at the top.

Section A - Information About the Deceased

1. Give the deceased's full name.

2. Give the deceased's date of birth.

3. Give the date of death.

4. Give the deceased's legal residence. The legal residence is the city and state where the deceased lived when he/she died.

5. Give the deceased's Social Security Number. If you don't know the number, write "unknown."

6. Give the deceased's CSA claim number if the deceased was a Civil Service annuitant. If the deceased was retired and receiving a monthly annuity check from the Civil Service Retirement System, the CSA claim number will identify the retirement file. The CSA number appears on the monthly checks from the U.S. Treasury and on all correspondence from OPM to the annuitant. If you don't know the number, write "unknown." If the deceased wasn't a Civil Service annuitant, write "not applicable."

7. Give the name of the department or agency where the deceased was employed at death, retirement, or final separation from Federal government employment. If you don't know, write "unknown."

8. Give the location of the employment shown in item 7. If you don't know, write "unknown."

9. Give the date the department or agency separated the

SF-2800

deceased from employment. If you don't know, write "unknown."

10. a. Show if the deceased applied for or was receiving payments from Office of Workers' Compensation Programs (OWCP). The Department of Labor, OWCP, makes recurring payments to workers who are injured or survivors of workers who die because of an on-the-job injury. Recurring payments for OWCP and Civil Service survivor annuity benefits usually are not payable for the same period of time.

   b. Give the deceased's OWCP claim number. It appears on the U.S. Treasury checks and correspondence from OWCP. If you don't know the number, write "unknown."

11. Give the name of the deceased's husband or wife at the time of death. If the deceased wasn't married at the time of death, write "none."

12. a. List all former spouses of the deceased, if known. If the deceased had no former marriage, write "none." If you don't know, write "unknown." If you married the deceased after he or she retired and if the deceased was married to someone else before marrying you, we may need proof that the previous marriage ended (such as a death certificate of the previous spouse or a divorce decree). If such proof is readily available, attach a copy of the proof to this application and send it to us, unless you know we already have it.

   b. Show whether the marriage ended by death or divorce/annulment. If you don't know, write "unknown."

   c. Give the date the marriage ended. If you don't know the exact date, give the approximate date followed by a question mark (?) or write "unknown."

Section B - Information About the Applicant

1. Give your full name.

2. Give your date of birth.

3. Give your Social Security Number.

4. a. Show whether you are a U.S. citizen.

   b. If you checked "No," give your citizenship.

5. Give your relationship to the deceased: for example, if the deceased was your father, write "son" or "daughter," as applicable. If you are appointed by the court to settle the estate of the deceased, enter "executor" or "administrator" and attach a copy of your court appointment.

6. Show if you are the widow or widower of the deceased. If you are, complete items 7-12. Otherwise go to Section C. (Note: If your most recent marriage to the deceased ended in divorce or annulment, you are not the deceased's widow or widower and items 7-12 do not apply to you.)

7. Show what type of official performed your marriage to the deceased. If you were married by a priest, rabbi, pastor, Justice of the Peace or other person empowered by the State to perform marriages, check "clergy/justice of the peace." If you were NOT married by someone empowered by the State to perform marriages, check "other" and explain (for example, "common law" or "tribal marriage"). Proof of marriage (such as a copy of your marriage certificate) may be necessary to complete processing of your claim. If such proof is readily available, please attach a copy to this application.

8. Give the date of your marriage to the deceased. If you married the deceased more than once, give the date of the most recent marriage.

9. Give the city and state where you were married on the date in item 8. If you were married outside the United States, give the city and country.

10. Show whether you were married to the deceased more than once.

    a. Give the date(s) of any prior marriage(s) between you and the deceased and attach a copy of your marriage certificate(s) for each prior marriage, if available.

    b. Give the date(s) of any divorce or annulment of a marriage between you and the deceased and attach a copy of the final decree of divorce or annulment.

11. Show whether you have married since the date given in Section A.3.

    a. Give the date you remarried and attach a copy of the proof of your current marriage.

12. a. Show if you have ever applied for a survivor annuity based on the Federal service of a deceased spouse other than the spouse you named in Section A of this application. If "Yes," complete items 12 b-e.

    b. Give the name of the former spouse.

    c. Give the former spouse's date of birth.

    d. Give the name of the retirement system, for example, Civil Service, Foreign Service, TVA, etc.

    e. Give the claim number assigned to you by that system.

Section C - Information About the Deceased's Dependent Children

1. a. List in order of birth all the surviving unmarried, dependent children of the deceased. List all such children you know of, no matter where they live. A dependent child is a son or daughter who is unmarried and:

    - was under age 18 at the time of the deceased's death, including any:
      - adopted child;

SF-2800

- stepchild or recognized child born out of wedlock who lived with the deceased in a regular parent-child relationship; or
- recognized child born out of wedlock if there was a judicial determination of support or if the deceased made regular and substantial contributions for the support of the child;
- is age 18 or older but became mentally and/or physically disabled before age 18 and who because of the disability is incapable of self-support. For each son or daughter attach a physician's statement describing the nature of the disability, the date it began, and the complete name and address of the physician we may contact if more information is needed;
- is between age 18 and 22 and is a full time student in school.
- DO NOT list foster children or grandchildren; they are not eligible for a monthly benefit.

b. Give each child's date of birth. If you don't know, write "unknown." If available, please attach a copy of the birth certificate of each child whose benefit should be paid to you.

c. If the unmarried dependent son or daughter is 18 or over, show if he or she is a full-time student and/or disabled.

d. Put an "X" in the proper blocks to show how each child is related to the deceased.

e. Give each child's Social Security Number. If you don't know the number, write "unknown."

2. Show whether, on the date in Section A.3, there was an unborn child of the deceased. If the child is now born, attach a copy of the birth certificate if you are applying for the child's benefits. If the child is born after you submit this application, the mother of the child, the legal guardian, or the person who is responsible for the child should send us the birth certificate and tell us the name and address of the person who should be paid.

3. Show if you have the responsibility for ALL the children in Section C.1. If "Yes," go to Section C.4. If "No," complete a-c. Usually, the person the children live with is the person who is responsible.

    a. Give the name and address of the person(s) who are responsible for the children named in Section C.1. If you don't know, write "unknown."

    b. Give the children's names.

    c. If the person(s) in 3.a is(are) court appointed, indicate by checking the "legal guardian" box. If there is no court appointment, check "other" and write in the relationship, for example, mother, father, sister, etc.

4. Show if a legal guardian (other than one already shown in Section C.3) has been appointed for any child listed in Section C.1.

    a. Give the name and the address of the legal guardian(s).
    b. Give the names of children for whom the legal guardian has responsibility.

Section D - Information About Other Heirs

We also must have information about other relatives who may be able to inherit from the deceased, even if you don't think they will get a payment from us. Be sure to make an entry in this section. If you can't give complete information, do the best you can. List only persons who were living when the deceased died and who have the following relationships to the deceased.

- Widow(er) unless named in Section B.1.
- Children of the deceased not included in Section C and the children of any deceased children.
- If there is no living widow(er) or child, list the deceased's parents.
- If there are no living relatives of the deceased as described above and no court-appointed fiduciary as described in Section E, list other blood relatives who can inherit from the deceased. In-laws (people related by marriage) are not relatives.
- If there are no other heirs as described above, enter "None."

Section E - Information About the Deceased's Estate

1. Show if a court appointed someone to be responsible for the estate of the deceased. State law determines whether the person appointed is called executor, administrator, or some other term, such as "personal representative." If someone was named as executor/administrator in the deceased's will, but hasn't been appointed by the court, check "No." If you have been appointed by a court, attach a copy of the court appointment.

2. Give the name and address of the person the court appointed.

3. Show if a court will be appointing an executor, administrator, or other official.

Section F - Active Military Service

Complete this section only if (1) you are the surviving spouse of a deceased employee (not an annuitant), (2) the deceased employee had at least 18 months of Federal civilian service, and (3) you were married to the deceased employee for at least 9 months before his or her death, you are the parent of a child born of the marriage, or the death was accidental.

SF-2800

Active military service includes active duty service in any of the following:

- Army, Navy, Marine Corps, Air Force, or Coast Guard of the United States;
- Regular Corps or Reserve Corps of the Public Health Service after June 30, 1960;
- As a commissioned officer of the National Oceanic and Atmospheric Administration (formerly Coast and Geodetic Survey and Environmental Science Services Administration) after June 30, 1961.

1. Provide the information listed below if it is available.

   a. Branch of service.

   b. Deceased's serial number.

   c. Dates deceased performed active duty service.

   d. Last grade or rank.

2. Check "No" or "Yes." If you check "No," you must attach OPM Form 1519, Surviving Spouse's Military Deposit Election, to this application. You may obtain OPM Form 1519 from the agency where the deceased was employed when he or she died.

   In order to obtain full and continuing credit for military service performed after December 31, 1956, an employee may make a deposit of 7% of basic military pay earned (plus interest, if applicable) to the employing agency. If an employee (not an annuitant) dies without making (or completing) this deposit, the surviving spouse may make the deposit with the employing agency. The deceased employee's employing office will provide information about how making (or not making) the deposit will affect the survivor annuity and how the survivor makes the deposit.

3. Show whether the deceased was receiving retired pay from any branch of the military.

   a. Check "No" or "Yes." Subject to Social Security considerations, the active military service will be used in the computation of the surviving spouse's monthly benefit, UNLESS the surviving spouse instructs OPM to exclude all the active military service.

Section G - Certification

Sign your name in ink. Please note that OPM will not accept the signature of someone who has a power of attorney for the applicant named in Section B. A court-appointed fiduciary can apply on behalf of the applicant, provided a court-certified copy of the court appointment is attached to the application for death benefits. If there is no court-appointed fiduciary and the applicant is not competent, a relative or person responsible for the applicant may sign. OPM will arrange later for the appointment of a representative payee to manage benefit payments after the applicant's incapacity is verified. Enter the current date and give your correct mailing address as you want it to appear on your check. Give a daytime telephone number so we can reach you if we need more information. If you do not complete this section, the processing of your claim may be delayed.

SF-2800

APPLICATION FOR DEATH BENEFITS
CIVIL SERVICE RETIREMENT SYSTEM

CSRS — Civil Service Retirement System

Form Approved
OMB No. 3206-0156

Section A - Information About the Deceased

1. Full name of deceased *(Last, first, middle)*	2. Date of birth *(Month, day, year)*	3. Date of death *(Month, day, year)*
4. Legal residence at time of death *(City, State)*	5. Social Security Number	6. CSA Number *(If applicable)*
7. Department or agency in which last employed, including bureau or division	8. Location of last employment *(City, State)*	9. Date of final separation *(Mo, dy, yr)*

10a. Was the deceased applying for or receiving workers' compensation from the Office of Workers' Compensation Programs (OWCP), Department of Labor? ☐ No ☐ Yes ⟶ 10b. OWCP Claim Number

11. Name of deceased's spouse at time of death

12a. Name of deceased's spouses from all former marriages	12b. How did each marriage end?	12c. Date each marriage ended *(Mo, dy, yr)*
	☐ Death ☐ Divorce/Annulment	
	☐ Death ☐ Divorce/Annulment	

Section B - Information About the Applicant

1. Full name of applicant *(Last, first, middle)*	2. Date of birth *(Month, day, year)*	3. Social Security Number

4a. Are you a citizen of the United States of America? ☐ Yes ☐ No ⟶ 4b. What country are you a citizen of? | 5. Relationship to deceased

6. Are you a widow or widower of the deceased? ☐ Yes ⟶ Complete items 7-12 below ☐ No ⟶ Go to Section C

7. Marriage performed by ☐ Clergy/Justice of the Peace ☐ Other *(Explain)*	8. Date of marriage *(Month, day, year)*	9. Place of marriage *(City, State)*

Were you married to the deceased more than once? ☐ No ☐ Yes ⟶ | 10a. Date of prior marriage | 10b. Date marriage ended

11. Have you married since the date given in A.3.? ☐ No ☐ Yes ⟶ | 11a. Date you married

12a. Have you ever applied for a survivor annuity based on the Federal service of a deceased spouse other than the one named above in A.1.? ☐ No ⟶ Go to Section C ☐ Yes ⟶ Complete items 12 b-e below

12b. Name of deceased former spouse	12c. Date of birth *(Mo, dy, yr)*	12d. Retirement system	12e. Claim number

Section C - Information About the Deceased's Dependent Children

1. Are there any unmarried dependent children as defined in the instructions? ☐ Yes ⟶ Complete Section C ☐ No ⟶ Go to Section D

a. Name(s) of Unmarried Dependent Children *(List in order of birth)*	b. Date of Birth *(Month, day, year)*	c. Age 18 or over (Student / Disabled)	d. Child's relationship to deceased (Child of marriage at death / Child of previous marriage / Adopted child / Stepchild / Child born out of wedlock)	e. Social Security Number

2. Is there a child of the deceased not yet born? ☐ Yes ☐ No

Office of Personnel Management   NSN 7540-00-634-4249   Previous editions are not usable   Standard Form 2800

SF-2800

Your Financial Guide

3. Do you (the applicant) have responsibility for all the children in C.1.?

☐ Yes → Go to C.4.   ☐ No → Complete a-c below

a. Name and Address of Person Responsible	b. Name(s) of Children	c. Custodian's Relationship to Child
		☐ Legal Guardian ☐ Other → Specify
		☐ Legal Guardian ☐ Other → Specify

4. Has a legal guardian (other than any shown in C.3) been appointed for any child listed in C.1.?

☐ Yes → Complete a-b below   ☐ No → Go to Section D

a. Name and Address of Legal Guardian	b. Name(s) of Children

Section D - Information About Other Heirs

List other relatives who can inherit from the deceased as explained in the instructions.

1. Full Name of Relative	2. Complete Address	3. Relationship to Deceased

Section E - Information About the Deceased's Estate

1. Has an executor, administrator or other official been appointed by the court to settle the estate of the deceased?

☐ No → Go to 3 below   ☐ Yes →

2. Full name and address of person appointed *(Street, city, state, ZIP Code)*

3. If an executor, administrator or other official has not been court appointed, will one be appointed?   ☐ Yes   ☐ No

Section F - Active Military Service

(Complete ONLY if deceased was a Federal employee covered under the Civil Service Retirement System at the time of death AND if you are the surviving spouse)

1. If the deceased performed active, honorable service in the Armed Forces or other uniformed service as described in the instructions, complete 1a-d below and attach a copy of the discharge certificate or other certificate of active military service (if available).

a. Branch of Service	b. Serial Number	c. Dates of Active Duty		d. Last Grade or Rank
		From *(Mo, dy, yr)*	To *(Mo, dy, yr)*	

2. If any of the above listed service was performed after 12/31/56, was a deposit to the Retirement Fund made for the service?   ☐ Yes   ☐ No → Complete and attach OPM 1519 *(See instructions)*

3. Was the deceased receiving military retired pay at the time of death?   ☐ No → Go to Section G   ☐ Yes →

3.a. Do you want the military service used to compute your Civil Service annuity?   ☐ No   ☐ Yes

Section G - Certification

I hereby certify that all statements made in this application are true to the best of my knowledge and that no evidence necessary to the settlement of this claim is withheld. I have read and understand all of the information provided in the instructions to this application.

1. Signature of applicant named in Section B. *(Sign in ink; do not print.)*	2. Mailing address	**WARNING:** Any intentionally false or willfully misleading statement or response you provide in this application is a violation of the law punishable by a fine of not more than $10,000 or imprisonment of not more than 5 years or both. (18 USC 1001)
3. Telephone number *(including area code)*		
4. Date		

SF-2800

WARNING – Do not fill out this form until you have read all instructions.

DESIGNATION OF BENEFICIARY
CIVIL SERVICE RETIREMENT SYSTEM

OMB Approved:
No. 3206-0142

A. INFORMATION CONCERNING THE DESIGNATOR

1. Name *(Last, first, middle)*
2. Date of birth *(Month, day, year)*
3. Social Security Number
4. Department or agency in which ☐ presently or ☐ last employed, including bureau or division *(Check one block)*
5. Claim number if retired

   CSA–

I, the employee or former employee identified above, canceling any and all previous designations of beneficiary heretofore made by me, do now designate the beneficiary or beneficiaries named below to receive any lump-sum benefit which may become payable under the Civil Service Retirement law after my death. I understand that this designation of beneficiary will not affect the rights of any survivors who may qualify for annuity benefits after my death, and that this designation will remain in full force and effect unless or until canceled by me in writing.

B. INFORMATION CONCERNING THE BENEFICIARY OR BENEFICIARIES

Type or print first name, middle initial, and last name of each beneficiary	Type or print address *(including ZIP code)* of each beneficiary	Relationship	Share to be paid to each beneficiary *(See example)*

I hereby direct, unless otherwise indicated above, that if more than one beneficiary is named, the share of any deceased beneficiary or beneficiaries who may die before a lump-sum benefit becomes payable shall be distributed equally among the surviving beneficiaries, or entirely to the survivor. If none of the beneficiaries are alive when the lump-sum benefit becomes payable, this designation shall be void.

Date of this designation *(Month, day, year)*

Signature of designator *(Do not print)*

C. WITNESSES *(A witness is not eligible to receive payment as a beneficiary.)*

We, the undersigned, certify that this instrument was signed in our presence.

Signature of witness *(Do not print)*

Number and street

City, state, ZIP code

Signature of witness *(Do not print)*

Number and street

City, state, ZIP code

Print or type your name and address *(including ZIP code)* to insure return of copy.

(Reserved for receiving stamp of Office of Personnel Management)

COMPLETE THIS FORM AND THE DUPLICATE COPY.
MAIL BOTH COPIES TO THE OFFICE OF PERSONNEL MANAGEMENT, CIVIL SERVICE RETIREMENT SYSTEM, BOYERS, PA 16017

SF-2808

Important — The filing of this form completely cancels any designation you may have previously filed. Be sure to name in this form all persons you wish to designate as beneficiaries.

EXAMPLES OF DESIGNATIONS

HOW TO DESIGNATE ONE BENEFICIARY

Type or print first name, middle initial, and last name of each beneficiary	Type or print address (*including ZIP code*) of each beneficiary	Relationship	Share to be paid to each beneficiary	
SARAH M. JONES	22 Elm Street Lima, Ohio 45801	Sister	All	Do not write name as S. M. Jones or as Mrs. George L. Jones.

HOW TO DESIGNATE MORE THAN ONE BENEFICIARY

Type or print first name, middle initial, and last name of each beneficiary	Type or print address (*including ZIP code*) of each beneficiary	Relationship	Share to be paid to each beneficiary	
MARY A. SMITH	4902 Oak Street Judson, North Dakota 58548	Aunt	One-half	Be sure that shares to be paid to the beneficiaries add up to 100%.
ANNA D. BROWN	50 Duke Street Judson, North Dakota 58548	Cousin	One-fourth	
HENRY G. BROWN	50 Duke Street Judson, North Dakota 58548	Cousin	One-fourth	

HOW TO DESIGNATE A CONTINGENT BENEFICIARY

Type or print first name, middle initial, and last name of each beneficiary	Type or print address (*including ZIP code*) of each beneficiary	Relationship	Share to be paid to each beneficiary
CATHERINE J. ANDERSON, if living	91 Adams Avenue Syracuse, New York 13206	Niece	All
Otherwise to: JOHN L. JONES	69 Harris Avenue Cleveland, Ohio 44104	Nephew	All

HOW TO CANCEL A DESIGNATION OF BENEFICIARY

Type or print first name, middle initial, and last name of each beneficiary	Type or print address (*including ZIP code*) of each beneficiary	Relationship	Share to be paid to each beneficiary	
Cancel Prior Designation				You may want to cancel a beneficiary you have named if your circumstances change and you want the benefit payable under the Civil Service Retirement law order of precedence. (See back of duplicate.)
				SF 2808

SF-2808

WHO SHOULD USE THIS DESIGNATION OF BENEFICIARY?

This designation may be used only by persons who 1) are or were covered by the Civil Service Retirement System (CSRS) and 2) want to designate that any lump sum which may become payable after their death should be paid other than according to the order of precedence which follows. This designation may also be used by a person who wants to cancel a prior Standard Form 2808 that is on file with OPM. If you are covered by the Federal Employees' Retirement System (FERS), you must use Standard Form 3102 to designate a beneficiary for any lump sum which may become payable from that retirement system. To designate a beneficiary for any life insurance benefits payable under the Federal Employees' Group Life Insurance Program, all persons covered by the Program must use Standard Form 2823. Employees under CSRS and FERS must use Standard Form 1152 to designate a beneficiary for any unpaid compensation payable by their employing agency if the employee should die while on the agency's rolls. To designate a beneficiary for amounts payable by the Thrift Savings Plan, use form TSP-3.

CIVIL SERVICE RETIREMENT LAW ORDER OF PRECEDENCE

If there is no designated beneficiary living, any lump-sum benefit which becomes payable after the death of an employee or former employee will be payable to the first person or persons listed below who are alive on the date title to the payment arises.

1. To the widow or widower.
2. If neither of the above, to the child or children in equal shares, with the share of any deceased child distributed among the descendants of that child.
3. If none of the above, to the parents in equal shares or the entire amount to the surviving parent.
4. If none of the above, to the executor or administrator of the estate of the decedent.
5. If none of the above, to the next of kin under the laws of the State in which the decedent was domiciled at date of death.

It is not necessary for any employee or former employee to designate a beneficiary unless he or she wishes to name some person or persons not included above or have payment made in a different order.

PURPOSE OF DESIGNATING A BENEFICIARY

A designation of beneficiary is for lump-sum benefit purposes only and does not affect the right of any person who qualifies to receive *survivor annuity* benefits. Such benefits are payable either by operation of law or as a result of an election made by a retiring employee. Survivor annuity benefits are never based on this form.

DESIGNATING A TRUST AS A BENEFICIARY

If you wish to designate a trust fund as your beneficiary, see your agency personnel office for information before filling out this form.

INSTRUCTIONS

1. The examples printed on the back of the first page may be helpful to you.
2. Type or print all entries except signatures.
3. Fill out and mail both copies to the Office of Personnel Management, Civil Service Retirement System, Boyers, PA 16017. The designation of beneficiary must be received by the Office of Personnel Management prior to the death of the employee or former employee to be valid.
4. Cancellation of a prior designation may be effected without the naming of a new beneficiary by making out a new Standard Form 2808 and inserting in the space provided for name of beneficiary the words "Cancel Prior Designation." All designations of beneficiary filed before September 1, 1950, have been canceled by law. It is not necessary to file a new form to cancel a designation made before that date.
5. This form is not intended as a will, and miscellaneous provisions, such as payment of just debts, payment on the monthly installment plan, etc., will not be recognized.
6. A designation free of erasures or alterations should be filed in order to avoid a possible contest after death.
7. The duplicate will be returned to you as evidence that the original has been received and filed. When you receive the duplicate, file it with your important papers. After your death, the beneficiary, or someone acting for the beneficiary, should request the Office of Personnel Management to furnish a form on which to make application for any lump-sum benefit which may be payable.

LAW AND REGULATIONS

1. By law, the designation of beneficiary shall be in writing, signed by the designator and witnessed. To be valid, the signed and witnessed form must be officially received at OPM before the death of the designator. A designation of beneficiary form delivered to OPM on a non-work day or after working hours cannot be officially received until the next work day. Also, facsimile copies, including those transmitted by telephone, are not acceptable and cannot be used to meet the filing deadline.
2. By law, no change or cancellation of beneficiary in a last will or testament, or in any other document not witnessed and filed as required by these regulations, shall have any force or effect.
3. A witness to a designation of beneficiary is ineligible to receive payment as a beneficiary.
4. Any person, firm, corporation, or legal entity may be named as beneficiary.
5. A change of beneficiary may be made at any time and without the knowledge or consent of the previous beneficiary, and this right cannot be waived or restricted.

PRIVACY ACT STATEMENT

Solicitation of this information is authorized by the Civil Service Retirement law (Chapter 83, title 5, U.S. Code). The information you furnish will be used to determine who will receive a lump-sum benefit in the event of your death, to identify records properly associated with your service, to obtain additional information if necessary, and to maintain a uniquely identifiable file. The information may be shared and is subject to verification, via paper, electronic media, or through the use of computer matching programs, with national, state, local or other charitable or social security administrative agencies in order to determine benefits under their programs, or to obtain information necessary for determination of benefits under this program. It may also be shared and verified, as noted above, with law enforcement agencies when they are investigating a violation or potential violation of the civil or criminal law. Executive Order 9397 (November 22, 1943) authorizes the use of the Social Security Number. Furnishing the data requested is voluntary, but failure to do so may delay or make it impossible for OPM to determine who is eligible to receive a lump-sum benefit in the event of your death.

PUBLIC BURDEN STATEMENT

We think this form takes an average 15 minutes per response to complete, including the time for reviewing instructions, getting the needed data, and reviewing the completed form. Send comments regarding our estimate or any other aspect of this form, including suggestions for reducing completion time, to the Paperwork Reduction Project, OMB Clearance Number 3206-0142, Office of Management and Budget, Washington, D.C. 20503.

SF-2808

CSRS
Civil Service Retirement System

APPLICATION TO MAKE VOLUNTARY CONTRIBUTIONS
CIVIL SERVICE RETIREMENT SYSTEM

To avoid delay:
(1) Read carefully the instructions below and the information on the attached page;
(2) Typewrite or print in ink;
(3) Complete application in full.

1. Name (Last, first, middle)
2. Date of birth (Month, day, year)
3. List all other names you have used (Including maiden name, if applicable)
4. Address (Number, street, city, state, and ZIP code)
5. Department or Agency (Including bureau, branch, or division where employed)
6. Location of employment (City, state, and ZIP code)
7. Title of present position
8. Social Security Number

9a. Do you have any civilian government service during which no Civil Service Retirement deductions were taken from your salary? ☐ Yes ☐ No
9b. Have you made a deposit to the Civil Service Retirement and Disability Fund to cover this non-deduction service? ☐ Yes ☐ No

10a. Do you have any service during which Civil Service Retirement deductions were taken from your salary and later refunded to you? ☐ Yes ☐ No
10b. Have you made a redeposit to the Civil Service Retirement and Disability Fund of the amount refunded to you? ☐ Yes ☐ No

11a. Have you ever made voluntary contributions before and later received a refund of them? ☐ Yes ☐ No
11b. Have you since been separated from the government service for a period of more than 3 calendar days? ☐ Yes ☐ No

If your answer to question 9b, 10b, or 11b is "NO", do not file this application. See Eligibility Instructions below.

I hereby apply to make voluntary contributions to the Civil Service Retirement and Disability Fund for the purpose of purchasing additional annuity at retirement and certify that I am currently employed in a position subject to the Civil Service Retirement System or I am an applicant for Civil Service retirement.

Applicant's signature (Do not print) _____ Date _____

Agency Certification

I certify that the applicant is currently employed by the agency shown below in a position subject to the Civil Service Retirement System.

Agency Address _____ Signature _____
_____ Official Title _____
_____ Telephone Number _____ Date _____

INSTRUCTIONS

Eligibility

1. Voluntary contributions may be made *only* if you are an employee who is serving under the Civil Service Retirement System or a former employee who is an applicant for retirement under the Civil Service Retirement System. You are not eligible if you are serving under the Federal Employees' Retirement System.

2. You must not owe a deposit for non-deduction service or a redeposit for refunded retirement deductions. Application to Make Deposit or Redeposit (Standard Form 2803) may be obtained from your employing agency.

3. If you have previously been paid a refund of voluntary contributions, you must have been separated from Government employment for more than 3 calendar days before you can again make voluntary contributions.

Limit on Contributions

Your total voluntary contributions cannot exceed 10 percent of the total of your basic civilian salary received during your Federal career.

Filing of Application

If you are an employee, you must submit the completed form to your agency personnel office which must complete the agency certification box and forward your application to the Office of Personnel Management. If you are already separated for retirement and are waiting for your retirement application to be approved, no agency certification is needed and you should send the application directly to the Office of Personnel Management. Send the application to the following address: Office of Personnel Management, Employee Service and Records Center, Boyers, PA 16017. **Do not send any payment with this application; if you do it will be returned.** OPM will send full instructions on how to make deposits once your application is accepted.

Additional Information

Important information regarding voluntary contributions is provided on the attached sheet. It is important that you read and understand this information **before** you make application. Further information, if needed, may be obtained from the personnel office of the agency in which you are employed. If this source of information is not available to you, contact the Office of Personnel Management, Retirement and Insurance Group, Washington, D.C. 20415.

Office of Personnel Management
FPM Supplement 831-1

Previous editions are unusable.
NSN 7540-00-634-4253

2804-107

SEE ATTACHED SHEET FOR MORE INFORMATION

Standard Form 2804
Revised August 1990

SF-2804

Your Financial Guide 157

Privacy Act Statement

Title 5, U.S. Code, Chapter 83, Civil Service Retirement authorizes the solicitation of this information. The data you furnish will be used to identify records properly associated with this application, to obtain additional information if necessary, and to determine if you are eligible to make voluntary contributions to the Civil Service Retirement and Disability Fund. This information may be shared and is subject to verification, via paper, electronic media, or through the use of computer matching programs, with national, state, local or other charitable or social security administrative agencies to determine and issue benefits under their programs or to report income for tax purposes. It may also be shared and verified, as noted above, with law enforcement agencies when they are investigating a violation or potential violation of the civil or criminal law. Executive Order 9397 (November 22, 1943) authorizes use of the Social Security Number. Furnishing the Social Security Number as well as other data is voluntary; however, failure to supply all of the requested information may delay or prevent approval of your application.

SF-2804

Designation of Beneficiary
Federal Employees' Group Life Insurance Program

FEGLI – Federal Employees Group Life Insurance

Form Approved
OMB No. 3206-0136

Warning
Read instructions on back of duplicate before filling in this form.

Information Concerning The Insured: If you have not assigned your insurance, YOU are "the Insured", as used throughout this form.

Name of Insured (Last, first, middle)	Date of birth of Insured (Month, day, year)	Social Security number of Insured

The Insured is:
Place an "X" in the appropriate box.

- [ ] An employee
- [ ] Retired or an applicant for retirement
- [ ] Receiving OWCP benefits or an applicant for OWCP benefits

If the Insured is retired or receiving Federal Employees' Compensation, give "CSA", "CSI", or OWCP claim number.

Department or agency in which the Insured is presently employed (If retired, former department or agency):

Department or agency	Bureau	Division	Location (City, state and ZIP code)

I am canceling any and all previous Designations of Beneficiary under the Federal Employees' Group Life Insurance Program and am now designating the beneficiary or beneficiaries named below to receive any amount of Life Insurance and Accidental Death Insurance due and payable at the Insured's death.

I understand that if I have previously validly assigned my insurance, any designation completed by me is not valid and has no force and effect.

I understand that this Designation of Beneficiary, if valid, will remain in full force and effect, unless or until canceled by me in writing, or until such time as it is automatically canceled (see back of Part 2). If this designation form is determined invalid for any reason, the next prior valid designation form will be given full force and effect. If no such prior form exists, the proceeds will be distributed under the order of precedence, or, if the insurance has been assigned, to the assignee(s).

Information Concerning The Beneficiary or Beneficiaries (See examples of designations on reverse side):

Type or print first name, middle initial, and last name of each beneficiary	Type or print address (Including ZIP code) of each beneficiary	Relationship	Percent or fraction to be paid to each beneficiary

Statement of Insured or Assignee

Print or type your name and address (Including ZIP code)

Please check:
I:
- [ ] have
- [ ] have not

elected Living Benefits.

Check only one:
I am:
- [ ] the Insured
- [ ] an Assignee

Please check:
- [ ] I have not assigned my insurance.
- [ ] I have signed this form in the presence of the two witnesses who have signed below.
- [ ] Neither witness is named as a beneficiary.
- [ ] If I designated shares to be paid to more than one beneficiary, the shares add up to 100%. (Dollar amounts are not acceptable.)

For each type of insurance (Basic Life, Option A-Standard, and Option B-Additional): (1) I hereby direct, unless otherwise indicated above, that if more than one beneficiary is named, the share of any beneficiary who may predecease me or become disqualified for any reason from receiving a share of the benefits shall be distributed equally among the surviving beneficiaries, or entirely to the survivor.

(2) I understand that if none of the designated beneficiaries is living at the time of the Insured's death, the proceeds will be distributed under the order of precedence, or, if the insurance has been assigned, to the assignee(s).

I hereby specifically reserve the right to cancel or change this designation of beneficiary at any time without knowledge or consent of the beneficiary(ies).

Signature of Insured/Assignee (Only the Insured/Assignee may sign. Signatures by guardians, conservators or through a power of attorney are not acceptable.)	Date of execution (Month, day, year)

Witnesses To Signature (A witness is not eligible to receive payment as a beneficiary):

Signature of witness	Number and street	City, state and ZIP code
Signature of witness	Number and street	City, state and ZIP code

Receiving agency	Date of receipt	Signature of authorized agency official	Title

See back of Part 2 for instructions on where to file this form. Do not file with the Office of Federal Employees' Group Life Insurance.

PART 1-Original

U.S. Office of Personnel Management
NSN 7540-01-231-6226
The FEGLI Handbook for Personnel and Payroll Offices

2823-102
Previous editions not usable

Standard Form 2823
Rev. July 1995

SF-2823

Important - the filing of this form, if valid, will completely cancel any Designation of Beneficiary you may have previously filed under the Federal Employees' Group Life Insurance Program. Be sure to name in this form all persons you wish to designate as beneficiaries of any life insurance payable under the Program.

Examples of Designations

1. How to designate one beneficiary Do not write names as M.E. Brown or as Mrs. John H. Brown. If you want to designate your estate as beneficiary, enter "My estate" in the beneficiary column.

Type or print first name, middle initial, and last name of each beneficiary	Type or print address (Including ZIP code) of each beneficiary	Relationship	Percent or fraction to be paid to each beneficiary
Mary E. Brown	214 Central Avenue Muncie, IN 47303	Niece	100%

2. How to designate more than one beneficiary Be sure that the shares to be paid to the several beneficiaries add up to 100 percent.

Type or print first name, middle initial, and last name of each beneficiary	Type or print address (Including ZIP code) of each beneficiary	Relationship	Percent or fraction to be paid to each beneficiary
Alice M. Long	509 Canal Street Red Bank, NJ 07701	Aunt	25%
Joseph P. Brady	360 Williams Street Red Bank, NJ 07701	Nephew	25%
Catherine L. Rowe	792 Broadway Whiting, IN 46394	Mother	50%

3. How to designate a contingent beneficiary

Type or print first name, middle initial, and last name of each beneficiary	Type or print address (Including ZIP code) of each beneficiary	Relationship	Percent or fraction to be paid to each beneficiary
John M. Parrish, if living	810 West 180th Street New York, NY 10033	Father	100%
Otherwise to: Susan A. Parrish	810 West 180th Street New York, NY 10033	Sister	100%

4. How to designate different beneficiaries for basic life and optional coverages*

Type or print first name, middle initial, and last name of each beneficiary	Type or print address (Including ZIP code) of each beneficiary	Relationship	Percent or fraction to be paid to each beneficiary
John D. Jones	124 Elm Street Dayton, OH 45420	Son	100% Basic Life
Jane M. Smith	421 Spring Avenue Portland, ME 04101	Niece	100% Opt. A-Standard
Elizabeth J. Allen	234 Fifth Avenue New York, NY 10029	Daughter	50% Opt. B-Additional
Ann J. Borden	678 Ninth Street Philadelphia, PA 19123	Daughter	50% Opt. B-Additional

5. How to cancel a designation of beneficiary and effect payment under the order of precedence (See back of Part 2)

Type or print first name, middle initial, and last name of each beneficiary	Type or print address (Including ZIP code) of each beneficiary	Relationship	Percent or fraction to be paid to each beneficiary
Cancel prior designations			

* If a beneficiary for Basic Life, Option A-Standard, or Option B-Additional predeceases the insured, and there is no surviving beneficiary or contingent beneficiary for that type of insurance, payment   that type of insurance will be made under the order   recedence or, if the insurance has been assigned, to the assignee(s) (See back of Part

SF-2823

Your Financial Guide

This Designation of Beneficiary Form is to be used solely for the disposition of proceeds of insurance under the Federal Employees' Group Life Insurance Program and is not to be confused with Standard Form 2808, *Designation of Beneficiary, Civil Service Retirement System*, Standard Form 3102, *Designation of Beneficiary, Federal Employees' Retirement System*, Standard Form 1152, *Designation of Beneficiary, Unpaid Compensation of Deceased Civilian Employee*, or RI 76-10, *Assignment of Federal Employees' Group Life Insurance*.

If you have not assigned your insurance, YOU are "the Insured", as used throughout this form.

Order of Precedence

If the insurance HAS BEEN assigned and there is no valid Designation of Beneficiary, the amount of group life insurance and group accidental death insurance in force at the date of the Insured's death shall be paid to the assignee(s).

If the insurance HAS NOT BEEN assigned and there is no valid Designation of Beneficiary, the amount of group life insurance and group accidental death insurance in force at the date of death shall be paid to the person or persons surviving at the date of death, under the following order of precedence:

1. To the widow or widower.
2. If none of the above, to the child or children, with the share of any deceased child distributed among the descendants of that child.
3. If none of the above, to the parents in equal shares or the entire amount to the surviving parent.
4. If none of the above, to the duly appointed executor or administrator of the estate.
5. If none of the above, to the other next of kin who are entitled under the laws of the domicile of the Insured at the date of death.

It is not necessary to designate a beneficiary unless you wish payment to be made in a way other than the order of precedence shown above.

Regulations

(a) The Designation of Beneficiary shall be in writing, signed and witnessed, in writing, by two people, and received in the employing office (or in the Office of Personnel Management, in the case of (1) a retired employee or (2) an employee whose insurance is continued while receiving benefits under the Federal Employees' Compensation Law because of disease or injury and who is held by the Department of Labor to be unable to return to duty) prior to the death of the Insured.

(b) A change or cancellation of beneficiary in a last will or testament, or in any other document not witnessed and filed as required by these regulations, shall not have any force or effect.

(c) A witness to a Designation of Beneficiary is not eligible to receive payment as a beneficiary.

(d) Any person, firm, corporation or legal entity (except an agency of the Federal or District of Columbia governments) may be named as beneficiary.

(e) A change of beneficiary may be made at any time and without the knowledge or consent of the previous beneficiary. This right cannot be waived or restricted.

(f) A Designation of Beneficiary is automatically canceled 31 days after the employee stops being insured.

(g) If a valid Designation of Beneficiary provides that a designated beneficiary shall be entitled to the proceeds of the insurance only if the beneficiary survives the Insured for a period of time (not more than 30 days) as specified by the designator, no right to the insurance shall vest as to such beneficiary during that period. In the event such beneficiary does not survive the specified period, payment of the proceeds of the insurance will be made as if the beneficiary had predeceased the Insured.

Instructions

1. If you have validly assigned your insurance (that is, you completed an RI 76-10 Assignment form) either as an employee or as an annuitant or as an assignee reassigning insurance, your Designation of Beneficiary is invalid. Only the assignee(s) may complete a Designation.
2. Only the Insured or Assignee may sign the Designation of Beneficiary. The signature of a guardian, conservator or other fiduciary (including, but not limited to, those acting pursuant to a Power of Attorney or a Durable Power of Attorney) is not acceptable.
3. The examples printed on the back of the first page of this form may be helpful to you in filling out this form to name a beneficiary or to cancel a prior Designation of Beneficiary. More than one beneficiary can be designated. Unless you direct otherwise in the Designation, the person(s) named will be considered as beneficiary (or beneficiaries) for *(both)* Basic Life and optional coverages. The total insurance can be divided by showing what share is to be paid to each beneficiary (example 2), or different beneficiaries may be designated for Basic Life and optional coverages (example 4).
4. If you have elected a full Living Benefit, any designation of Basic insurance cannot be honored--you no longer have any Basic to designate.
5. Complete this form in duplicate. All entries on the form except signatures should be typed or printed in ink (typewriting preferred).
6. It is not necessary to file a new Designation of Beneficiary when your name or address or that of the Insured or the beneficiary changes or when the Insured changes employing offices or retires.
7. This form must be free of erasures or alterations.
8. Properly completed designations are not valid unless they are received prior to the death of the insured by the Office specified below under *Where to File Completed Form*.

IMPORTANT: If you wish to designate a trust as beneficiary, ask the Insured's employing office or retirement system for instructions.

Where to File Completed Form

If the Insured is an employee, file the form with the employing agency. If the Insured is a retired employee or is receiving Federal Employees' Compensation, file the form with the Office of Personnel Management, Retirement Operations Center, Validation Section, Boyers, PA 16017. If an application for retirement or compensation is pending, file the form with your employing agency if still employed, or with the Office of Personnel Management if no longer employed. Receipt of the designation form will be noted on the bottom of the form and the duplicate (Part 2) will be returned to you as evidence that the original has been received and filed. It is suggested that the duplicate be kept with the RI 76-21 (RI 76-20 for Postal Employees), the *Federal Employees' Group Life Insurance Description and Certification of Enrollment*.

Privacy Act and Public Burden Statements

Title 5, U.S. Code, chapter 87, Life Insurance, authorizes solicitation of this information. The data you furnish will be used to determine your beneficiary(ies) for your life insurance and accidental death insurance. This information will be shared with the Office of Federal Employees' Group Life Insurance in the event of your death. It will also be shared with the Office of Personnel Management and be placed in your Official Personnel Folder. This information may be disclosed to other Federal agencies or Congressional offices which may have a need to know it in connection with your application for a job, license, grant or other benefit. It may also be shared and is subject to verification, via paper, electronic media, or through the use of computer matching programs, with national, state, local or other charitable or social security administrative agencies to determine and issue benefits under their programs. In addition, to the extent this information indicates possible violation of civil or criminal law, it may be shared and verified, as noted above, with an appropriate Federal, state, or local law enforcement agency.

We also request that you provide the Insured's Social Security Number so that it may be used as an individual identifier in the Federal Employees' Group Life Insurance Program. Executive Order 9397, dated November 22, 1943, allows Federal agencies to use the Social Security Number as an individual identifier to distinguish between people with the same or similar names.

While the law does not require you to supply all the information requested on this form, doing so will assist in the prompt processing of your designation.

Agencies other than the Office of Personnel Management may have further routine uses for disclosure of information from the records systems in which they file copies of this form. If this is the case, they should provide you with any such uses which are applicable at the time you complete this form.

We think this form takes an average of 15 minutes to complete, including the time for reviewing instructions, getting the needed data, and reviewing the completed form. Send comments regarding our estimate or any other aspect of this form, including suggestions for reducing completion time, to the Office of Personnel Management, OPM Reports and Forms Officer, Washington, D.C. 20415.

Designations should be kept current. With changes in family status (marriage, divorce, death, birth etc.), you may wish to make changes in your designation(s).

SF-2823

THRIFT SAVINGS PLAN
WITHDRAWAL REQUEST

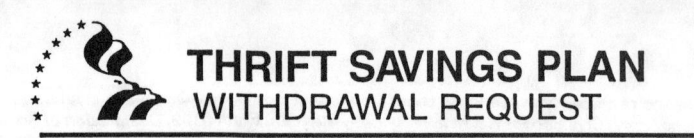

TSP-70

Use this form when you are ready to request a withdrawal of your Thrift Savings Plan (TSP) account, but not before you separate from Federal service. **Read the instructions on the back before completing this form.** Type or print the information requested.

I. INFORMATION ABOUT YOU

1. Name _____
   Last / First / Middle
2. ___-___-_____ Social Security Number
3. _____ Date of Birth (Month/Day/Year)
4. (___) ___-____ Daytime Phone (Area Code and Number)
5. Address _____
   Street address or box number
6. City _____ 7. _____ State/Country 8. _____ Zip Code
9. I am separated from Federal service **and** I expect my separation to exceed 31 full calendar days from the date of my separation. ☐ Yes ☐ No (**STOP.** See back of form.)

II. YOUR WITHDRAWAL ELECTION

10. ☐ Make my withdrawal as soon as possible **or** ☐ Make my withdrawal in ___/___ Month/Year

I choose to withdraw my TSP account as indicated below (Check **either** Item 11 **or** 12 **or** 13):

11. ☐ A life annuity
    The Annuity Request Package will be sent to you. (CSRS participants skip to Section IV. FERS participants skip to Section VI.)

or 12. ☐ A single payment

or 13. ☐ A series of monthly payments
(Check and complete a **or** b **or** c):
a. ☐ Payments for _____ months **or**
b. ☐ $ _____ per month **or**
c. ☐ Payments based on IRS life expectancy table

III. TRANSFER

14. ☐ I want all or a portion of my single payment or of each monthly payment to be transferred to an Individual Retirement Arrangement (IRA) or other eligible retirement plan. (See back of form for restrictions on transfer of monthly payments.) **Also complete Form TSP-70-T.**

IV. SPOUSE INFORMATION

15. Are you married, even if separated from your spouse?
    ☐ Yes (Complete this section.) ☐ No (Skip to Section VI.)
16. Spouse's Name _____
    Last / First / Middle
17. Spouse's Social Security Number ___-__-____
18. Spouse's Address _____
    Street address or box number (If same as yours, write "SAME.")
19. City _____ 20. _____ State/Country 21. _____ Zip Code
22. ☐ Check here if you do not know your spouse's address. (See back of form.)

V. SPOUSE WAIVER OF ANNUITY BENEFIT

Married FERS participants only

Your withdrawal election in Section II does not provide for a joint life annuity with 50 percent survivor benefit, level payments, and no cash refund, as required by law. Therefore, this election cannot be processed unless your spouse waives the right to that annuity.

Spouse: I give up my right to the prescribed joint life annuity by signing below.

23. _____ Spouse's Signature
24. _____ Date Signed
25. ☐ Check here if you cannot obtain your spouse's signature. (See back of form.)

VI. YOUR SIGNATURE AND CERTIFICATION

I certify that the information provided above is true to the best of my knowledge. **Warning:** Any intentional false statement in this application or willful misrepresentation concerning it is a violation of the law that is punishable by a fine of as much as $10,000 or imprisonment for as long as 5 years, or both (18 U.S.C. 1001).

26. _____ Participant's Signature
27. _____ Date Signed

WEB1.0 10/4/96   Form TSP-70 (11/94)

INFORMATION AND INSTRUCTIONS

Make a copy of this form for your records. Mail the original to:

Thrift Savings Plan Service Office
National Finance Center
P.O. Box 61500
New Orleans, LA 70161-1500
Telephone number: (504) 255-6000
TDD: (504) 255-5113

Read the booklet *Withdrawing Your TSP Account* and the notice "Important Tax Information About Payments From Your Thrift Savings Plan Account" before you make your withdrawal election. Your agency must give you these materials when you separate from service. If it has not done so, ask your agency for them.

Accounts of $3,500 or less. When your agency reports that you have separated from service, the TSP will notify you about automatic cashout procedures or leaving your money in the TSP. If the TSP receives a properly completed Withdrawal Request before issuing your cashout notice, your election will be processed, and a cashout notice will not be sent to you.

Accounts of more than $3,500. If you wish to leave your money in the TSP, you do not need to submit any forms. If you wish to withdraw your account, spouse notice or waiver requirements apply (see instructions for Sections IV and V).

SECTION I. 9. Separation from Federal service. If either part of this item is not true, you are not eligible to withdraw your account at this time; do not submit this Withdrawal Request. If you have separated but anticipate being rehired after a break in service of more than 31 full calendar days, see the withdrawal booklet for important information about rehired participants and withdrawal restrictions.

SECTION II. 10. Date of withdrawal. Check the appropriate box to indicate whether you want your withdrawal as soon as it can be processed or at a specific future date. The timing of your withdrawal depends on when we receive this form and when your agency submits your separation information. If you choose a specific date more than four months in the future, the TSP will notify you before that date and will provide current withdrawal and tax information.

Note: You cannot request a withdrawal for a future date that is later than March of the year following the year you become 70½.

11. Life annuity. Your account balance must be $3,500 or more before an annuity can be purchased. The TSP will send you the Annuity Request Package (Form TSP-11-A-B-C) four months before the date you choose in Item 10, or immediately, if you request a withdrawal to be made as soon as possible. Spouse notice or survivor annuity requirements will apply when you complete your annuity election.

12. Single payment. Your entire account balance will be paid out at one time.

13. Series of monthly payments. You can have monthly payments determined in one of three ways. Choose carefully, because you cannot change the way your payments are determined once they begin. For 13a or 13b, your monthly payments must be at least $25.

You may choose **one** of the following:

a. Number of monthly payments. Indicate the number of monthly payments you wish to receive. At the beginning of each year, the TSP will recalculate your monthly payment amount based on your account balance at the end of the preceding year and the number of payments remaining.

b. Monthly payment amount. Indicate the dollar amount of your monthly payments. You will receive payments in this amount until your entire account balance has been paid.

c. Payments based on IRS life expectancy table. (Table V, 26 CFR §1.72-9). At the beginning of each year, the TSP will recalculate your monthly payment amount based on your account balance and your age.

SECTION III. 14. Transfer to an IRA or other eligible retirement plan. Check Item 14 if you want the TSP to transfer all or part of your single payment or all or part of each monthly payment to an IRA or other eligible retirement plan. **You must also submit Form TSP-70-T, Transfer Information.** If you request a transfer at a date more than four months in the future, do not submit Form TSP-70-T at this time. The TSP will mail you a notice several months before your chosen withdrawal date to remind you to submit current transfer information. If Form TSP-70-T is not then received, your election will be cancelled.

Note: The TSP cannot transfer annuity payments, monthly payments based on the IRS life expectancy table, or monthly payments expected to last 10 years or more (i.e., 120 or more months). If you are choosing monthly payments in a specific dollar amount (13b above), see the withdrawal booklet to estimate whether your payments will be eligible for transfer.

SECTIONS IV and V. Spouses' rights apply to accounts that are more than $3,500 at disbursement. If your account balance is $3,500 or less, you do not need to complete these sections.

Spouses' Rights

Classification	Requirement	Exceptions
FERS	Spouse is entitled to a survivor annuity unless he or she waives that right.	Whereabouts unknown or exceptional circumstances
CSRS	Spouse is entitled to notification by TSP of participant's election.	Whereabouts unknown

22. Cannot provide spouse's address. If you are a married CSRS participant and you do not know the whereabouts of your spouse, you must submit Form TSP-16, Exception to Spousal Requirements, with the required documentation. (If you are a married FERS participant, you must complete Items 15 – 17, but you do not need to provide your spouse's address.)

25. Cannot obtain spouse's signature. If you are a married FERS participant and you cannot obtain your spouse's signature because his or her whereabouts are unknown or you believe that exceptional circumstances apply, you must submit Form TSP-16, Exception to Spousal Requirements, with the required documentation. (If your current spouse has previously waived the right to a survivor annuity, this section does not have to be completed.)

SECTION VI. 26 – 27. Signature and certification. You must sign and date this section; otherwise, this form will not be accepted.

PRIVACY ACT NOTICE. We are authorized to request this information under Title 5, U.S. Code Chapter 84, Federal Employees' Retirement System, Subchapter III, Thrift Savings Plan. Executive Order 9397 authorizes us to ask for your Social Security number, which will be used to identify your account. We will use the information you give us to process the withdrawal of your TSP account. This information may be shared with other Federal agencies in order to administer your account or for statistical, auditing, or archiving purposes. It may also be shared with Federal, state, and local agencies to determine benefits under their programs, to obtain information necessary under this program, or to report income for tax purposes. In addition, we may share this information with the Parent Locator Service, Department of Health and Human Services, for the purpose of enforcing child support obligations against the TSP participant. We may share this information with law enforcement agencies when they are investigating a violation of civil or criminal law. We may give this information to financial institutions, private sector audit firms, annuity vendors, current spouses and, to a limited extent, former spouses and beneficiaries. Finally, this information may also be disclosed to others on your written request. While the law does not require you to give any of the information we are asking for on this form, it may not be possible to process the actions you request by this form if you do not give us this information.

WEB1.0 10/4/96   Form TSP-70 (11/94)

THRIFT SAVINGS PLAN
DESIGNATION OF BENEFICIARY

TSP-3

Use this form to designate a beneficiary or beneficiaries to receive your Thrift Savings Plan (TSP) account after your death. **Read the instructions on the back to assist you in completing this form.** Type or print the information requested. Do not alter this form or the information you enter; if you need to make a correction or change your entries, start over on a new form.

I. INFORMATION ABOUT YOU

1. Name _____ Last / First / Middle
2. _____ Social Security Number
3. _____ Date of Birth (Month/Day/Year)
4. (___) ___-____ Daytime Phone (Area Code and Number)
5. Address _____ Street address or box number
6. City _____
7. _____ State
8. _____ Zip Code

II. DESIGNATING YOUR BENEFICIARIES

Indicate in whole percentages or fractions the share of your TSP account to be paid to each beneficiary.

1. _____ Beneficiary Name (Last) (First) (Middle)   Share: _____
   _____ Street address or box number
   _____ City / State / Zip Code
   _____ Social Security Number/EIN / Date of Birth (Month/Day/Year) / Relationship

2. _____ Beneficiary Name (Last) (First) (Middle)   Share: _____
   _____ Street address or box number
   _____ City / State / Zip Code
   _____ Social Security Number/EIN / Date of Birth (Month/Day/Year) / Relationship

3. _____ Beneficiary Name (Last) (First) (Middle)   Share: _____
   _____ Street address or box number
   _____ City / State / Zip Code
   _____ Social Security Number/EIN / Date of Birth (Month/Day/Year) / Relationship

☞ ☐ Check here if additional pages are used. Number of additional pages _____ . (See back of form.)

III. YOUR SIGNATURE

Sign and date this section. Your signature must be witnessed in Section IV.

_____ Participant's Signature   _____ Date Signed

IV. WITNESSES TO SIGNATURE

This form is valid only if it is witnessed by two persons. The witnesses must be age 21 or older. (A witness cannot be a beneficiary of any portion of your TSP account.) By signing below, the witnesses affirm that the participant (a) signed Section III in their presence, or (b) informed them that the signature in Section III is the participant's own signature.

Witness 1 _____ Typed or Printed Name of First Witness   _____ Signature of First Witness

Witness 2 _____ Typed or Printed Name of Second Witness   _____ Signature of Second Witness

WEB 1.0 10/4/96   Form TSP-3 (Revised 10/96)
PREVIOUS EDITIONS OBSOLETE

Your Financial Guide

INFORMATION AND INSTRUCTIONS

Make a copy of this form for your records. Mail the original to:

> Thrift Savings Plan Service Office
> National Finance Center
> P.O. Box 61135
> New Orleans, LA 70161-1135
> Telephone number: (504) 255-6000
> TDD: (504) 255-5113

Your semiannual Participant Statement will show the date of your most recent designation.

Designating a beneficiary. This Designation of Beneficiary form applies **only** to the disposition of your Thrift Savings Plan (TSP) account after your death. It does not affect your FERS Basic Annuity, your CSRS annuity, or any other benefits.

It is only necessary to designate a beneficiary if you want payment to be made in a way other than the following order of precedence:

1. To your widow or widower.
2. If none, to your child or children equally, and descendants of deceased children by representation.
3. If none, to your parents equally or to the surviving parent.
4. If none, to the appointed executor or administrator of your estate.
5. If none, to your next of kin who is entitled to your estate under the laws of the state in which you resided at the time of your death.

In this order of precedence, a child includes a natural child and an adopted child, but does not include a stepchild whom you have not adopted; parent does not include a stepparent, unless your stepparent has adopted you. "By representation" means that if one of your children dies before you do, that child's share will be divided equally among his or her children.

Making a valid designation. To name beneficiaries to receive your TSP account after you die, you must complete this form, and it must be received by the TSP on or before the date of your death. Do not submit a will to designate beneficiaries for your TSP account; a will is not valid for the disposition of a TSP account. You may, however, designate an estate or trust on Form TSP-3.

You are responsible for ensuring that your Form TSP-3 is properly completed, signed, and witnessed (see the Instructions for Section II in the right-hand column). Do not submit an altered form; if you need to correct or change the information you have entered on the form, start over on a new form.

Changing or cancelling your designation of beneficiary. This Designation of Beneficiary will stay in effect until you submit another valid Form TSP-3 naming other beneficiaries or cancelling prior designations.

Keep your designation (and your beneficiaries' addresses) current. If your family status changes due to marriage, birth or adoption of a child, divorce, or death, you may want to change your designation.

If your beneficiaries predecease you. The share of any beneficiary who dies before you die will be distributed proportionally among the surviving designated TSP beneficiaries unless a designated contingent beneficiary is alive at your death. If none of your designated beneficiaries is alive at the time of your death, the standard order of precedence will be followed.

INSTRUCTIONS FOR SECTION II. You may name as a beneficiary any person, corporation, trust, or legal entity, or your estate. Note: If the beneficiary is a minor child, benefits will be made payable directly to the child.

If you need additional space, use a blank sheet of paper. Enter your name, Social Security number, and date of birth, and number the pages. You must sign and date **all** additional pages; the same two witnesses who signed the form must also sign each additional page.

Enter the share for each beneficiary as a whole percentage or a fraction. Percentages must add up to 100 percent; fractions must add up to 1.

The examples show you how to name a beneficiary or cancel prior Designations of Beneficiary.

- For each person you designate as a beneficiary, enter the full name, share, address, Social Security number (SSN), date of birth, and relationship to you. If you do not have all the requested information, you must provide at least the beneficiary's name, the beneficiary's share, and either the SSN or date of birth.

- You may designate one or more contingent beneficiaries, but **only** to receive a beneficiary's share if that beneficiary dies before you do.

- If the beneficiary is a corporation or other legal entity, enter the name of the entity on the name line. Enter the legal representative's name and address on the address lines. Enter the Employer Identification Number (EIN). Leave the date of birth and relationship blank.

- If the beneficiary is a trust, enter the name of the trust on the name line. Enter the trustee's name and address on the address lines. Enter the EIN, if available. Leave date of birth blank. Enter "Trust" on the relationship line. Note: Filling out this form will not create a trust.

- If the beneficiary is an estate, enter the name of the estate on the name line. Enter the executor's name and address on the address lines. Enter the EIN, if available. Leave date of birth blank. Enter "Estate" on the relationship line.

INSTRUCTIONS FOR SECTION IV. Do not ask the individuals you name as beneficiaries of your TSP account to witness your Form TSP-3. A person named as a TSP beneficiary who is also a witness cannot receive his or her share.

PRIVACY ACT NOTICE. We are authorized to request this information under 5 U.S.C. Chapter 84. Executive Order 9397 authorizes us to ask for your Social Security number, which will be used to identify your account. We will use the information you provide to determine who your beneficiaries are for amounts due and payable from your TSP account. This information may also be shared with other Federal agencies to administer your account or for statistical, auditing, or archiving purposes. In addition, we may share the information with law enforcement agencies investigating, prosecuting, or enforcing a violation of civil or criminal law or with other agencies for the purpose of implementing a statute, rule, or order. It may also be shared with Congressional offices, the TSP annuity vendor, retirement plan sponsors, auditing firms, spouses, former spouses, beneficiaries, persons responsible for your care, and representatives of your estate. It may also be released in response to a court subpoena or to appropriate parties preparing for or engaged in litigation affecting your TSP account. You are not required by law to provide this information, but if you do not provide it, it may not be possible to process your Beneficiary Designation.

WEB 1.0 10/4/96   Form TSP-3 (Revised 10/96)

TSP

FEDERAL RETIREMENT THRIFT SAVINGS PLAN

TSP-17

APPLICATION FOR ACCOUNT BALANCE OF DECEASED PARTICIPANT

See Privacy Act Notice on Reverse

SECTION A - IDENTIFICATION OF DECEASED.

1. NAME OF DECEASED PARTICIPANT (Last, first, middle)
2. DATE OF DEATH — Month | Day | Year
3. DATE OF BIRTH — Month | Day | Year
4. SOCIAL SECURITY NUMBER

Legal Residence of Participant at Time of Death

5. FIRST LINE ADDRESS
6. SECOND LINE ADDRESS
7. CITY
8. STATE/COUNTRY
9. ZIP CODE

SECTION B - IDENTIFICATION OF APPLICANT.

10. APPLICANT NAME (Last, first, middle)
11. RELATIONSHIP TO DECEASED
12. ADDRESS
13. CITY
14. STATE/COUNTRY
15. ZIP CODE
16. DAYTIME PHONE (Area Code and Number)

17. Was the participant married at the time of death? If yes, skip Blocks 18 through 21 and complete Section C. If no or do not know, go to Block 18.
    - [ ] Yes [ ] No [ ] Do Not Know

18. Are there any children of the deceased as defined in the instructions? If yes, skip Blocks 19 through 21 and complete Section C. If no or do not know, go to Block 19.
    - [ ] Yes [ ] No [ ] Do Not Know

19. Are either of the deceased participant's parents living? If yes, skip Blocks 20 and 21 and complete Section C. If no or do not know, go to Block 20.
    - [ ] Yes [ ] No [ ] Do Not Know

20. Has an executor or administrator been appointed by the court to settle the estate of the deceased? If yes, skip Block 21 and complete Section C. If no or do not know, go to Block 21.
    - [ ] Yes [ ] No [ ] Do Not Know

21. Will an executor or administrator be appointed? If yes, complete Section C. If no or do not know, go to Section D.
    - [ ] Yes [ ] No [ ] Do Not Know

SECTION C - ADDITIONAL INFORMATION.

If you checked "Yes" for any of the questions in Blocks 17 through 21, you must complete this section. See reverse for instructions.

SECTION D - CERTIFICATION.

I hereby certify, under penalty of perjury, that all statements made on this application are true to the best of my knowledge and that that I have not withheld any evidence necessary to settle this claim. **Warning:** Any intentional false statement in this application or willful misrepresentation concerning it is a violation of the law that is punishable by a fine of not more than $10,000 or imprisonment of not more than 5 years or both (18 USC 1001).

22. APPLICANT'S SIGNATURE
23. DATE SIGNED

FORM TSP - 17 (8/87)

TSP-17

INSTRUCTIONS FOR COMPLETING
APPLICATION FOR ACCOUNT BALANCE OF DECEASED PARTICIPANT

This application is to be used by persons applying for a deceased participant's Thrift Savings Plan account. This application will not be processed unless an original certified copy of the death certificate is attached.

Please type or print the information on this form. Send completed forms to:

Thrift Savings Plan Service Office
National Finance Center
P.O. Box 61135
New Orleans, LA 70161-1135

SECTION A - IDENTIFICATION OF DECEASED

Block 1, Name of Deceased Participant. Enter the deceased participant's name.

Block 2, Date of Death. Enter date of death. A certified copy of the death certificate must be attached.

Block 3, Date of Birth. Enter the deceased participant's date of birth.

Block 4, Social Security Number. Enter the deceased participant's 9-digit social security number.

Blocks 5 through 9, Legal Residence of Participant at Time of Death. Enter the participant's legal residence at time of death.

SECTION B - IDENTIFICATION OF APPLICANT

Block 10, Applicant's Name. Enter the applicant's name.

Block 11, Relationship to Deceased. Enter the applicant's relationship to the deceased participant. If the applicant is appointed by the court to settle the estate of the deceased, enter "executor" or "administrator" and attach a copy of the court appointment.

Blocks 12 through 15, Address. Enter the applicant's address.

Block 16, Daytime Phone Number (Area Code and Number). Enter the applicant's daytime area code and phone number.

Block 17. Was the participant married at the time of death? If yes, skip Blocks 18 through 21 and complete Section C. If no or do not know, go to Block 18.

Block 18, Are there any children of deceased as defined in the instructions? This includes adopted children, but not stepchildren who were not adpoted. It also includes decendents of deceased children. If yes, skip Blocks 19 through 21 and complete Section C. If no or do not know, go to Block 19.

Block 19, Are either of deceased participant's parents living? If yes, skip Blocks 20 and 21 and complete Section C. If no or do not know, go to Block 20.

Block 20, Has an executor or administrator been appointed by the court to settle the estate of the deceased? If yes, skip Block 21 and complete Section C. If no or do not know, go to Block 21.

Block 21, Will an executor or administrator be appointed? If yes, complete Section C. If no or do not know, go to Section D.

SECTION C - ADDITIONAL INFORMATION.
Enter the names, social security numbers, addresses, and daytime phone numbers of persons referred to in Section B, if known, along with any other information that may help in processing this application. Enter the persons' relationship to the deceased (spouse, son, daughter, mother, father, executor, etc.). If additional space is needed, continue on a separate sheet of paper and attach it to this form.

SECTION D - CERTIFICATION.

Block 22, Applicant's Signature. Sign your name.

Block 23, Date Signed. Enter the date you signed Block 22.

PRIVACY ACT NOTICE

We are authorized to request this information under Title 5, U.S. Code Chapter 84, Federal Employees' Retirement System, Subchapter III, Thrift Savings Plan. Executive Order 9397 authorizes us to ask for the employee's social security number, which will be used to identify the employee's account. We will use the information given us in administering the Thrift Savings Plan. We may share this information with the Office of Personnel Management. The information may be shared with other Federal agencies or Congressional offices for certain official purposes. It may also be shared with national, state, and local agencies to determine benefits under their programs, to obtain information necessary under this program, or to report income for tax purposes. In addition, we may share this information with law enforcement agencies when they are investigating a violation of civil or criminal law. Finally, we may give this information to financial institutions, private sector audit firms, annuity vendors, beneficiaries, current spouses and, to a limited extent, former spouses. While the law does not require you to give any of the information we are asking for on this form, it may not be possible to process the form if you do not give us this information.

TSP-17